Gary Gentile started his diving career in 1970. Since then he has made thousands of decompression dives, over 100 of them on the *Andrea Doria*. He was instrumental in merging mixed gas diving technology with wreck diving. In 1994, he participated in a mixed diving expedition to the *Lusitania*, at a depth of 300 feet.

Gary has specialized in wreck diving and shipwreck research, concentrating his efforts on wrecks along the east coast, from Newfoundland to Key West, and in the Great Lakes. He has compiled an extensive library of books, photographs, drawings, plans, and original source materials on ships and shipwrecks.

Gary has written dozens of magazine articles, and he has published thousands of photographs in books, periodicals, newspapers, brochures, advertisements, corporate reports, museum displays, postcards, film, and television. He lectures extensively on wilderness and underwater topics, and conducts seminars on advanced wreck diving techniques and high-tech diving equipment. He is the author of more than two dozen books, both novels and nonfiction works, the latter on diving and nautical and shipwreck history. The Popular Dive Guide Series will eventually cover every major shipwreck along the east coast.

In 1989, after a five-year battle with the National Oceanic and Atmospheric Administration, Gary won a suit which forced the hostile government agency to issue him a permit to dive the USS *Monitor*, a protected National Marine Sanctuary. Media attention that was focused on Gary's triumphant victory resulted in nationwide coverage of his 1990 photographic expedition to the Civil War ironclad. Gary continues to fight for the right of access to all shipwreck sites.

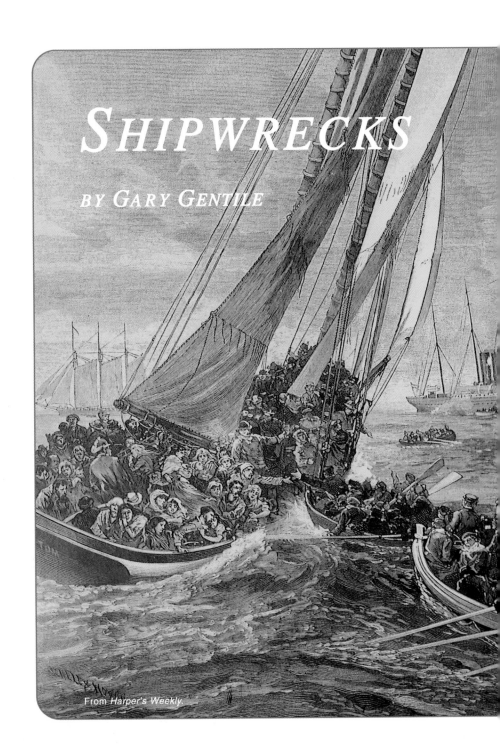

SHIPWRECKS

BY GARY GENTILE

From *Harper's Weekly.*

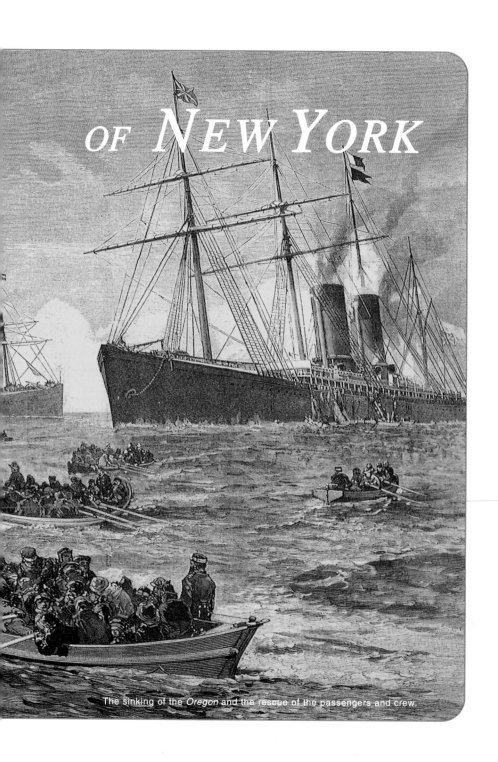

OF *NEW YORK*

The sinking of the *Oregon* and the rescue of the passengers and crew.

Gary Gentile Productions
P.O. Box 57137
Philadelphia, PA 19111

Additional copies of this book may be purchased from the same address by sending a check or money order in the amount of $20 U.S. for each copy (postage paid).

Picture Credits

The upper front cover photograph of the *Lexington* burning is courtesy of the Library of Congress. The lower front cover photograph of the *Peter Rickmers* aground is courtesy of the Long Island Maritime Museum. Every attempt has been made to contact the photographers or artists whose work appears in this book, if known, and to ascertain their names if unknown; in some cases, copies of pictures have been in public circulation for so long that the name of the photographer or artist has been lost, or the present whereabouts are impossible to trace. Any information in this regard forwarded to the author will be appreciated. Apologies are made to those whose work must under such circumstances go unrecognized. Uncredited photographs, including all marine life examples typical to the area, were taken by the author. Back cover photographs: the helm is from the *Coimbra*, the Guion Line and the Cunard Steamship Company crests are from china from the *Oregon*.

The author wishes to acknowledge Drew Maser and Pat Stewart for proofreading the galleys.

International Standard Book Number (ISBN) 1-883056-04-7

First Edition

Printed in Hong Kong

CONTENTS

INTRODUCTION

Sunk off New York's eastern shores is a rich trove of maritime history. Since the colonization of America, the New World's largest and most active port—New York City—has seen the arrival and departure of more vessels of more descriptions than any other port on the North American continent. In that context it is not difficult to understand why so many ships have come to grief in such a geographically small area. Nor is it difficult to perceive how the chronicles of a nation from fledgling to maturity have come to be represented by a multitude of wrecked ships whose sunken carcasses litter the coastal sea bed like prehistoric bones in the ground, each with its story to tell.

For hundreds of years ships have set their courses for New York harbor: first for the purposes of exploration, then for immigration and trade. Where the shipping lanes converge at the approaches to the harbor entrance there have been numerous collisions and strandings. Many of those are covered in *Shipwrecks of New Jersey*, by this author. Those which occurred above an arbitrary line bisecting the channel and extended approximately southeast are included here. Of necessity, there is some overlap of wrecks which could conceivably be covered in either volume.

Long Island Sound has likewise provided a trade route, between New York City and ports in New England, especially at a time when the way around Montauk Point was fraught with danger from winter storms, and when the rivers between the various islands of which New York City is now comprised, were unbridged. I have used the political boundary along the east-west corridor of the Sound as the means of separating shipwrecks into the geographic organization embraced by the state specific titles used to categorize the Popular Dive Guide Series. Those wrecks which lie or are suspected to lie south of the border are included here; those north of the border will be found in *Shipwrecks of Rhode Island and Connecticut*. By this system a certain amount of arbitrariness results.

During the golden age of sail and early steam, some of the most dramatic rescues of the Life-Saving Service occurred off Long Island's south shore, evoking the heroic drama which has come to symbolize that Service and those who served in it, and whose traditions are carried on today in the guise of the U.S. Coast Guard. Wherever possible I have quoted from Life-Saving Service reports and records in order to give the reader an idea of how these devoted men understated their extraordinary efforts to rescue sailors from precarious and often life-threatening situations. You may not see good English construction or proper spelling or grammar, but remember that these men were being paid to save lives, not to compose literature. They did the job for which they were trained, and they did it well. In the same vein, the newspaper reporters who recounted events so much more graphically and grammatically correct probably would not have made very good life-savers. Each was an expert in his chosen field of endeavor.

Conspicuous by its absence is one wreck which is perhaps the most frequently dived site off Long Island's south shore: the *San Diego*. Many summer weekends will find as many as three or four charter vessels anchored on the wreck. Since I have devoted an entire volume to the *San Diego*, replete with black and white historical and color underwater photographs, a single chapter included within these covers would serve only as an injustice to a story rich in character and historical events. Therefore, I refer interested readers to *U.S.S. San Diego: the Last Armored Cruiser*. See the last page of this book for instructions on how to order it.

Also absent is the paddle wheel steamer *Savannah*, the first ship to cross the Atlantic Ocean under steam, which feat was accomplished in 1819. The *Savannah* incorporated a design unique in sidewheel steamers: paddles that could be unshipped and folded up in order to reduce drag when sailing with the wind. In fact, the *Savannah's* steam engine was more an auxiliary than the primary means of propulsion. Most of the famous crossing was made under sail. After the voyage her engine was removed and thereafter she glided through the seas much as any other windjammer. On November 5, 1821, the *Savannah* ran aground on Fire Island and became a total loss. Many have sought to locate her aged ribs but none has succeeded. For a full account of this historic ship, read Frank Braynard's book *S.S. Savannah: the Elegant Steam Ship*.

The title of the volume in hand is overly inclusive. In order to maintain conformity with my Popular Dive Guide Series, which is intended to cover all major shipwrecks along the Atlantic seaboard, I have titled this book *Shipwrecks of New York*. More precisely it could be called "Shipwrecks of Long Island," for it does not include the western shores of New York State which border the Great Lakes of Erie and Ontario. Perhaps someday, when I run out of east coast wrecks, I will get around to recounting the adventures of those ships which wrecked in the world's Eighth Sea.

A note about wrecking companies. As you read this volume you will undoubtedly be confused by the variety of company names by which the salvage outfits went, depending upon chronology. What exists today as the Merritt-Chapman & Scott Salvage Corporation is a conglomerate of several different salvage companies which merged throughout the years. It all started in 1860 when Captain Israel J. Merritt founded the Coast Wrecking Company. He later changed this name to the Merritt Wrecking Company. In 1881, William E. Chapman formed the Chapman Derrick and Wrecking Company. In 1897 the two companies merged into the Merritt & Chapman Derrick & Wrecking Company, whose long and rather cumbersome name was often abbreviated by writers and reporters into any number of variations. Due to the large number of salvage jobs in the Long Island area, Captain Thomas A. Scott established his own company in 1903, with offices in Connecticut. In 1922, Scott joined Merritt & Chapman. Thus was born—or rather, reborn—Merritt, Chapman & Scott.

Now learn about the first tank ship ever built to carry petroleum in bulk, vessels from the Revolutionary War and both world wars, tall ships from the majestic days of sail, paddle wheelers, warships, merchant ships, tankers, freighters, and fishing vessels. They are all part of New York's rich maritime history as seen from the decks of ships which wrecked off Long Island's sandy shores.

Courtesy of Sharon Reese.

ACARA

Built: 1898
Previous names: None
Gross tonnage: 4,193
Type of vessel: Freighter
Builder: Palmer's Company, Ltd., Newcastle, England
Owner: James M. Wood
Port of registry: Liverpool, England
Cause of sinking: Ran aground
Location: 26800.9

Sunk: March 1, 1902
Depth: 25 feet
Dimensions: 380' x 47' x 29'
Power: Coal-fired steam

43750.8

Local divers and fisher folk know the *Acara* as the Tea Wreck, a name which has come down through history because her cargo consisted largely of Chinese leaves intended to flavor the hot water of American cups: perhaps not "all the tea in China," but at least 50,000 cases of it, enough to create quite a brouhaha in Jones Inlet at the time of the calamity.

"It was a dark and stormy night," as the saying goes, when the *Acara* approached New York on the final leg of a voyage that began months before in Oriental splendor. The recently constructed freighter was on a routine voyage from Shanghai and other Eastern ports, carrying not only tea and a small miscellaneous cargo, but ingots of tin. When she left Shanghai on December 27, 1901, Captain George Kilgour commanded a crew of fifty-nine hands; also aboard was the captain's wife. The *Acara* reached Bermuda on February 24, where she coaled, and left the following day.

"All went well till the 28th, when soundings were taken in 20 and 23 fathoms, but observations were imperfect owing to hazy weather. When observations were obtained at night by the Pole star, they threw the vessel out of her presumed position considerably, whereupon the captain decided to trust to his dead reckoning. At 1 15 a.m., a bell buoy was seen, whereon the captain, who had gone below shortly before, having been on deck since the early morning, came on deck and altered the vessel's course."

The wind was blowing strong from the south-southwest and the seas were running high. As so often happens when a vessel is navigated by dead reckoning, the reckoning was off. The *Acara* strayed from her intended course and stranded on the Jones Inlet Bars. The ship was hard aground, and no amount of backing could bring her off the sandy shoal. The engine strained in reverse to no avail. With waves crashing across the exposed deck, the crew wasted no time in launching lifeboats before the ship broke up in the battering surf.

Meanwhile, ashore, a lookout from the Short Beach Life-Saving Station noticed the wreck. The time was two a.m., the date March 1, 1902. The lookout raced back to the station and notified the keeper of the vessel's plight, starting a course of events which, before the long night was over, resulted in the saving of many lives. The station keeper "burned a Coston signal and telephoned to Zachs Inlet station for aid. The life-savers then started in the surfboat for the stranded ship. At outer point of beach they encountered the Zachs Inlet surfboat and three of her men shifted to the Short Beach boat, the heavy sea running making a strong crew imperative. The Short Beach boat, thus reenforced, then pulled to the *Acara*, and lay by for a favorable chance to board.

"Meantime two boats launched from the wreck, one containing forty-four, the other seventeen persons, started for the shore. The former, being a large lifeboat, weathered the seas and landed in safety, but a the latter, a smaller boat, capsized in the breakers. Of the seventeen men thus thrown out of her the Short Beach crew rescued thirteen, and the Point Lookout crew, just arrived on the scene, saved the remainder.

"The *Acara* being now abandoned, the life-savers devoted their attention to the care of the shipwrecked, many of whom were in a pitiable condition. Two of them required two hours of incessant work to insure their recovery. Shelter and relief were afforded at the station to the master, his wife, the first officer, and chief engineer, while the crew were carried to Fairport for transportation to New York. Several of the seamen were supplied with clothing, as was also the master's wife, from the stores of the Women's National Relief Association. The *Acara* was subsequently turned over to wreckers, and a portion of the cargo saved, the ship becoming a total wreck."

Thus the hardy members of the Life-Saving Service succinctly described their heroic efforts in the nighttime surf.

The *Acara* eventually broke up where she grounded. Since she hit the shoal head-on at full speed, the momentum drove her halfway over to the other side of the bar until only her middle was supported by the sandy spit. The bar acted as a fulcrum, and the weight of her cargo and machinery at the bow and stern became levers. The incredible stresses pried the hull apart like a dry twig snapped over a fire-starter's knee, and the wreck broke in two amidships. While this act of destruction was proceeding, however, wreckers did all they could to save the vessel and her valuable cargo of Celestial seasonings.

Lighters were brought alongside on March 3, after the storm moderated, so the process of offloading cargo from the holds could begin. However, strong winds and heavy seas prevented immediate salvage. The following day, a preliminary survey of the hull revealed that she was "broken from bridge to main deck and damaged on starboard side bottom, engine-room full of water, very difficult to board." By that afternoon the disintegration was accelerating rapidly. The wreckers telegraphed to the owners: "Engines shifted, both bridge main deck broken, plates badly buckled in wake brake, number one eighteen feet water, number four full, three dry; cannot sound two and five." Not only were the holds breached, but the hull was imbedded in fifteen feet of sand and the engine room was flooded.

Another communiqué gave more bad news in detail: "The vessel is broken high amidships and to-day water is pouring through the great cracks in her hull. The engine room is submerged and two of the water-tight compartments are reported to have given way. The Merritt Company is now working on cargo. Vessel and cargo insured. Nearly all the cargo in the hold of the steamer is damaged by the salt water and will be practically worthless." The wreckers were forced off the site by bad weather until the 6th; then, by working all night and long into the next day, they removed most of the cargo from the dry hold forward and conveyed it to New York aboard the barges *Richards* and *John W. Chittendon*, under tow of the tug *I.J. Merritt*. "None of the cargo in the after compartments could be saved, as water nearly twenty feet deep was washing through the big split in the vessel's hull amidships, flowing toward the stern, which was settled down to the level of the sea." By then the hull was cracked right down to the turn of the bilge on both sides abreast the boilers.

On March 10 it was reported that "Nearly all the tea, consisting of 30,000 chests, has been taken out, although some of it was damaged by the salt water, and yesterday the wreckers commenced to unload the rolls of matting stored between decks." By that time the after hatches had been washed off by the sea and the hull was completely severed and bent like a partially folded jackknife. The stern drooped down until the upper deck was awash.

On March 12 the Liverpool Salvage Association issued a progress report: "Tin in bottom of vessel, much cargo must be removed to recover. Merritt's now working, no cure no pay, settlement when finished." And on March 13: "Cargo landed sound about 20,000 chests tea, 2,500 packages (or cases) matting, 4,000 packages (or cases) general . . . Remainder cargo reported submerged. Ship still opening."

Courtesy of Sharon Reese.

Despite the condition of the wreck, which now lay in two separate parts, Merritt's still hoped for total hull salvage: "The portions of the vessel will be towed to New York and then to a shipyard." Alas, this was never to be. Lightering went on till the middle of April, when it was reported that the "Tug *Wm F Cooley* with barge *Henry Seymour*, laden with part of cargo of steamer *Acara* (Br), arrived at New York on April 16." By that time a considerable amount of the cargo had been removed, although not all of it was salvageable. Wet tea is, after all, used tea, and not recyclable. Perhaps the loss of the *Acara* gave someone the idea of the flow-through tea bag.

The Board of Trade held an inquiry on April 22 and 23, in Liverpool, England. Charged with accountability for the *Acara's* loss were Captain Kilgour and second officer William James Freer, who was on the bridge at the time of the grounding. "The Court, in delivering judgment, found that the stranding and loss of the vessel were due to the careless navigation of her by her master, George Kilgour, whose certificate the Court suspended for a period of six months. . . . The lead was not used after 8 p.m. on February 28 last, and the omission to use it was, in the opinion of the Court, a grave one. . . . The master totally ignored the results of the Pole star observations and made no attempt whatever to verify them; in fact, he went off the bridge to the chart-house very shortly after the first one was obtained, leaving the second officer in charge, but without telling him that the course being steered was leading direct on to the land, or giving him any instructions, except as to being called in case of change of weather."

According to the court records, Captain Kilgour assumed full responsibility during the hearing, "and would have been given a longer suspension had he not been completely honest in his testimony."

Over the years the *Acara's* decks and hull plates were pounded into an indescribable pile of bent and twisted steel, while her once-straight beams were converted into pretzel-like art forms. For more than half a century the wreck lay in quiet repose, the slow collapse given spurts of disintegration during winter gales. The wreckage provided living quarters for a multitude of fish, crabs, and lobster. Unlike many other sunken hulls, the *Acara* was not forgotten, largely because her remains were, and still are, visible above the surface. At extreme low tide pieces protrude through the troughs when the waves run high; at high tide the current creates swirls over her grave site. Thus the wreck is easily found by anglers who desire to make their catch close to shore, and by divers searching for souvenirs and the occasional ingot of tin.

In the 1960's the *Acara* became the subject of a lawsuit. The case was heard in Federal Court in the Eastern District of New York, and the final decision was rendered in May 1967. The circumstances of the case were summarized in the court records. According to stipulations in the case, Robert Rickard dived the *Acara* in 1962 and found the massive bronze propeller intact and still secured to its shaft. This is unusual in that bronze propellers found in much deeper water enjoy a relatively a short life span: not because the metal decomposes in the ocean environment (in fact, bronze is particularly resistant to salt water corrosion, which is why it is employed with such profusion in ocean-going vessels) but because commercial salvors consider them to be easy pickings, and have long since raised them and sold them for scrap. Marine bronze is a valuable alloy and brings high prices at the scrap yards and foundries. Rickard, however, entertained far loftier goals than reducing the ancient propeller to a molten state in a crucible or melting pot. He thought it was far more valuable as an antique whose worth lay in its historic significance.

By scraping off the encrustation, Rickard found the inscription "Manufactured by Stones Bronze Company of London, England." Through research he learned that the manufacturer's successor company was still in operation, under the name J. Stone Company (Propellers) Ltd. When he contacted the British company and reported his find, the company professed a strong interest in acquiring the propeller for its heritage value, both as an example of the company's early products and as proof of its long-lasting workmanship. Thus the propeller, if Rickard could salvage it, could become a monument to the achievement of nineteenth century metallurgy, rather than a puddle of bronze to be recast in new form.

That autumn Rickard began salvage operations, and throughout the winter of 1962-1963 and the following spring, he worked incessantly. He buoyed the wreck both bow and stern, then "purchased special machinery, equipment and supplies" to the tune of nearly $2,000 "for the specific purpose of removing" the propeller. After he finally "succeeded in detaching and removing" the propeller from the shaft, he "departed from the scene of said salvage operation to make arrangements to engage machinery for the purpose of lifting to the surface and transporting the blades of the propellor which were of great size and weight."

It was at this time, with the task nearly completed and with all the hard work done, that Rickard's ten-months effort was nearly lost. To quote the court records, "Jay E. Porter, in the month of July, 1963, with full knowledge that Libellant was engaged in said salvage operation as aforesaid, transported the respondents, Allan Boehm, Ronald Pringle and Carl Helwig on board the vessel, *Jess Lu III* to the scene of the said salvage operation, and said respondents, with full knowledge that the Libellant was temporarily absent from the said scene, dragged part of the propellor by means of a winch on board said vessel, *Jess Lu III*, along the bottom of the water to Freeport, New York, and appropriated the same to their own use and possession.

"With full knowledge that the Libellant had salvaged the said propellor from the derelict, *Acara*, and was engaged in the salvage work thereon, and that the said Libellant had not abandoned the salvage operation, all of the respondents acted in concert to remove, and did remove part of the said propellor, dispose of, sell the same and divided the proceeds from the said sale, and in fact did remove, dispose of, sell and divide among themselves the proceeds from the sale of part of the said propellor for its mere metal content."

District Judge Matthew T. Abruzzo found that the "defendants wrongfully interfered with the plaintiff-salvor's possession of the propeller of the *Acara* and have no rights in the said propeller." Judge Abruzzo elaborated, "A strong inference can readily be drawn from the facts stated in the Complaint that the

Defendants' conduct indicated that they must have been watchful of the Plaintiff's efforts, for they readily pounced upon this propeller at a time when they saw that the plaintiff had temporarily departed from his salvage operation. It wasn't coincidental that the Defendants were at the site where the Plaintiff was working on this wreck, at the time that they moved in with their boat and attached lines to the propeller and dragged it to Freeport, since when they started to drag the propeller they could see from the buoys that someone had been working there."

The judge further wrote that the "Plaintiff is clearly entitled to a decree in his favor." The litigants agreed to settle the amount of the award out of court, so it was not entered in court documents. However, the judge duly noted, "Public policy is to encourage volunteers in the salvage of derelict, abandoned or distressed property. For this reason salvage awards in generous amounts have traditionally been given to successful salvors. . . . Salvage awards are not intended merely as compensation for work and labor performed. Public policy intends them as rewards in the nature of a bounty to encourage voluntary services by seamen and others to save imperiled lives, ships and their cargoes."

Active work ceased after the removal of the propeller so that, according to the centuries-old law of salvage, the *Acara* subsequently lapsed back to a condition of abandonment. However, before you decide to dredge away the sand in order to expose and recover the remaining tin ingots, you should know that with the passage of the Abandoned Shipwreck Act of 1987, whose authority extends to the territorial limits of the United States (three miles offshore), the *Acara* was nationalized in the guise of historic preservation. Although the State of New York has enacted no local legislation with respect to the Abandoned Shipwreck Act, ownership has now technically been taken over by the government. Your tax dollars at work.

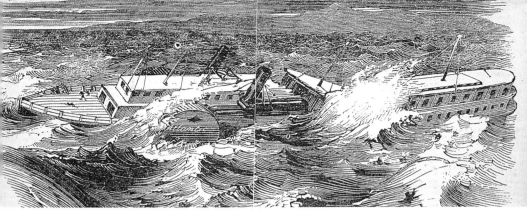

From *The Illustrated London News.*

ATLANTIC

Built: 1846
Previous names: None
Gross tonnage: 1,112
Type of vessel: Side wheel excursion steamer
Builder: Bishop & Simonson, New York, NY
Owner: Norwich & New London Steam Boat Company
Port of registry: New London, Connecticut
Cause of sinking: Boiler explosion

Sunk: November 26, 1846
Depth: Unknown
Dimensions: 320' x 36' x 12'
Power: Coal-fired steam

Location: Fisher's Island

The *Atlantic* is one of those ships whose dramatic loss was only briefly related when it occurred, and whose history has since been submerged in anonymity. Yet at the time of the occurrence it was a grave and heartfelt event because forty-two people lost their lives. The year was 1846, six years after the awful tragedy of the *Lexington* (q.v.).

The *Atlantic* was a paddle wheel steamer designed to provide passenger service between New York City and New England. She was needed to serve as an important link in the transportation chain to Massachusetts by ferrying people through the Long Island Sound to and from Providence, Rhode Island, which was connected by railroad to Boston. Her hull was built by Bishop & Simonson; her 600 horsepower engine was built by T.F. Secor at the Novelty Works.

The following notice appeared in the May 8, 1846 issue of the *New York Tribune*: "The new steamer *Atlantic* will be launched tomorrow morning at 8 o'clock, from the ship yard of Bishop & Sons, foot of Sixth-st., East River. If it is a fine day (which we most devoutly hope for,) there will be thousands to witness the spectacle. It is true that launching fine vessels is a matter of every day occurrence in New York, but the *Atlantic* is one of the noblest of her class and it is worth a visit to see her take the water."

The vessel was fitted out during the next three months. She began service on August 18, 1846, but her short career ended after running for only three months.

At midnight of November 25, the *Atlantic* left Providence in the teeth of a winter storm which had already disrupted rail service. High winds caused the snow to accumulate in deep drifts on the tracks. Thus the steamboat's staterooms were packed with passengers who might otherwise have taken the train all the way to New York. After traversing Narragansett Bay she rounded Point Judith, then hugged the north shore of Block Island Sound and passed between Fisher's Island and Connecticut, whereupon she pulled into New London to take on additional passengers. "The snow fell thick and fast, and stuck as it fell."

She left New London at about one o'clock in the morning, slipped down the Thames, and turned west. "The weather was now very rough, the sea running high, but the wind was still north-east, and therefore right aft, so that the speed of the boat enabled her to run ahead of the sea and make good weather of it."

The *Atlantic* got only nine miles from the mouth of the Thames when there occurred the awful calamity which was so common in the early days of steam propulsion: the boiler exploded; more specifically, "the steam-pipe running into the steam-chest burst."

The explosion of compressed steam was so violent that it completely wrecked the boiler and nearby machinery, and blew out the adjacent side of the hull. Escaping steam scalded numerous crew members and passengers, particularly men on duty in the boiler and engine rooms, and passengers in staterooms immediately above. Ships in those days were lighted meagerly by candles and gas lanterns, and all these were extinguished by the whoosh of air, plunging the vessel into an abysmal darkness from which rose shrieks and cries of pain of the injured vying to be heard above the raging tempest outside. Some passengers were crushed when the cabins they occupied tumbled into the void opened by the collapsing deck. The dead and dying lay amid the ruin of splintered timbers.

Without motive power or forward momentum, the *Atlantic* was slowly shoved aside by the wind and the following sea until she broached to. The hull wallowed sideways in the troughs of tremendous waves, and water cascaded over the sides and washed relentlessly across the upper deck and down into the exposed holds and bilges. "The wind changed almost instantaneously to N.W., placing the powerless steamer in the vortex of the storm." The anchors were dropped overboard and, once they grabbed the bottom, helped to swing the ship around so her head faced the oncoming seas. In such uncertainty the *Atlantic* rode out the night.

There was no medical attention for the injured, and no way to reach many of those who lay screaming in the wreckage of the darkened decks below. Death offered the only surcease from searing torment.

Dawn found the anchors dragging. The *Atlantic* was then five miles from Fisher's Island, with the strong winds blowing the hulk toward the island's western shore. "Two steamers, the *New Haven* and the *Mohegan*, made ineffectual attempts to get to her assistance, but the high sea prevented their approach." What is stated in a few words took all day to take place. By sundown the *Atlantic* lay within six hundred feet from shore, still dragging inexorably toward the rocks. There seemed no way to prevent further catastrophe. Yet she clung to her precarious position until midnight, when her anchors again began to drag.

At 4:30 in the morning, November 26, the steamboat's stern struck a submerged reef some two hundred feet from the water's edge, where jutting rocks protruded above the tumultuous surface of the sea. At the time, passenger Captain Hanna stood upon the upper saloon with the *Atlantic's* master, Captain Isaac Dustan. Hanna quoted the captain as saying "She has gone" when the hull grated against the granite bottom.

The after half of the ship smashed against the rocks with such severity that the hull was bilged and the holds were flooded. The great ship listed awkwardly. Many of the remaining survivors were knocked off their feet; then, huge waves stove in the upper decks and swept people helplessly off the ship and against the rocks, where they were battered to death or drowned.

Captain Hanna raced toward the bow not a moment too soon. The *Atlantic* split in two just abaft the boiler room. Hanna lowered himself into the water and "was thrown by the sea over the reef, and among the rocks on shore. He managed to scramble up on to the beach. He was considerably bruised, and suffered much from cold." He thought he was the only survivor among those who had gathered on the upper saloon deck to await their fates, for the *Atlantic*, once pierced by the rocks, immediately went to pieces until very little remained above the surface. It was later reported, perhaps with too great a touch of dramatic license, that "the sole relic of the ill-fated vessel on the following day was one upright beam, upon which hung a bell tolled by the sea."

About thirty people managed to reach the safety of shore. The number who found eternal peace was estimated to be between forty-two and forty-five.

Because boiler explosions were so prevalent and the cause of so many fatalities, the loss of the *Atlantic* became another hardened statistic which forced Congressional investigation into the matter. The Commissioner of Patents solicited inventors for ways of preventing such explosions, and the second session of the 30th Congress, in 1848, reported accumulated findings and discussed legislation for regulating steamboat inspections and for providing passengers with greater safety at sea. This has come down in the form of the Steamboat Inspection Service and, ultimately, the vessel inspections required and conducted by the U.S. Coast Guard.

Although the story of the *Atlantic's* bell being tolled by the sea comes across as a droll reporter's dramatic license, it is likely not far from the truth, for another reporter wrote that he heard the bell "tolling a solemn requiem for the souls lost as the waves dashed against the wrecked ship." As late as 1944 the bell hung "over the main entrance to the Seaman's Church Institute at 25 South Street, N.Y. city and rings the half hours in ship's time. . . . For 98 years . . . the *Atlantic's* bell has summoned seamen to worship, having been hung after the wreck in the belfry of the Floating Church of the Holy Comforter for sailors, the Institute's second floating church, later transferred in 1883 to the chapel at the Institute's North River Station and taken to its present place in 1927."

Ask not for whom the bell tolls. It tolls for thee and for those who perished on the excursion steamer *Atlantic* in 1846.

Entering Havana Harbor. (Courtesy of the Peabody Essex Museum.)

BLACK WARRIOR

Built: 1852
Previous names: None
Gross tonnage: 1,556
Type of vessel: Side wheel steamer
Builder: William Collyer, New York, New York
Owner: Livingston, Crocheron & Company
Port of registry: New York, NY
Cause of sinking: Ran aground
Location: 26951.8

Sunk: February 20, 1859
Depth: 35 feet
Dimensions: 225' x 37' x 18'
Power: Coal-fired steam

43755.3

The *Black Warrior* was a large and innovative ship for her time. She had a wooden hull and bore three masts, and was adequately powered by a vertical beam engine with a single 65-inch cylinder whose stroke was eleven feet. Each of her paddle wheels was thirty-two feet in diameter—as tall as a three story building—and could churn the water at a prodigious rate. She cost $200,000 to build, one quarter of which was spent on cabins and furniture for the comfort of the passengers.

When she first entered service she was owned by the New York and Alabama Steamship Company (which itself was owned by Livingston, Crocheron & Company), which also owned her running mate, the *Cahawba*. The two ships ran regular service between New York and Mobile, Alabama, with stopovers in Havana, Cuba.

Some ships get into the news more than others. It was in 1854, on February 28, when the *Black Warrior* first ran into trouble that seemed to plague her short career. What became known as "the *Black Warrior* incident" was only one of a long list of political insults which hampered diplomatic relations between the U.S. and Spain for more than a century, and which finally culminated in war. On that day the *Black Warrior* made her usual stop in Havana for coal. As was customary, her agents cleared her for customs the day prior to her arrival so she could depart as soon as her bunkers were full. In her holds were 960 bales of cotton destined for consignees in New York, plus $34,000 in specie and "a quantity of merchandise in boxes." None of the cargo was intended to be offloaded in Havana. The port was used simply a coaling station. Therefore, for customs clearing purposes, the vessel was listed as being "in ballast," meaning that she had no cargo, which under these circumstances meant that she had no cargo for Havana, the way station, and that any cargo on board was in transit and intended for another port of call. This was not a new procedure, but one which had been established for years, and which had been considered proper on the *Black Warrior's* thirty-six prior visits to Havana.

It was also customary for the suspicious Spaniards in Cuba to place on board all arriving vessels "two custom-house guards and an unlimited number of policemen, public and secret, . . . to watch every passenger or package on the ship." This time, however, the Spaniards laid a neat trap for the *Black Warrior*. After requesting to see the holds and observing the cotton, they declared that local law had been violated. The *Black Warrior* was seized, the cotton was confiscated, and Captain James Bullock, master, was fined an amount double the value of the cotton. This despite the fact that the *Black Warrior* could not possibly have offloaded any of the cargo as she was moored at the coaling wharf.

Captain Bullock protested, of course, but to no avail. He appealed to the U.S. consulate, William Robertson, who immediately went to see the Captain General of the island in order to rectify the situation. At the same time, Charles Tyng, the local agent for the *Black Warrior*, hurried to the custom house in order to take advantage of the clause which allowed twelve hours for alterations to be made on a vessel's manifest; but this he was not permitted to do. Nor did Robertson meet with any success with the Captain General.

Matters quickly came to a head. As Robertson explained in a dispatch to Secretary of State William Marcy, in Washington, the Spaniards detailed a work party to remove the cotton. "The officer at the head of the party demanded of the captain the delivery of the cargo, which Captain Bullock declined, remarking to the officer that if he took by force, as he must do, one single bale of the cargo, he, the captain, would instantly haul down his colors and abandon his ship to them. This seemed to make the officer hesitate. He suspended his operation and came on shore, no doubt to lay the facts before his superiors and receive their directions. He soon returned on board, opened the hatches and commenced the discharge; whereupon Captain Bullock hauled down his flag, and, with his officers and crew, abandoned the vessel to the Spanish authorities." Robertson agreed that the course which Captain Bullock took was the only dignified and proper one.

The fourteen passengers also disembarked, with their luggage. All passengers and crew departed Havana on March 2 aboard the U.S. steamer *Fulton*. Captain Bullock left on the U.S. coastal survey steamer *Corwin* along with official dispatches.

Lest the seizure of the *Black Warrior* appear as an isolated event rather than a consistent program of insults instituted by Spain against foreign shipping, and particularly against American shipping, consider the letter of protest submitted to Secretary of State Marcy by Livingston, Crocheron & Company. "The company also complain, that, in the month of February, 1853, soon after leaving Havana, a Spanish brig-of-war ran down upon the *Black Warrior*, fired a gun, and instantly, without allowing time to hoist the United States ensign, fired a shot directly at the steamer, which passed within a few inches of the fore-stay, and then, without apology or explanation, bore away and left the steamer." This was in addition to an occasion in 1852 and another in 1853, where the company was forced to pay tonnage dues, "in defiance of all law and usage," in excess of $5,000. "The company beg leave to represent, that they have suffered great loss from the seizure, to the amount of at least *three hundred thousand dollars*—the cargo in the ship being estimated at *one hundred thousand dollars*, the ship at *two hundred thousand dollars*, besides which they have lost their entire business, which will be worth to them at least *fifty thousand dollars*, during the time that they are deprived of the use of their ship; that they will be debarred from trading with the island of Cuba, which is open to the vessels of all other nations, and that such trade is worth to them a large amount of money; that they now place themselves under the protection of the United States, and, by the right of every American, demand that their government insist upon a redress of these injuries, and insure them a full restoration of their property, with sufficient damages for the several outrages committed upon them; that they claim the sum of *three hundred thousand dollars* as their lawful right, for loss of business, property, and for detention in the harbor of Havana."

On March 14, 1854, the President of the United States, Franklin Pierce, addressed the House of Representatives about the seizure of the *Black Warrior*. He said, in part, "There have been, in the course of a few years past, many other instances of aggression upon our commerce, violations of the rights of American citizens, and insults to the national flag, by the Spanish authorities in Cuba, and all attempts to obtain redress have led to protracted, and, as yet, fruitless negotiations. The documents in these cases are voluminous, and, when prepared, will be sent to Congress. Those now transmitted relate exclusively to the seizure of the *Black Warrior*, and present so clear a case of wrong, that it would be reasonable to expect full indemnity therefor, as soon as this unjustifiable and offensive conduct shall be made known to her Catholic Majesty's government; but similar expectations, in other cases, have not been realized. The offending party is at our doors, with large powers for aggression, but none, it is alleged, for reparation. The source of redress is in another hemisphere; and the answers to our just complaints, made to the home government, are but the repetition of excuses rendered by inferior officials to their superiors, in reply to representations of misconduct."

Pierce was obviously incensed with Spain's longtime protocol of insults, for he finished his address with a suggestion of waging war. "In view of the position of the island of Cuba, its proximity to our coast, the relations which it must ever bear to our commercial and other interests, it is vain to expect that a series of unfriendly acts infringing our commercial rights, and the adoption of a policy threatening the honor and security of these States, can long consist with peaceful relations. In case the measures taken for amicable adjustment of our difficulties with Spain should unfortunately fail, I shall not hesitate to use the authority and means which Congress may grant, to insure the observance of our just rights, to obtain redress for injuries received, and to vindicate the honor of our flag. In anticipation of that contingency, which I earnestly hope may not arise, I suggest to Congress the propriety of adopting such provisional measures as the exigency may seem to demand."

As Erik Heyl summed up the aftermath, "The American Secretary of State mailed a sharply worded protest to the Spanish government in Madrid which did not sit well. In fact, the American note only aggravated the situation as the Spanish Court had been considerably irritated by the appointment of Pierre Soule as Minister to Spain because of co-sponsorship of the Ostend Manifesto demanding that Spain voluntarily sell Cuba to the United States or else the island would be 'forcibly detached'. The dispute became acrimonious and was not settled until after Soule's return home, when calmer counsels prevailed. Spain not only repaid the fine but also an additional $53,000—compensation for the detention of the *Black Warrior*." And you thought that only today's bureaucrats were troublemakers!

In 1856, service to Mobile ceased, and New Orleans became the turnaround port in its place, at which time the shipping line's name was changed to the New York and New Orleans Steamship Company. Livingston, Crocheron & Company remained the parent company.

Courtesy of the Long Island Maritime Museum.

The *Black Warrior* was nearly lost in January 1857, during a passage from Havana to New York. Three days of northerly travel found her in the vicinity of the Virginia Capes with nothing untoward to report. Then she ran into a gale "which caused the steamer to pitch and roll with great violence. . . . A succession of violent snow-squalls followed, so that they could not see the ship's length in any direction. Ice was making all over the vessel."

Because it proved impossible to keep the ship's head to the sea, a drogue or sea anchor was fashioned "by lashing the topmast and topsail-yard together, with a six-pounder cannon and 600 pounds of grate bars attached to sink them, which was paid out at the end of sixty fathoms of hawser. Although this was found of some service, it was not sufficient to prevent the steamer from falling off into the trough of the sea, where she labored heavily, the sea occasionally breaking with tremendous force over her. The fore-topmast backstay parted, and the head of the foremast, with topmast, top-sail-yard and fore-yard, went by the board, carrying with them the main-topmast. The mizzen-mast is but a slight spar, and remained standing. A heavy sea boarded her forward, smashing their yawl-boat to a thousand pieces, and carrying two other metallic boats away from the after davits."

The sails were blown to ribbons so that what remained of the masts were bare poles. The port wheel house was carried away, "and everything movable washed off the forward deck; the vessel was also so badly loaded up with ice that it was impossible to get about." When they ran out of coal to fire the boilers, "the spars, and all the woodwork of the forward state-rooms were cut up for fuel—the cargo was broken out to get at the dunnage—large quantities of orange-boxes were emptied of their contents; in fine, everything that would burn, and could be spared from the interior woodwork of the ship was cut up and used in generating steam. . . . all hands, including passengers being kept constantly plying their axes to everything within reach to supply fuel."

A day and a half passed before the storm blew itself out. When the weather cleared, the *Black Warrior* lay wallowing in the Gulf Stream one hundred miles from shore, although Captain J.W. Smith, master, did not know the distance until he steered westward and sighted land at Nag's Head, North Carolina many hours later. He turned the ship to the north, "making the best possible use of every combustible article on board. When the ship finally reached the mouth of the Chesapeake "the engine, like a tired giant, gave up the contest and stopped, every splinter of fuel having been consumed; the anchors were let go, and during the forenoon the propellor *Piedmont* came alongside and towed them up to Point Comfort, where they anchored near Fort Monroe. The passengers, during this protracted scene of suffering and danger, bore themselves most creditably. The women passengers also—of whom there were several on board—manifesting great courage and fortitude during the trying ordeal. When the anchors were well down, and the vessel and her passengers were once more safe, there was a general scrambling for the bunks and a good long watch below."

This I can readily believe, as the ordeal of the *Black Warrior* reminds me of a few dive trips I have made.

"During the gale, and until the vessel was at her anchors, Capt. Smith was constantly at his post, never leaving the deck, or scarcely changing his clothes. Most of the officers and crew were more or less frost-bitten." Nor were their troubles over. "The officers at Fort Monroe generously contributed from their own private stores several tons each of coal, which, with what they were able to purchase, gave them sufficient to make the trip to New York."

Extreme cold and strong winds tormented the *Black Warrior* during the three days she was laid up off Fort Monroe, waiting for coal. During that time she dragged at her anchors due to the amount of ice flowing down Hampton Roads, and went aground on the Rip Raps. After finally getting under way, she "encountered immense fields of heavy ice all the way from Cape Henry to Barnegat," New Jersey.

It goes without saying that when the *Black Warrior* arrived in New York she required a complete refit. Her interior was totally gutted because the partitions between staterooms had gone to feed the fires. She had to be refurbished throughout. She needed new masts, sails, and rigging. She needed boats, deck houses, hatches, and skylights. When the overhaul was complete, the *Black Warrior* was a brand new ship.

Captain Smith was still in command of the *Black Warrior* when she met her premature end on Rockaway Bar, as she was negotiating the passage into New York harbor. On the morning of February 20, 1859 she was proceeding slowly through calm seas and dense fog, with a harbor pilot at the helm, when she gently ground to a halt on the sandy shoal. There was no panic aboard as the ship did not seem to be in dire straits. Wrecking tugs were called to pull the steamer off the bar but, strain as they might, the *Screamer* and the *Achilles* were unequal to the task. The *Black Warrior* had gone aground at the worst possible time of the day—high tide.

The passengers, at least, were not too long inconvenienced; the *Screamer* took them and their baggage off the *Black Warrior* and carried them ashore. Also aboard the *Screamer* were all nonessential crew members, and $208,000 in gold Mexican dollars which were consigned to four local companies. Elsewhere it was reported that the passengers were brought ashore in the pilot boat *Edwin Blunt*.

All might have ended well had not foul weather complicated salvage operations. With her bow swung to eastward and ten feet of water in her hold, the *Black Warrior* was in a bad way. Soon the full fury of a winter storm was upon the ship. Westerly gales beat against her stern, and huge combers rolled completely across her exposed deck. All day long on the twenty-first the ship was pounded unmercifully. The New York Times reported with prescience, "Captain Boune, the underwriter's agent, was on board, making every exertion with the aid of a strong party of wreckers to save the vessel, but with small hopes of success unless very favorable weather should intervene. Wrecking steamers were on hand to take out the coal as soon as it should be found possible to go alongside. The probability is that she will not come off, as she went on at the top of a high easterly tide, and she was steadily sinking into the sand. The prevalence of the westerly gales of the last forty-eight hours have caused lower tides than have been known for several months, which render it almost certain that the steamer will leave her bones on the spot where she now lies. In that event her machinery will probably be saved, as no time will be lost in getting that out, as soon as it is ascertained that she is a hopeless case."

The ship stayed, and the wreckers must have been successful as no sign of the massive engine is evident among the wreckage. A single boiler, half buried in the mud, presents the highest point of relief. Otherwise, the wreck consists of flattened low-lying debris, encrusted timbers (some with brass fastening spikes protruding), a section of the keel still sheathed in copper, part of a mast (pointing north, toward shore), and the remains of one of the paddle wheels. Despite the evident lack of interest, the *Black Warrior* is a good digging wreck. For the diver willing to fan away the sand the rewards may be commensurate with the time invested, as occasionally small brass objects such as brass sheathing nails, padlocks, and door latches are found, and rarely, a utensil with the ship's name engraved on the handle. The best time to dive is during slack tide, since otherwise a fast rip might make exploration difficult.

The sand continually shifts on the wreck, so it can in no way be said to be "picked over." Winter storms often disturb the bottom, and may wash away a foot or more of sand, thus exposing objects never seen before. This occurred in 1994, when the wreck's 1,500 pound anchor was suddenly exposed. A salvage operation conducted by Dan Berg recovered the anchor successfully by raising it with two 2,000-pound liftbags and towing the entire arrangement to shore.

Ocean pout.

As a sub chaser during World War Two. (Courtesy of the Naval Historical Center.)

BRONX QUEEN

Built: 1942
Previous names: *SC-635*, *Air Eider*, *Yank*
Gross tonnage: 99
Type of vessel: Wooden hulled fishing boat
Builder: Mathis Yacht Building Company, Camden, New Jersey
Owner: EDJAC Fishing & Enterprises, Bronx, NY
Port of registry: New York, NY
Cause of sinking: Foundered
Location: 26968.8

Sunk: December 2, 1989
Depth: 35 feet
Dimensions: 107' x 18' x 14'
Power: Twin diesel engines

43735.1

The *Bronx Queen* was originally built for the U.S. Navy as a submarine chaser, one of more than a thousand of a class of 110-footers which patrolled the east coast during the dark days of World War Two when German U-boats lurked under every wave and sank Allied and neutral ships indiscriminately and without warning. Sub chasers were so numerous that they were not given names, so when she was commissioned—on October 23, 1942—she received the official designation *SC-635*. Armed with guns and depth charges, she served in her capacity as sub chaser and escort vessel until the end of the war.

With peace temporarily in the offing, the Navy was left with a vast fleet of surplus auxiliaries for which it had no immediate need. Many smaller craft were sold off: some to foreign countries, some for commercial enterprise, some for scrapping. The *SC-635* was transferred to the U.S. Coast Guard and renamed *Air Eider*. The Coast Guard kept her for little more than a year. She was decommissioned on January 20, 1947, stripped of her armament, and sold civilian, on September 30 that same year. She was renamed the *Yank* by her new owner, Harry Tonks.

In 1952, ownership of the *Yank* passed to a company eponymously named M.V. Yank. In 1956, she was owned by the Land & Sea Service Company. Finally, on November 6, 1956, she was registered as the *Bronx Queen* under a company name which evolved gradually and which eventually was recorded in Coast Guard records as the EDJAC Fishing & Enterprises.

For the next thirty-three years the *Bronx Queen* ran fishing excursions from New York harbor, operating as what is commonly called a "head boat." People wishing to go out for a relaxing day of fishing would arrive at the dock prior to the established time of departure, pay a "head" fee, and walk on the boat with their rods and reels and perhaps a cooler holding a six-pack or two. For more than a generation the *Bronx Queen* was a well known and much respected member of New York's fishing fleet, during which time hundreds of thousands of people stood out to sea on her deck for a much needed break from the workaday city routine.

Sub chasers were constructed much stronger than their better known and smaller cousins, the plywood PT boats. Oak frames were laid on with planks of yellow pine two and a half inches thick. The hull was segregated into eight watertight compartments, each separated by steel bulkheads which extended to the main deck. Modifications were made when she was converted to a head boat, with particular attention paid to cutting down her lazarette (the aftermost compartment) in order to reduce her tonnage from 115 to 99, probably because an ocean operator's license required to operate a vessel which grosses 100 tons and over is more difficult to obtain than a license to operate a vessel which grosses less than 100 tons.

Despite these alterations, the integrity of the watertight compartments remained. Furthermore, since the *Bronx Queen* was licensed to carry 121 passengers she had the requisite number of life preservers plus four life rafts which could accommodate a total of sixty-eight people. The vessel was inspected regularly by the Coast Guard, and recommended repairs were always completed to the satisfaction of the inspectors. Even though the *Bronx Queen* was an old boat, she was considered safe enough to carry passengers on daily trips outside the harbor.

December 2, 1989 dawned much like any other. The sky was slightly overcast, the wind was mild, and the air was crisp, with the temperature hovering around the freezing point. The *Bronx Queen* pulled out of her dock in the Bronx at 8:30 in the morning. On board were nineteen people: 26-year-old Captain Jack Chale, crewmen Elliot Lopez and James Frierson, cook and concessionaire Greta Fowle, her son, one guest, and thirteen paying customers. The *Bronx Queen's* route took her down the East River, under the Verrazano-Narrows Bridge, and out the Ambrose Channel to the vicinity of the Scotland Buoy, where she anchored in sixty feet of water. Wave heights in the harbor were about one foot, but offshore they tended toward ten feet. The water temperature was 38° F.

Breakfast was served on the way out, then lunch was made available from 11 o'clock on.

Nothing untoward occurred during the day. The passengers fished, the concessionaire dispensed food and drink, and the crewmen helped the customers by supplying bait and by replacing lost rigs. The captain remained in the wheel house, and several times he moved the boat to a different spot. The fishing continued until 3 o'clock in the afternoon, by which time the wind was picking up and spray was washing across the deck. One passenger donned rain gear to keep dry. Then the anchor was weighed and the *Bronx Queen* headed for home.

Just outside the Ambrose Channel there came what was described as a loud "thump" near the stern of the vessel. Captain Chale called crewman Elliot Lopez on the public address system and asked him to come to the wheel house, whereupon Chale directed Lopez to check out the stern. Lopez did as instructed and found two feet of water in the lazarette compartment; he went to the engine room, turned on the pump, then reported the situation to the captain. Minor leaks are not unusual, so Chale instructed Lopez to keep an eye on the water level, and the *Bronx Queen* continued on as planned.

Shortly thereafter, Lopez saw that the water had risen despite the action of the pump, so he turned on a second pump. Even with two pumps going the compartment was not dewatering as it should. Lopez reported again to the captain, who turned over the helm to Lopez while he went to investigate for himself. By this time the water had risen to a depth of four feet. Chale wasted no time now. He ordered the passengers to don life preservers and he called the Coast Guard on the radio to report his predicament. The situation became desperate with the telescoping speed that often accompanies such dire events.

A following sea with wave heights from seven to ten feet pounded the vessel's stern fiercely. Then an outbound freighter on a parallel but opposite course drove a wake which, combined with the high seas, created a very large wave which "struck the starboard stern quarter of the M/V *Bronx Queen* and broke onto its after deck. A huge wall of water swept forward with such force that it "tore loose benches and the large bait tank on the after deck." The bait tank smashed "into the dog house entrance to the after cabin destroying the doors. Following this wave, subsequent waves came onto the deck of the vessel and the stern of the vessel appeared to the master to be rapidly settling." Fortunately, all the passengers were in the main cabin at the time the great wave struck, else they would have been seriously injured or washed overboard. Crewmen directed the passengers to leave the cabin and make their way to the bow.

Captain Chale recognized the seriousness of the situation. He threw the helm to starboard and cut across Ambrose Channel in an attempt to reach the closest point of land—Breezy Point—where he could beach the foundering fishing vessel. "At that time both engines continued to run but appeared to be laboring under a load." Just as the *Bronx Queen* exited the channel "the vessel lost all power."

Help was already on the way. The Coast Guard dispatched three vessels: two 41-foot utility boats and one 44-foot motor surf boat. In addition, the pilot ship *New Jersey* picked up the distress call and responded immediately by heading for the *Bronx Queen's* radioed position. Less than fifteen minutes passed from the time the Coast Guard received Captain Chale's urgent request for help and the time the first cutter arrived on site. By that time the *Bronx Queen* was down by the stern with only forty feet of the bow remaining above the surface. Considering that the depth of water was only thirty-five feet, it is likely that the stern was already resting on the bottom and that air trapped in the forward compartments was keeping the bow afloat.

Crowded on that small section of dry deck were the passengers and crew, except for Captain Chale, who "remained at the entrance to the wheelhouse talking to the Coast Guard over the radio." The ocean was full of debris which was washing off the after deck, and the prevailing wind carried it toward the bow of the *Bronx Queen*. The coxswain of *CG41382* "determined that the waves and debris would make it extremely hazardous to bring the *CG41382* right up to the sinking vessel. The debris was identified as hoses, life preservers, large coolers, large boxes and lots of wood."

The *CG41382* approached to within forty feet of the fishing vessel, which was as close as she could get without fear of damaging her hull or fouling her propeller, and one of her crew "yelled over to the *Bronx Queen* that they would have to go into the water." The crew of the Coast Guard cutter decided "to send a line over to the sinking vessel and ferry the people to the *CG41382* through the water one at a time."

According to the Coast Guard investigation, "The people from the sinking vessel started slipping into the water one at a time. The master made one last radio transmission to the Coast Guard and then made his way to the bow to assist the passengers into the water. When the master arrived on the bow, a couple of the passengers had entered the water. All seemed calm and the people were entering the water one by one, some being assisted. After assisting some of the people, the master put both buoyant apparatus that were stored on the bow into the water for the people to hang onto.

"As the people were being assisted into the water, the master determined that one of the passengers, Raymond Kupczynski, would require assistance. He had an artificial arm and was unable to swim. The master told James Frierson to enter the water with Raymond Kupczynski and to assist him. James Frierson entered the water with Raymond Kupczynski and attempted to assist him. Almost immediately, James Frierson was struck in the face by a wave and became separated from Raymond Kupczynski. He was unable to get back to Raymond Kupczynski and even struggled to keep himself afloat. As James Frierson struggled in the water, he noticed a plastic bucket float by. He reached out for it, dumped the water from it, inverted it, and used the air trapped under it as buoyancy to keep himself afloat.

"After Frierson and Raymond Kupczynski entered the water, Elliot Lopez entered the water with the cook's son, followed by Greta Fowle, and then the master. The master was the last person to leave the M/V *Bronx Queen*. The *CG41382* had already rescued the first of the passengers from the water before the master had abandoned the M/V *Bronx Queen*.

"On the *CG41382*, there was surprise that the people were entering the water before the directions had been completed; however, there was little time to think about it. The coxswain pivoted the *CG42382* around and approached the closest person in the water stern first. This person was swimming toward the *CG41382*. When the person in the water could be reached by the crew in the well deck of the CG41382, the coxswain placed the engines in neutral and left the helm to assist bringing the person aboard. The freeboard at the aft deck of the *CG41382* was approximately two (2) feet, nine (9) inches. To bring the person in the water on board the Coast Guard crew had to physically reach over the side of the boat and grab him by the arms and pick him up. After a strenuous effort the Coast Guard personnel managed to lift the person over the transom into the well deck. The rescued man was then directed to go up into the forward cabin of the *CG41382* where blankets were available. This process took a matter of only a couple of minutes. The coxswain then returned to the helm and maneuvered the *CG41382* toward the nearest person in the water."

After the second rescue was carried out in a similar fashion, one Coast Guardsman, dressed in an exposure suit, yelled, "The girl over there is in trouble. I've got to go get her" with which he jumped overboard.

The three men in *CG41382* continued rescue operations in the manner described above. They brought aboard a third person with great difficulty because of his weight—over 200 pounds—and a fourth person required the strength of all three Coast Guardsmen because he weighed even more. The fifth person was so huge, and so stiffened by hypothermia that he could not help himself, that the best they could do "was hang on to him partly out of the water."

In the mean time another rescue craft arrived. This was a rigid hull inflatable (RHI) launched from the M/V *New Jersey*, and manned by Drew Barry and two other men from the pilot ship. The RHI has an inflatable outer hull with a rigid inner hull. It is driven by jet propulsion and is capable of making some thirty knots; it is more maneuverable than a cutter. The RHI drew alongside people in the water and picked them up much quicker than was possible from the *CG41382*; the low freeboard allowed the men on the RHI to roll people over the pontoon with relatively little effort, despite the fact that the survivors were so benumbed that they could not help themselves. In short order the RHI rescued ten people, including two women and Captain Chale, and also picked up the Coast Guardsman in the exposure suit.

At 3:47, the *Bronx Queen* slipped beneath the surface of the heaving sea.

Then came the *CG41421*. This cutter picked up James Frierson, who was nearly unconscious due to the cold. They next strained to get the one-armed Raymond Kupczynski, but his life preserver tore off at the shoulders and he fell back into the water. When he was finally brought aboard he was unconscious, "his face was pale and his lips had started to turn blue." He was given two-person CPR, but without avail.

The men on the *CG41382* were still struggling with the man they could not lift over the transom. They waved to the RHI, which approached the stern of the cutter and took the man aboard. Coast Guardsman Pechasek also jumped aboard the RHI from the *CG41382* because he was an emergency medical technician and his expertise was needed for a man who had stopped breathing. "Pechasek determined that the man had asthma and was lapsing in and out of consciousness. His breathing was labored." Pechasek loosened his clothing and massaged his chest, and "attempted to calm the individual down as he talked him into breathing in and out in a relaxed manner."

The third cutter arrived and took part in rescue operations. Two people were plucked from the raging sea by the *CG44306*, in addition to which two others were transferred aboard from where they were floating in the water while clinging to the side of the overcrowded RHI. The RHI then sucked up some debris into the water intake of the jet portion of the propulsion unit, which disabled the engine. Drew Barry called for the pilot ship to pick up the boat, but "this attempt failed with the larger M/V *New Jersey* drifting by the RHI." The *CG44306* maneuvered alongside the RHI and effected the transfer of all the survivors despite the heavy sea running. Then the CG41382 took off the two Coast Guardsmen from the RHI, and "maneuvered the RHI over to the M/V *New Jersey* which hoisted the RHI back on board."

A Coast Guard helicopter flew overhead, circled around, then hovered over the CG44306 and "hoisted the individual with the respiratory problems."

Emergency medical units gathered at the Sandy Hook Coast Guard Station. As the cutters arrived with the survivors from the *Bronx Queen* they were whisked off to the hospital for treatment from their exposure to the frigid water. In addition to Kupczynski, who had drowned, Charles Little was pronounced dead at the Monmouth Medical Center, the cause being listed as "hypothermia due to floating in cold water."

The sinking of the *Bronx Queen* resulted in what is perhaps the most dramatic ocean rescue operation of the decade, and serves as a fine example of the common heroism displayed by Coast Guard personnel in the face of peril, as well as the willingness of individuals untrained in the ways of life-saving methods to exert all effort to save lives when humanitarian duty calls. Coast Guard personnel received recommendations for bold action above and beyond the call, and civilian participants from the *New Jersey* "were recognized and presented with awards at a 21 June 1990 testimonial dinner."

Two days after the loss of the *Bronx Queen*, a Coast Guard helicopter flew over the spot where the vessel had gone down, and sighted a sheen of oil above the sunken hull. In consequence of this, a civil penalty case was initiated for violation of the Clean Water Act. Imagine being taken to the hospital after a highway accident, then being fined for littering because your vehicle, which was totaled, was left behind!

"On December 6, 1989, Randive, Inc., a commercial diving company, was hired by the National Transportation Safety Board (NTSB) to survey the M/V *Bronx Queen*. The vessel was found on the bottom in thirty-five (35) feet of water. The vessel lay on a hard sandy bottom with a twenty degree port list. The vessel had numerous planks missing from its hull, particularly in the after section of the vessel. A large section of the after portion of the vessel was detached from the main part of the vessel from the turn of the bilge on the port and starboard sides up to and including the main deck. This detached portion included a section of the transom and extended fifteen (15) feet forward. The forward bulkhead of the lazarette was not in position and could not be found by the diver. The after bulkhead of the engine room was in place. Due [to] the extent of the damage found, the diver was unable to distinguish any damage that may have been identified as the initial source of flooding. The diver was also unable to distinguish any damage consistent with the vessel having struck something. The diver did not find any damage done to the propellers and the rudders."

Although Captain Chale believed that he had struck a submerged object, the official position taken by the Coast Guard was that "the proximate cause of this casualty was the structural failure of the hull of the vessel in the area of the lazarette. The exact cause to the structural failure cannot be determined; however, the most probable cause was the failure of the frames at the turn of the bilge on the starboard side in the lazarette." One possible reason given for the structural failure was the tonnage reducing modification made so long before. Contributing factors were adverse following sea conditions and "the operator's decision to keep the seas oriented on the stern of the vessel after the flooding was discovered. The vessel had the reserve buoyancy available to withstand the flooding of that aftermost compartment. This decision exposed the stern to the waves which caused the bait tank to destroy the entrance to the aft cabin and set into action the progressive flooding which eventually sank the vessel." The "thump" that was experienced was concluded to be the "actual catastrophic failing of the frames in the lazarette."

If you have ever wondered why the Coast Guard is so rigid in its inspections of passenger carrying vessels, now you know.

Neither the captain nor the crew of the *Bronx Queen* were found guilty of "actionable misconduct, inattention to duty, or negligent or willful violation of law or regulation."

Despite the fact that she sank such a short time ago, the wreck of the *Bronx Queen* has suffered measurably from the ravages of the hostile environment in which it resides. This is partly due to the Army Corps of Engineers reducing the least depth over the wreck because it presented a menace to navigation. The hull has collapsed into a what can best be described as a gigantic wood pile. The now-rotted timbers are completely overgrown with large flowering sea anemones and other species of filter feeders, to the point that the wreck does not even closely resemble the vessel it once was. Only the hard metal parts such as the engines and shafts show distinguishing features. The bronze propellers were recovered by Dan Berg. What remains of the wreck is gorgeously painted with marine encrustation, and it has become a virtual haven for fish and lobster. In that respect the wreck is a perfect site for marine life observers, underwater photographers, shell collectors, anglers, and those who like to shoot fish or catch lobsters.

CAPITOL CITY

Built: 1852
Previous names: *City of Hartford*
Gross tonnage: 1,306
Type of vessel: Side-wheel excursion steamer
Builder: Samuel Sneeden, Greenpoint, New York
Owner: E.H. Williams, Middletown, Connecticut
Port of registry: Hartford, Connecticut
Cause of sinking: Ran aground
Location: Passengers Rock off Parsonage Point near Rye in Long Island Sound

Sunk: March 31, 1886
Depth: 25 feet
Dimensions: 259' x 33' x 11'
Power: Coal-fired steam

The *Capitol City* began her career in 1852 as the *City of Hartford*, and for thirty-one years was owned and operated by the Hartford & New York Steamboat Company to run between the eponymous ports. Her construction represented the most advanced engineering designs of the time, including a nearly full-length above-deck truss, called a hogging arch, which added structural support to the wooden frame and hull. The single cylinder of the vertical beam engine was five feet across and had a stroke of twelve feet. The paddle wheels that churned the water at her sides were thirty-five feet in diameter—nearly as tall as a four story building. Twin stacks forward of the engine provided draft for the boilers and added grace and balance to her profile.

As an excursion steamer she was fitted out sumptuously for her passengers' every comfort. Thirty-nine staterooms with two berths each catered to those with expensive tastes who could afford the extra cost. Otherwise, berthing space was available for 194 cabin class passengers traveling more economically. According to one description, accommodations included "spacious cabins and saloons laid with Brussels carpeting; silk curtains; rosewood chairs, sofas and settees; marble-topped tables and sideboards; great crystal chandeliers." If a person had to make the 150-mile passage across the Long Island Sound, this was the way to go. There was no Victorian splendor on horseback or stagecoach.

In 1853 the *City of Hartford* was given a running mate, the *Granite State*, and between them they shared the duties of shuttling passengers between ports.

Regular service continued unabated during the hostilities between the States, and many a Union soldier planted newly shod feet on the steamer's wooden decks in order to speed his advance to the South. For a quarter of a century the *City of Hartford* provided steady, reliable service with hardly a break in the routine. She was practically a treadmill between growing population centers. Eventually, though, competition arrived in the form of what the Indians called the Iron Horse: trains steaming along steel railroads, which were less luxurious than their waterborne counterparts but also less weather dependent; it took a storm of major proportions to wash out the tracks.

So on March 29, 1876, the *City of Hartford* took it upon herself to retard rail service by butting her bridge against that of the Middletown railroad, with disastrous results for both contestants. Racing downstream from Hartford along the Connecticut River in flood, the excursion steamer approached the draw bridge in Middletown with frightening speed. Several loud blasts of the steam whistle signaled for the tender to open the bridge, which he did in time. But the current pushed the *City of Hartford* out of the proper channel. Instead of charging through the opening unopposed, she veered to the wrong side of the pier and crashed into the western span. The gentle slope of the hogging arches acted as wedges. As the steamer's momentum carried her forward, the span was lifted up off its piers. With a raucous rending of torn metal the bridge truss broke completely free of its fastenings and was carried away on top of the steamer like a giant steel derby: bridge to bridge, so to speak, and truss on truss. Then the jagged beams of the span collapsed around the ship's sides, wrapping around the wheel house and the superstructure and hull. So perfectly balanced was the weight of the bridge on the centerline of the steamer that the *City of Hartford* took only a slight list to starboard.

The wheel house was totally wrecked. Erik Heyl described beautifully the *City of Hartford's* condition: "The vessel came to rest a short distance below the bridge, her nose weighted down with the iron bridge girders which were draped across the hull like wet spaghetti. The usual and inevitable recriminations and counter accusations of negligence between the steamboat company and the railroad followed as a matter of course." And you thought that the ludicrous lawsuit syndrome was a pathology of twentieth century absurdity! One could hardly blame a bridge for jumping in the way of a ship. And confusion over signal lanterns displayed on the bridge is hardly an excuse for the pilot to mistake the proper interpretation of lights. After all, it was not as if the bridge had been built overnight; it had been there for years.

Both the Middletown bridge and the *City of Hartford* were repaired and put back into service. In the future, the steamer confined its river excursions to the channel that flowed through the section of the bridge that could be drawn. And she exercised great care in staying out of the way of the newly constructed western span. One bridge abutment was enough.

Wearing the Middletown Bridge. (Courtesy of the Steamship Historical Society of America.)

Repaired and renamed. (Courtesy of the Steamship Historical Society of America.)

The Hartford & New York Steamboat Company fell on hard times. Ticket sales went down and operating expenses went up. By 1882, the company could no longer keep its head above water, so it was forced out of business. The *City of Hartford* was sold at auction for $25,000, as was her running mate, the *Granite State*. Her new owner, E. H. Williams, had both ships completely rebuilt and modernized. They were back on the run in 1883 not only under new management, but under new names. The *City of Hartford* became the *Capitol City*, and the *Granite State* became the *City of Lawrence*.

Then came that fateful day when the *Capitol City* met her end. It had become her routine to stop off at Saybrook to pick up passengers, freight, and mail bound for New York City, "but the fog was so thick that only two passengers took the boat, the others preferring to continue their journey by rail." Captain J.N. Russell, master of the *Capitol City*, took no chances in the clinging fog. He reduced speed from the usual fifteen knots to ten. By 5:30 in the morning (of March 31, 1886) "he did not know where the vessel was. Neither did Pilot J.H. Gaines, who had the wheel. They were steering the vessel's course by compass, and thought they were two miles clear from the shore, with plenty of free water ahead of them. No one dreamed of Passengers Rock till the steamboat was on it, and then there was not very much time for dreaming."

According to local legend, Passengers Rock was so named when a schooner went aground there and the passengers clambered onto the rock near Parsonage Point for safety. Soon a re-enactment of that historic event took place.

"The moment the bow of the boat struck Capt. Russell rang the bell for the engineer to back water, but before Assistant Engineer L.B. Wright, who was in charge, could obey orders the steamer gave another lurch forward, dragging her entire length over the rocks, and the engines stopped of their own accord. The boilers of the boat were on each side of the main deck, forward of the paddle wheels. The firemen raked out the hot coals at once, to prevent an explosion. Then the crew of 40 men (including nine officers) bustled around to see what could be done about getting ashore, and to take in the real situation. Some of the men cut away the guard rails with axes and got afloat in the lifeboats. The fog was still so thick that they could not discover that they were within 200 feet of a Westchester County farm.

"The steamboat filled with water so rapidly that it seemed as though half the 4-inch planks on the flat bottom had been torn away, and in a few minutes from the time she struck she had settled solidly on the rock."

Only two passengers were aboard at the time of the grounding. H.D. Chronister reported that the sudden shock threw him from his berth. After this rude awakening he waded through waist-deep water to the baggage compartment to retrieve his valise. "It was nearly four hours after the boat struck before the fog lifted so that Capt. Russell could see the shore, though he was only a few feet from it." Chronister and the other passenger, Louis Pfahler, requested to be put ashore. Captain Russell obliged them, whereupon they "knocked at the doors of the country residence of George H. Van Wagenen, of Brooklyn. There was no one there, so they went to Rye and took the first train to" New York City. Two more discontented passengers lost to the rails!

"It was obvious to Capt. Russell that he could not get his steamer off the rocks, so he set the crew at work saving as much of the freight as possible. There was about $30,000 worth of it—miscellaneous stuff from manufactories in the valley along the Connecticut River. Much of it was damaged by water. In the after hold of the vessel was the dining saloon, the berths for sleeping, and the crew's quarters. These all filled with water and settled the steamer on the rocks with her bow high in the air. The main deck, where the bulk of the freight was stored, sloped at an angle of about 20 degrees. The freight was all rolled forward out of the wet, and the furniture and bedding was carried from the ladies' saloon and lower staterooms to the upper decks.

"The wind, which kept increasing in force every minute, was in the most unfavorable position for the unfortunate steamer. The waves came rolling in upon her from the open Sound, sweeping away her light rigging, wrenching her hull from stem to stern, sweeping through the windows that had been broken by the shock into the carpeted cabins, and bumping her about on the rocks generally in a way that threatened soon to tear her to pieces. It was well along in the afternoon before the *Hegerty* and the *Fly*, from the Chapman Wrecking Company, got in sight of Rye Beach, and then the steamer was so close inshore that they could not get near her. When the tide was full the water rose about four feet over the sunken vessel's main deck and set afloat everything that was lying around loose. The boat rocked to and fro like a cradle, snapping the huge hog frames and throwing the upper deckwork all out of shape. People came down from the shore towns and stood for hours on the beach, expecting every minute to see her go to pieces."

By the end of the day "the freight was all in a wet heap on the forward decks, though the *Eleanor Peck* was waiting to transfer it to this city [New York] if she could get hold of it. Everybody was waiting for something and nobody doing anything in particular. Soon after dark it began to rain heavily and the storm increased. Though the steamer was falling away, piece by piece, and the men did not know how soon they might be swamped with water, they prepared to spend an uncomfortable and somewhat dangerous night on board."

The weather did not moderate for more than a week, by which time little was salvageable of either the *Capitol City* or her cargo and furnishings, all the more frustrating with the wreck only one hundred feet from shore. Wrote Allison Albee in *The Quarterly Bulletin*, "The waves washed over the helpless ship, rocking it continuously upon the ledge where it was caught like a fly in a spider's web. As quickly as possible hawsers were run beneath the hull and made fast to the salvage vessels alongside. These boats then started their pumps and began to draw water from the steamer's hull. The plan proved successful as long as the tide was ebbing but when it started rising again the pumps proved insufficient to keep the water from rising inside the wrecked boat. It was then reluctantly admitted additional leaks that were unknown, caused the defeat of this effort. Within a week it became evident that the salvage of the vessel now would be a long time operation at best, if salvage was possible. Independent reports said the hull was broken in two. The point where the steamer rested and all along the adjacent shore was now covered with litter and debris. A great quantity of white paper envelopes had gone adrift and the shore was lined with a layer of paper whipped into a pulp by the waves. Cases of tobacco emerged from the wreck and floated ashore where they were carried away by men and boys. People came from far and wide to see the wreck lining the shore all the following Thursday, Friday, and Saturday, some coming from great distances. Local boatmen did a thriving business transporting visitors out to her."

The *Capitol City* was valued at $100,000 and insured for $75,000. In order to recoup some of the loss, the machinery was dismantled and the walking beam engine was removed, and bit by bit the useful portions of the hull and fittings were salvaged.

One eyewitness to subsequent events, Henry Bird, reported that "during the day people came by the thousands. They arrived from everywhere by train and hired rigs and other conveyances. The whole local population also turned out. There must have been 10,000 people. Among the items in the cargo were lumber, harness and a fabulous number of small spindles (bobbins) of cotton thread.

"The insurance people finally took over the wreck which settled lower in the water as time passed. Oystermen who had lived all their lives by the honest sweat of their brows now found a new use for their long rakes. Instead of oysters, loads

A bergall swimming past a sea anemone.

of harness were brought ashore and left in secluded places to dry. Various others tramping through the nearby woodland fell upon these strange items and became the new owners of fine harness. . . . More interesting is the fate of the thread wound spindles. As time passed thousands of them washed ashore in the immediate vicinity of the wreck. Sightseers not wishing to return home without a souvenir found the spindles not only symbolic but handy. More often than not an extra one or two was taken for a friend or relative. As in most instances no arrangements for return to the [railway] station had been made by these people, this journey was made on foot.

"As they walked their pockets became heavier and their thoughtfulness for relative and friend lessened considerably. Extra spindles were cast by the way more than once seemingly with a thread end still attached to the visitor. In this manner the spindle unwound as the walk continued. Aided by the wind and small boys' efforts the resulting strange phenomenon was that of a giant cotton web spread over the entire countryside in the region of the route from the wreck.

"Further changes in the otherwise quite lives of Milton's inhabitants resulted. For at least a whole generation the spirit of the *Capitol City* lived on. Evidence of her reincarnation was to be found in almost every building of a minor nature in the Milton Point area. These structures included sheds, leantos, chicken coops and even dog houses. The steamer's bow, a massive wooden piece lasted longest. It came ashore and lasted fifteen or twenty years before being finally chopped up for firewood. I have a stateroom door number and a pair of cabin door hinges as souvenirs."

From this description it is evident that not much of the *Capitol City* remains; at least, not much of her hull or machinery. Yet divers combing the area find a wide variety of odds and ends littering the bottom, such as fire brick, coal, dresser hardware, miscellaneous items of brass and copper, and china from shards to intact pieces. Visibility in the Long Island Sound is limited to a few feet, so do not expect clear Caribbean water.

A goosefish swimming over a field of sponges and starfish.

CIRCASSIAN

Built: 1856
Previous names: None
Gross tonnage: 1,742
Type of vessel: Iron-hulled, full-rigged ship
Builder: Robert Hickson & Company, Belfast, Ireland
Owner: T.A. de Wolf, Liverpool, England
Port of registry: Liverpool, England
Cause of sinking: Ran aground
Location: Bridgehampton Bar

Sunk: December 11, 1876
Depth: Unknown
Dimensions: 254' x 39' x 30'
Power: Sail

While the name of the builder of the *Circassian* may not sound familiar to most, it is appropriate to point that Robert Hickson & Company later became the well-known and highly respected shipbuilding yard of Harland & Wolff, which constructed some of the most famous ships in history. The *Circassian*, however, was more notorious than famous.

The *Circassian* was one of those wayward ships that led a checkered career, always seeming to get into trouble and, consequently, into the news. She entered service as a single-screw steamer whose engine could propel her iron hull through the water at a respectable nine knots. Marine engines were not always reliable in the early days of steam, so she was also fitted with three masts, multiple yards, and a huge spread of canvas. Her finely raked lines bespoke her speed under both steam and sail, and she certainly lived up to the meaning of her name, for the Circassians are Caucasian people inhabiting Circassia, a Russian region on the northeastern shore of the Black Sea, who are renowned for their striking physical beauty.

At the time of her construction the *Circassian* was the largest vessel ever built in Ireland, at slightly more than one hundred tons larger than her predecessor and close approximation in build, the *Khersonese*.

In 1857, the *Circassian's* maiden voyage for the North Atlantic Steam Navigation Company took her from Liverpool to St. John's to Halifax to Portland, and back along the same route. Nothing untoward occurred, and there was no hint within shipping circles that she would go on to become such an oceanic waif and ne'er-do-well.

The first hint of trouble began at the outset of the American Civil War, when the *Circassian* began her short career as a blockade runner. In an attempt to curtail the export of cotton from the Confederate States to European countries in need, and the import of materiel with which to prosecute the war (guns, ammunition, shoes, and so on), the Union blockaded the principal Southern ports with its ragtag navy. Every vessel that could float and that the Union could muster,

From *Harper's Weekly.*

was conscripted for the blockading squadrons, principally in the area of Hampton Roads, Virginia; Charleston, South Carolina; and Confederate ports in the Gulf of Mexico. All vessels attempting to breach the blockade, whether Southern or foreign, were considered by the Union as violators and were liable for capture or destruction.

This policy did not sit well with those foreign nations which recognized the sovereignty of the Confederate States of America, and which chose to trade with the newly formed nation. Chief among these was Great Britain, which needed cotton and which had great quantities of goods to sell. Foreign commerce was Great Britain's lifeblood.

What further infuriated the European nations was the Union's penchant for stopping foreign vessels in the vicinity of the Southern States, on suspicion, and vessels on the high seas. While technically a ship did not become a blockade runner until it ran the Union blockade—the legality of which the world's countries found lacking—it became the habit of the Union to stop all suspects in order to inspect their cargo manifests and their cargoes. Thus the *Circassian* was captured on May 4, 1862 off the coast of Cuba, by the USS *Somerset*. It was not an easy capture.

Wrote Lieutenant Earl English, captain of the *Somerset*: "I stood down for her, crossed her bow, rounded to, and hailed, having hoisted the American ensign. She had an English ensign flying. Ordered her to heave to, so as to allow me to send a boat alongside, to which he made no audible reply, but proceeded directly on his course. As she was much faster than this vessel, I fired a blank cartridge, then a shell to the right of her. Still he continued on his course, evidently endeavoring to escape me. I then fired a shell over, which exploded beyond him. Still he continued on his course, when I ordered a shell to be fired into him, which took effect in his fore rigging. He then stopped," whereupon the vessel was taken to Key West for internment as a prize of war.

On October 14 she was ordered to New York, and on November 8 the U.S. Navy Department purchased the *Circassian* from the prize court for $107,000, which amount was distributed among the officers and crew of the *Somerset*, as was the custom of the times. The ship was re-rigged as a bark and armed with four 9-inch Dahlgren smooth bore guns, one 100-pounder Parrott rifle, and one 12-pounder rifle. By spring of 1863 she was working hard for the Union as a troop transport, store vessel, and supply ship, but she also did her share of freebooting, capturing quite a few Confederate ships during her sojourn along the east coast and in the Gulf of Mexico.

At the conclusion of the Civil War the *Circassian* was sold at public auction since the Navy no longer had a need for her services, and because of the much depleted government coffers. On June 22, 1865, Arthur Leary paid $71,000 for the vessel (minus the armament), and converted her back to a full-rigged ship. This must have been a bargain for Leary since at the time of her loss eleven years later she was valued at $145,000, more than double her purchase price.

Quite a to-do was made of American ownership of the *Circassian* and of her return to the Atlantic transportation service. It seems that prior to and during the Civil War, the "mails, and the majority of all the passenger traffic, were carried under the British flag; and when the rebellion began to assume large proportions, the Germans and Frenchmen came in, and became the competitors of the Englishmen, who gloried in the fact that not one American ocean steamer could be found to venture out, lest it would be seized by an Anglo-rebel pirate. They soon became masters of the situation, and they have been reaping the benefits of our disasters. But now we see a practical proof that we are soon to contest this business, and again our flag will cover our mails and passengers, and a fair portion of the freight." In addition to this new-found patriotism, the *Circassian* was deemed "in excellent condition, very strong, staunch and remarkably seaworthy. She is well known and will, no doubt, accomplish all that is promised of her."

The latter sentiment was less than prescient for, according to the records of the Life-Saving Service, she "went ashore on Sable Island, and was got off by the Colombian Wrecking Company, under the charge of Capt. John Lewis, who finally lost his life upon her." Having once gotten a taste for grounding, she seemed bent on making a career of it. "She was subsequently purchased by a New York firm, and placed on the New Orleans route. Upon a voyage to New York, she again went ashore, this time at Squan, New Jersey, in December 1869. Being gotten off, she was laid up in dock about three years, and finally bought by a Liverpool house, and converted into a sailing-ship." Other sources indicate that she was removed from Squan Beach by Captain R.C. Perry of the Coast Wreck Company.

Then came the *Circassian's* final day of reckoning. No longer did she have the power of an engine to propel her effortlessly through the waves. Now she depended solely upon the wind to waft her to her destination. Unfortunately, her destination was now with destiny, with a few strange twists and a dramatic surprise ending. The sad saga of the *Circassian's* last days off Bridgehampton were unsparingly detailed in the records of the United States Life-Saving Service, which I can do no better than to reprint here as it was written.

"Her final wreck took place upon her first voyage since her alteration. She was then bound from Liverpool to New York with a crew of 37 persons, including her commander, Capt. Richard Williams, together with 12 passengers whom she had taken from a wreck at sea."

"On December 11, at ten minutes to eleven o'clock at night, owing, as her captain stated, to an error of the compass, she ran upon a bar about 400 yards from the shore, where she stranded; her size and her great draught of water, which was 19 3/4 feet, causing her to ground at this considerable distance. The night was dark; a northeast gale was blowing, with a thick snow-storm and heavy sea.

"The ship was immediately discovered by the patrol of Station No. 10 (Capt. Baldwin Cook, keeper), and the crew of the station promptly assembled. To have launched the boat in the heavy seas, which in that vicinity roll in numerous combing breaker from the outer bar to the beach, would have been fool-hardy. It was equally impossible to reach the ship at that time with the shot-line; her distance from shore, the resistance of the gale to the line, and the darkness, which would have prevented the men firing the mortar from seeing by the bowing of the line what allowance to make for the force of the wind in aiming, and also prevented the people on board from discovering the line if it fell over the rigging, being all elements of failure. It was, therefore, necessary to wait till dawn before commencing operations, when the life-saving crew would have the double advantage of light and a lower tide. The gear meanwhile was gotten in readiness for action, and the crews of the contiguous stations, Nos. 9 and 11, were summoned from a distance of several miles on either hand.

"At day-break the falling tide enabled the mortar to be planted lower on the beach and nearer the vessel, which also in the meantime had been driven considerably nearer to the shore by the force of the sea; and, at the third fire, the ball fell plumply upon the deck and connection was made with hawser and hauling-lines for the use of the life-car.

"The sea had now, however, subsided to such an extent that it was judged that more expeditious work could be done with the surf-boat, which was accordingly launched, and in seven trips the entire number of persons on board the vessel, forty-nine in all, were safely brought on shore.

"During the night there was the usual difficulty in prevailing upon those on board the ship not to attempt to land in their own boats—an attempt which would certainly have resulted disastrously. It was prevented, however, and the deliverance of all on board was accomplished without casualty."

At this point in the narrative it must be remembered that a dozen of the survivors had been wrecked and rescued twice, and that the ordeal of saving life had been engaged with the usual aplomb and professionalism by which the Life-Saving Service was known. The stranding and subsequent rescue was handled in such a routine fashion and so underplayed that the events escaped the notice of the press.

"The Coast Wrecking Company, of New York, were now engaged to save the vessel and cargo, and at once commenced operations under the general direction of Captain Perrin, an agent of the company, and the local agent, Captain Charles A. Pierson, of Bridgehampton. Captain John Lewis, of New York, had immediate charge of the work on board the vessel, assisted by three engineers from New York, and twelve men, ten of whom were members of an Indian tribe, now whalers and wreckers, resident at the neighboring village of Shinnecock. Beside these sixteen persons there were on board the ship sixteen of her regular company, including the master and officers, making a total of thirty-two in all. Captain Luther D. Burnett, of Southampton, owing to his great experience as a surfman, had been employed by the wrecking company to take charge of the boats employed in lightering the ship by removing her cargo.

"The ship lay across the bar with her head to the southeast. This transverse position, as events proved, was dangerous. Being of iron, very heavy, of great length, and lying thus substantially athwart a ridge, principally supported amidships, with her ends comparatively off the bottom in the deeper water, she had a constant tendency to sag and break in two. The object of the wrecking company was, of course, to work her off as speedily as possible into the open sea. In such cases the method usually adopted is to sink heavy anchors to seaward of the ship, the latter being held thereto by immense hawsers, and a perpetual strain being kept by the capstan upon these hawsers, the vessel, aided by the heavy swell and the rising tides, which tend to move and lift her, is gradually pulled toward the ocean. This course had been pursued with the *Circassian*, and within a fortnight she had been moved 98 yards upon the bar. She now lay a total distance from the shore of 308 yards at low tide.

"Under the circumstances, it would have been prudent to have kept a line stretched from the ship to the shore, thus retaining communication with the life-saving station for use in case of emergency. This, however, the agents of the wrecking company, upon repeated solicitations, steadily refused to do. It appears that the crew of twelve wreckers, including the ten Shinnecock Indians, had been engaged to remain on board the vessel until she floated off the bar. The coming easterly storm, with its accompanying high tides, was relied upon to aid in effecting the release of the ship, and the principal motive for refusing to allow a line to be run from the ship to the shore was the apprehension that the crew, fearing danger, might avail themselves of this means to leave the vessel during the storm, when their services would be most needed. Absolute dependence was placed upon the great strength of the ship to enable her to withstand the gale, and it was this miscalculation of her resistant power which led to the catastrophe.

"As early as the 26th of December an easterly storm was prevailing and the weather was very threatening. By the 29th, the storm had so increased that the lighters engaged in removing the cargo were unable to work with safety, and at ten o'clock in the morning the last cargo-gang, led by Capt. Luther D. Burnett, came ashore. This was the latest communication had with the vessel.

"It was expected that the ship would float at high water that night, and be taken to sea under canvas. During the day, however, the gale increased in violence, with snow and sleet, and the sea had become tremendous. By four o'clock in the afternoon the immense bulk of the ship was seen from the shore rolling and pounding heavily on the bar. It was also seen that the hawsers, bent to heavy anchors to seaward, had been slacked. This denoted that the hope of getting her out to sea at that particular time had been abandoned, and also that those on board were becoming apprehensive, and desired that she should be driven in toward the beach, where their peril would have been lessened. The slackening of her cables, however, had no effect, and it was seen later that she had settled in the water. This appearance was probably the result of her having already broken her hull, and explains why she did not move when her hawsers were eased.

"Darkness came on without any abatement of the tempest, and the ship continued to labor heavily. It was not, however, till seven o'clock that she made any signal of distress. Notwithstanding the general confidence in her stoutness, alarm for her safety began soon to prevail. The crews of the next stations, Nos. 9 and 11, were at once sent for, and Capt. Baldwin Cook and his men, of station No. 10, hastened to prepare for the forlorn attempt at rescue.

"Ordinarily, the beach presents the aspect of a broad, interminable avenue of sand, with the ocean on one hand, and a low line of hummocks and mounds, crowned with coarse grass, upon the other. Upon that night it presented an almost unprecedented spectacle. The broad space, usually bare, was flooded in the darkness by a furious sea, which momentarily broke all over it, with prodigious uproar and confusion, reaching in places as far as the beach hills, and pouring through their clefts or sluice-ways. So overswept was the beach with this seething water, that the keeper and his men could with difficulty find a place upon which to plant the mortar for an attempt to fire a shot-line to the wreck. The spot finally fixed upon was almost under the beach-hills, 72 yards farther back than the position chosen for the mortar upon the occasion of the original stranding of the *Circassian*. The vessel being at a distance of 308 yards, at low tide, as stated, the mortar was now 380 yards from her. Although the effort was resolutely and persistently made, it is evident that no shot-line could possibly have reached her at such a distance in the teeth of the hurricane which prevailed. If it had, it would have been useless at this time, her decks being now completely swept by the surges, her crew already up in the fore-rigging for safety, and no one in a position to haul upon a line from shore. No other means of reaching the wreck was possible. In the tremendous sea then hurling thousands of tons of water each moment upon the beach, no life-boat, even if unbroken by the weight of the surf, could have been propelled from shore.

"A red Coston light was burnt by the crew of the station to let the men in the fore-rigging of the wreck know that their peril was understood, and a large fire of driftwood was built upon shore, abreast of the ship, under the sand hills. The preparations for firing the mortar, which meanwhile actively continued, were much impeded at first by the difficulty of finding a place where the sea did not reach, and then by the wet, flying sand which covered the shot-line in spite of every effort to protect it. To keep the shot-line dry, free, and unsnarled, it is necessary for its efficient flight toward a wreck. It was now almost immediately soaked by the rain and spray, clogged by the drifting sand, and frozen. By eight o'clock, however, the gun was in readiness. In the mean time the mainmast had fallen, carrying with it the mizzen topmast. This was a sinister occurrence. It denoted the beginning of the breaking up of the vessel.

"The alarm and anxiety of the old captains and seamen on shore was now increased by an extraordinary circumstance. The mortar was just shotted and the line ready for the first fire, when the wind, which had been blowing furiously from the east-southeast all day, suddenly chopped around to the west-southwest, and became almost a tornado. So abrupt a change, with such an increase of fury in a gale, is almost unprecedented. it blew with such dreadful violence that it was nearly impossible to look to windward on account of the flying sand. A terrific cross sea at once ensued. The water swelled up in great heaps, and swept the decks of the wreck from every side. The surf flooded the beach still higher, cutting away the beach-hills, and at intervals tearing new gullies through them. added to all was a streaming torrent of rain. The bitter cold, the darkness, the frightful roar and commotion, the incessant hail of wet sand, the wind blowing so that men were thrown down by it, the general elemental pell-mell, made the scene indescribable.

"The effect of this sudden change in the direction of the gale was to force the gun from the position which had been obtained for it with so much difficulty. In firing toward a wreck, allowance must be made for the yawing of the shot-line by the wind, and the position, somewhat to the eastward of the ship, which had been chosen on this consideration, had now to be taken up to the westward. Considerable time was consumed in the effort to find a suitable place for the mortar, and there was also trouble to get the match-rope to burn. At length, however, the obstacles were surmounted and several shots were fired in succession toward the vessel. It was necessary the humane effort should be made, but as already remarked, it was impossible that any shot carrying a line could have reached her at such a distance and in such a gale, and equally impossible, even if it had reached her, that it could have been taken advantage of by the wretched men clinging to the foremast with the furious mob of waters rioting over the hull below them. In fact one of the survivors expressly declared, 'it would have been impossible for us to have used the line even if it had reached us.'

"Beyond the futile endeavor to reach the wreck by a shot-line, nothing further was or could be attempted. The only hope was that the wreck might hold together till daylight, when it was barely possible that something might be done to effect a rescue. The night was passed by those on shore in watching the vessel. What appeared to them, as some have said, the longest night ever known, must have seemed a miserable eternity to the hapless men upon the wreck. The storm never abated its violence. At midnight the tide fell. Lights were seen upon the deck, and the hull was apparently whole, but cleared of everything by the sea. At two o'clock (Saturday, December 30), it was descried by the glass that the men had left the foremast, and had taken to the mizzen rigging. At half past three the vest black hulk was seen to have broken in two; her forepart settling down outside, and her stern inside, the bar. The glass showed the mizzen-mast was still erect, and the rigging was full of men. At times, through the roar of the tempest, their cries were heard by those on shore. At four o'clock, the mizzen-mast, which was of iron, began to career to port with its living load. For half an hour the powerless watchers on the beach saw it gradually dipping toward the sea. At half past four it reached the monstrous water, into which it settled slowly, with the men that clung to the shrouds.

"It is to the credit of the life-saving crews that the dreadful catastrophe did not paralyze what further exertion was possible. Nothing was more unlikely than that any person could reach the shore from the wreck in that raging sea; but, in view of such a possibility, Capt. H.E. Huntting, the superintendent of the district, had organized a lantern squad of 18 or 20 men to search the surf about 40 yards apart, and immediately upon the disappearance of the mast, they scattered up the beach, with their lanterns, to the eastward. The set, or current, was running with great velocity outside the breakers to the east, which lessened the chances of any person reaching the shore. Suddenly, however, those in the rear heard a shout on ahead. A group of life-saving men was approaching through the darkness with their lanterns, supporting four drooping figures, which they had hauled from the surf. These were the only survivors. The remaining 28 had perished.

"The persons rescued were the first and second officers of the ship, the carpenter, and a seaman in the employ of the wrecking company. It appears that the two first named had obtained possession of a cylindrical piece of cork, 5 feet long and 11 inches in diameter, fitted it with straps and beckets, and arranged between themselves to cling to it for their last chance of life. When the mast

From *Frank Leslie's Illustrated Newspaper.*

dipped into the sea, they had sprung together as far forward as possible. They were at once immersed in the raging flood, and presently came to the surface clinging to the buoy. In a moment the seaman employed by the wrecking company clutched hold of the buoy, and then the carpenter, coming up near them, was seized and helped to a place beside them. Their salvation now was mainly owing to the perfect coolness, judgment, and resolution of the first officer of the ship, under whose management the escape was accomplished. This brave and steady man, under such circumstances, actually schooled his comrades in the course they were to pursue, and took command of their strange craft, as composedly as though he were assuming charge of the staunchest sea-boat. Under his direction the four men, side by side, locked legs with each other. This quadruple intertwining of their lower limbs bound them together, and served to steady the buoy to whose ropes they clung. They were now one mass in quaternion, tossed to and fro in the immense wash of the sea. Every other instant, in the thick darkness, they were flooded by the surge. At these times, under their gallant captain's word of command, they held their breaths and gripped the buoy-ropes hard, till their momentary release from the wave. In the influence of the surge, his order bade them relax their hold a little for rest and breath. There was but a bare chance for life, but these maneuvers economized their strength and breath, till, swept eastward by the current and forward by the surf, the moment came which flung them into the shoaling breakers. Then under his last shout of command, in the furious welter of the surf and undertow, they gave all their reserved force to the desperate plunge ahead for the beach, and in the midst of their convulsive struggle, half on their feet and half dragged down by the wave, the men of the life-saving service rushed in upon them, and tore them from the sea. They were almost drowned, but they were saved.

"In the common judgment of all present, old captains and seamen, this escape was little less than miraculous. There was hardly one chance in a thousand of its accomplishment, and it was unquestionably owing to the marvelous discretion and stout-heartedness of the first officer. The men were all terribly worn by their struggle. None of them could stand. The carpenter was nearly dead, and could not have been carried a mile without perishing. Fortunately, the station was near, and the four survivors were brought to it and put into warm beds near the stove as quickly as possible. The medicine-chest was at once brought into requisition, and with the aid of mustard-plasters, brandy, coffee, dry clothes, and active chafing and rubbing, the sufferers were revived. It was not until noon the next day that the carpenter was considered out of danger.

"The corpses of the twenty-eight persons lost were washed ashore within a fortnight afterward on Montauk Beach, and were buried by the town of East Hampton, except the ten Shinnecock Indians, who were brought off and buried by the Southampton people, and the bodies of Captain Lewis and the three engineers, which were taken to New York by the friends of the deceased."

Some details not included in the Life-Saving Service account were the names of the survivors: Henry Morrell (or Morel), first mate; John Rowlands, second mate; Alexander Wilson, carpenter; and Charles Campbell, a seaman in the employ of the Coast Wrecking Company. The names of the tugs used by the Coast Wrecking Company in attempting to pull the *Circassian* off the bar were the *Cyclops* and *Relief*. Note that John Lewis, who was in charge of the wrecking crew at Bridgehampton and who died on that fateful night when the hull broke in two, was the man responsible for pulling the *Circassian* off the beach at Sable Island (or off Squan Beach, according to another report, which is more likely).

The cargo of the *Circassian* at the time of her loss consisted of "332 tierces of soda ash, 110 tierces chloride of lime, 45 packages of merchandise, 100 cases sauce, 395 cases soda ash, 10 casks of gelatine, 41,660 Bath brick, 105 hogsheads soda ash, 280 barrels soda crystals, 44 tons and 253 tierces dye-wood, 87 casks bleaching-powder, 471 bales of rags, 281 bags hide pieces, 600 drums caustic soda, 15 cases of matches, and 600 boxes Bath brick. The cargo is insured for $90,000." One third of the 1,400 tons of cargo was lightered before the vessel's destruction. A small portion came ashore with the debris from the wreck. (A tierce, by the way, is a measure of liquid capacity equivalent to about 42 gallons; similarly, a hogshead equals about 63 gallons.)

Bodies began washing ashore the day after the collapse of the hull. People scoured the beach in search of the dead. "The shore is now strewn, from this point [Bridgehampton] to Awagausett, with bits of the wrecked vessel, cases, chests, boards, and spars. The casting up of this broken and unprotected litter attracted to the water's edge, in addition to the mourning relatives and friends of the lost, another class of hunters. While the poor men who live near the sea are as a rule strictly honest, they cannot quite conquer the prejudice which is bone of their bone and flesh of their flesh, that anything which comes to them from the sea, cast up on their shores, is their rightful prey and plunder. Obeying the dictates of this old prejudice, these old-fashioned wreckers have already begun their work upon the fragments of the wreck. Chests which have been thrown up have been broken open, their contents examined, and, in some cases, the locks and hinges broken and carried off. Cordage has been stripped from spars, brass-work and bolts have been secured wherever they could be detached without difficulty."

A relief fund was taken up for the wives and children of the ten Indians from nearby Shinnecock.

A British Naval Court was convened in order to determine the cause of the disaster. It agreed with the opinion of the deceased Captain Williams, master of the *Circassian*, that the spirit compass may have been in error. The alcohol used to dampen movement of the needle was made so viscous by subzero temperatures that the compass was "rendered less than useless." At that time vessels were generally unheated, and the wheel house was often exposed to the elements. Notwithstanding this finding, it also found fault with the captain and the pilot for not taking sufficient soundings upon approach to shore, "whereby the fatal calamity which befell the ship would doubtless have been avoided."

Somewhere under the sand off Bridgehampton lies the wreckage of one of the most tragic shipwrecks in the annals of New York shipping.

Official U.S. Coast Guard photograph.

COIMBRA

Built: 1937
Previous names: None
Gross tonnage: 6,768
Type of vessel: Tanker
Builder: Howaldtswerke A.G., Kiel, Germany
Owner: Standard (Socony-Vacuum) Transportation Company, Ltd.
Port of registry: London, England
Cause of sinking: Torpedoed by *U-123* (Kapitanleutnant Reinhard Hardegen)
Location: 26203.6

Sunk: January 15, 1942
Depth: 180 feet
Dimensions: 422' x 60' x 32'
Power: Oil-fired steam

43576.8

When the *U-123* torpedoed and sank the *Norness* off Block Island, on January 14, 1942, it heralded a terrible onslaught of death and destruction along the American east coast. The next night the *U-123* attacked the *Coimbra*; but whereas the entire crew of the *Norness* survived their ordeal, aboard the *Coimbra* the loss of life was severe, and horrible deaths they were. Details of the sinking are meager since most of the crew were burned to death when the cargo of oil caught fire and the tanker became a charnel house. As flames raged throughout the ship, half a dozen men managed to launch a lifeboat and make good their escape. Captain J.P. Barnard, master of the *Coimbra*, was among the thirty-six men who perished in such agony.

At the time, the *Coimbra* was on route from New York to the United Kingdom with 9,000 tons of lubricating oil. As in the case of the *Norness,* an alert pilot in a patrol plane spotted six men in what he described as a dory, south of Shinnecock Inlet. He radioed the information to base, but immediate rescue operations were hampered by a storm that was then raging across the south shore of Long Island. That the men managed to keep the lifeboat from foundering was a miracle.

Strangely reminiscent, and almost as a replay of the *Norness* incident of the previous day, a Navy blimp was dispatched to the vicinity and located the bow of the *Coimbra* protruding from the water. In the flight report filed by the pilot of the blimp, it is stated, "dropped restoratives and remained nearby until arrival of Navy Destroyers 402 and 435, which were directed to scene by plane."

Probably the fact that their condition was known gave as much encouragement as the restoratives to the men struggling for their lives in the heavy seas, and gave them the strength and courage to hang on until the destroyers *Grayson* and *Mayrant* hove into view and effected their rescue.

Due to the furor aroused by newspaper publicity following the sinking of the *Norness*, the Navy banned the release of information about the circumstances of the *Coimbra's* demise. Even the official records contain a paucity of information.

Adding to the sense of deja vu relevant to the *Norness* is the fact that the *Coimbra* was also a German-built ship. Thus, the first two vessels torpedoed by the *U-123* off the American east coast were constructed in German shipyards.

Courtesy of the National Archives.

It took six months for the U.S. Navy to chase the U-boats out of the Eastern Sea Frontier, that stretch of the Atlantic seaboard extending from the Canadian border to the north Florida coast. U-boats made a few skirmishes in subsequent years, but by and large they lost as many submarines as the Allies lost merchantmen. During that time the Germans sank one hundred twenty vessels, damaged many more, and killed over 2,400 men, women, and children. Germany also left a dozen U-boats on the bottom of the ESF, and most of their crews as well.

Due to the number of wrecks which littered the sea bed in the deadly wake of the U-boats, once the coast was fairly well protected from foreign incursion a program was undertaken to mark and identify these sunken hulks by means of underwater photography, which was then in its infancy. This was accomplished by means of a specially built camera housed in a pressure proof case, which was lowered by cable from a support vessel onto shipwrecks previously located by means of sonar. Hanging below the camera was a weighted trip wire which triggered the shutter when the weight touched the bottom and took the strain off the connecting wire. This "hit or miss" snapshot method proved quite effective on the *Coimbra*, for the camera was providentially positioned on the bow of the wreck where the tanker's name was spelled out in raised letters. Because the lens faced down, and the camera could not be situated to shoot sideways, only overhead pictures could be taken. This generally yielded results less than desirable since most wrecks were upright or upside down, but it was discovered that the *Coimbra* lay on its starboard side, so in this instance the camera captured a dramatic image.

Courtesy of J. Lamar Worzel.

While not much was written about the *Coimbra* at the time of her loss, she was very much in the news during the late '60's and '70's. This was brought about by the grounding of the *Torrey Canyon* off the coast of Cornwall, England, on March 18, 1967 . The subsequent spill of oil on British and French shores triggered worldwide awareness of the hazards of pollution. That same year, in direct response to this ecological catastrophe, the American government initiated what came to be known as the "Sunken Tanker Project." In the introduction to the report which was generated by the project, it is stated, "As a part of this study, the Secretary of Transportation directed the Commandant of the Coast Guard to contract for the investigation of one or more tankers sunk on the United States continental shelf by enemy action during World War II." Four tankers were chosen for underwater examination: the *Gulftrade*, *R.P. Resor*, *Varanger* (all sunk off the coast of New Jersey), and the *Coimbra*. The reason given was, "The tankers, most of which were carrying cargoes of petroleum products when sunk, were considered to pose a potential and substantial threat of pollution to the American shoreline should they still contain their cargoes and be in a position to release them as a result of the natural deterioration of their hulls."

Investigation soon disclosed that the tanks of the three tankers off the New Jersey coast had long since ruptured and contained no oil. "After determining the hull thickness with ultrasonic gauging equipment, a stud gun and plug would be used to penetrate the hull and sample the cargo." Ultimately, "no oil was found in sufficient quantities for analysis." But "the *Coimbra's* tanks are in good condition and appeared to be closed to the sea and yet even her cargo has somehow been released over the years, leaving only the slightest traces of residual oil. Attempts to penetrate the hull of the *Coimbra* failed, and indicate that corrosion has not occurred to an extent which would allow a mass release of entrapped petroleum. Best estimates are that the oil has escaped by rising through the tank ventilation systems. This would most likely have occurred gradually over an extended period of time, allowing the oil to be assimilated by the surrounding sea through bio-degradation of the persistent oils and evaporation of the volatiles to the atmosphere from the non-persistent oil cargoes."

A more detailed description of the survey, conducted between August 30 and September 5, 1967, is interesting: "Divers established that the *Coimbra* was split into three sections. . . . The center section is lying on its port side in 182 feet of water and inclines 75° degrees to port with only its starboard side above the mud line. The tanks are intact, two of which, located in the aft section, were closed to the sea. Divers attempted to penetrate the hull with their stud guns, but the excellent condition of the hull plate prevented its being more than dented with the force of the explosive. The explosive charge of the gun pushed the diver away rather than forcing the projectile through the plating, which was measured at 0.9" inch on the hull. Divers then entered the starboard tanks through hatches and found only a trace of residual oil. They took samples which also contained slight traces of oil. The port and center tanks were below the mud line and inaccessible. Intermittent oil seepage was observed on the surface of the water but its source could not be located."

In its conclusions, the Coast Guard found that, "Evidence gathered from this project indicates that tankers sunk during World War II do not present a potential pollution threat to the American coastline."

The matter should have ended there, but several years later the issue of sunken tankers releasing oil was raised again, specifically with respect to the *Coimbra*. The primary instigator was Henry Frey, associate professor at the Polytechnic Institute of New York. After making a bounce dive to the wreck, he concluded that the Coast Guard investigation of 1967, involving 41 surface supplied dives conducted by experienced commercial divers, was incomplete. He claimed that as many as "ten tank compartments remain closed to the sea and may still contain oil." His basis for this viewpoint was the oil slick reputed to have been observed in the vicinity of the *Coimbra*. Frey began a campaign for a complete re-examination of all tankers sunk off the American east coast during World War Two, a number calculated by the Coast Guard to be 105 in the Atlantic and in the Gulf of Mexico.

Frey lectured zealously on the subject, made proposals to government agencies, tried to get funding from private foundations and corporations, and sought publicity through the media. He claimed that each and every tanker was a "sunken time bomb" waiting to explode and deluge public beaches with black, viscous sludge. (This despite the fact that the *Coimbra* did not carry crude oil, but lubricating oil, which is light and nearly transparent.) His thesis relied upon the assumption that some of the wreck's tank compartments were intact and full of cargo, and that, instead of oil leaking out a drop at a time through valves and pinholes in the bulkheads, a massive quantity could gush out if a bulkhead let go suddenly.

Largely as a result of Frey's continued outspoken insistence, in 1975 the Coast Guard began dropping sealed drift cards over the wreck "at the rate of 20 a month for one year, to verify the institute's belief that the oil may reach Fire Island, Jones Beach and the Rockaways. The cards contain questions to be answered by those who find them, and should be returned to the school or the Coast Guard. They are designed to drift with the currents in patterns that are identical with the drift of oil slicks." No positive evidence was ever obtained that a catastrophic release of oil from the *Coimbra*, if indeed significant quantities remained within the wreck's tanks, would reach New York beaches. Frey maintained his stance for several years, but eventually the threat of oil from the *Coimbra* contaminating Long Island's white sandy shores fizzled out.

Today the *Coimbra* is a popular dive site among deep wreck divers. Despite the Coast Guard's description of the wreck, the hull actually lies on its starboard side, not its port, a fact which disoriented me and my fellow divers who explored the wreck in the '70's. Once we determined that the Coast Guard's interpretation, and the media illustrations based upon it, was reversed, navigation on the bottom became easier and the locations of the bow and stern made sense. It was also apparent to us that the cargo tanks had long since ceased to be oil tight.

The wreck lies with the bow pointing east. The hull is broken into three sections, but the breaks are not as large as one is led to believe by reading the Coast Guard reports. The two breaks that separate the center section from the bow and the stern are only ten feet across at the keel, twenty feet across at the place of the upper deck. Since the visibility is generally forty feet or better, the breaks do not present a problem with getting from one section to another.

The stern is the most intact portion of the three, and rises some thirty feet off the bottom. It lies at an angle of about 75°, as reported. The immense bronze propeller is exposed; each of its three blades is some six feet in length and is beautifully adorned with large sea anemones. The stern section is truncated about fifty feet forward of the fantail, as if it were sliced open with a huge knife, permitting access to the aft compartments. At the level of the sand is the galley, where china and flatware have been found.

Forward of the open space is the midship section, the aft portion of which consists of the forward end of the stern superstructure, much of which has slid off the hull and is lying in the sand. Portholes are found here. Forward of that is the midship section which is mostly comprised of tanks. It does not have the

An ornate brass ceiling fixture, whose glass cover is in the design of a porthole complete with dogs, hangs by a wire from the overhead.

same angle of tilt as the stern, as if the lack of structural support allowed the upper deck to fall back partially into the void. This goes on for several hundred boring feet, with very little to see other than the starboard gunwale topped by lots of steel plates.

But if you are watchful, you will see the remains of the wheel house off the wreck in the sand, as Bill Nagle did when he found the wooden helm and brass stand lying loose on the bottom. (See the back cover photo.) To my knowledge, nothing else has been recovered from the area.

The bow is undistinguished, existing largely of a structure of hull plates with very little of obvious interest to see, and for this reason receives much less attention than the stern.

Since so much of the *Coimbra's* underwater history has been concerned with oil pollution, it is appropriate to relate Rick Jaszyn's experience in removing a porthole from the stern section. From the upper hull he spotted an intact porthole complete with uncracked glass. Since portholes open only from the inside, he found a way through the cut into the compartment and knocked back the dogs with a hammer. When he was unable to move the porthole on its hinge pin, he then went back outside the wreck to where he could obtain more leverage, and shoved the porthole in. Unbeknownst to Rick, a layer of oil (not cargo, but fuel oil from the bunkers) had risen and collected at the top to the compartment. As soon as he managed to break the seal and force the porthole in, the black bunker oil burst out and engulfed his face and upper body. It completely coated his mask, and was an unholy mess to clean off enough so he could see his way back to the grapnel. He left black hand prints all the way up the anchor line, and soiled the boat to the great discomposure of the captain.

Nevertheless, a couple of bucketfuls of oil is nothing to be concerned about in the vast reaches of the sea. The amount still remaining on the *Coimbra* is undoubtedly much less than that pumped overboard by the average sized tanker or freighter when one cleans its bilges.

Crockery and stainless steel drawers lie atop a low partition, now horizontal, in the galley.

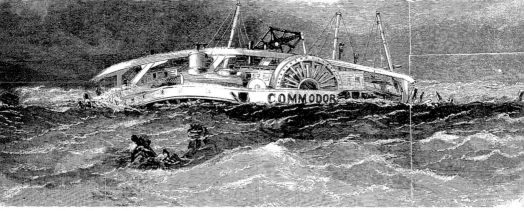

From *Harper's Weekly.*

COMMODORE

Built: 1848
Previous names: None
Gross tonnage: 984
Type of vessel: Wooden hulled sidewheeler
Builder: Simonson & Logan, New York
Owner: Stonington Line
Port of registry: New Haven, Connecticut
Cause of sinking: Beached to prevent foundering
Location: Horton's Point, Long Island Sound

Sunk: December 27, 1866
Depth: Unknown
Dimensions: 275' x 32' x 11'
Power: Coal-fired steam

The *Commodore* was constructed to provide passenger service across the Long Island Sound, between New York and New Haven, Connecticut, and served reliably in that capacity for seventeen years, carrying thousands of people on their errands between those two cities. Her walking beam engine turned her two massive paddle wheels with speed and efficiency considered admirable for the times. Service went unabated during the Civil War, and many a Union soldier began his journey to the battlefront aboard the well-known steamboat. This is not to say that she did not have her "fender benders" and occasional groundings and mechanical breakdowns, but somehow she managed to keep going after each adversity.

In October of 1866 the *Commodore* was condemned as unseaworthy by Captain William Bradford, Supervising Inspector in New York. Therefore, she was laid up in New Haven for repairs. According to the report issued by the Treasury Department, "Much of her timber work and planking was found to be rotten, which added to her age, rendered her at once unsound and unsafe; whereupon she was docked and subjected to an overhauling and repairing at a cost of $10,000. This it was believed rendered her sufficiently strong for Sound navigation, but even then she was regarded by Capt. Bradford as poorly adapted to withstand the severe weather of the Winter season." According to another account, she was "put on the dry-dock, engines secured, keelsons thoroughly repaired, and supplied with a shaft and two new life-boats."

Local inspectors at New London agreed with Bradford about the *Commodore's* condition, and even after the repairs stated above, refused to issue a conditional certificate to allow the steamboat to carry on her trade unless "she was properly equipped according to the law."

Apparently, the Stonington Line thought it had already invested enough money in refurbishing the steamboat and refused to invest any more. "It appears that she left the wharf at 4:10 P.M. on the 27th of December, and proceeded on her voyage; that at the time of leaving there was a lull; but previous to that it had been blowing heavily from west to west northwest during the entire day, attended with snow-squalls. The weather appeared cleared at the time she departed, and the captain, without consulting his barometer, was induced by the apparent favorable weather to put to sea. At 8 o'clock that evening, however, the breeze freshened from the northwest, and soon increased to a violent gale, with a heavy sea, and with a flood tide making against the wind. It became rougher at 10:30, the vessel heading east 1/4 by north, the wind nearly aft, and steering wildly broached to and was immediately thrown upon her beam ends, and in this condition she was driven by the wind across the sound, and was brought to an anchor, with two anchors down, near Horton's Point, on Long Island, when she soon righted.

"It was here discovered that she was leaking so badly that it was necessary to slip her cables and beach her, in order to save the lives of her passengers. This was fortunately accomplished without a casualty or the loss of a single life.

"The cause of the leak seems to have been the severe straining which her timbers and planks experienced when she broached to, and while being driven across the Sound on her beam ends, and not, as has been stated, by her taking the ground; for it was when she had righted at her anchors, her batts and seams, which had been sprung, being then brought under water, that the leak was discovered. It is very clear from the testimony that the *Commodore* was to-day unfit for the service in which she was engaged as well as by reason of her age as by her light draught of water. . . . Her light draught was in a great degree the cause of her steering so wildly, for the rudder not being thereby sufficiently immersed, and being frequently out of the water, could not perform its office, and the vessel was therefore in a measure at times uncontrollable.

"The crew seem to have been inadequate to the emergency, for some of them were totally unacquainted with the management of the boats. It is a wonder, therefore, that no lives were lost in landing. . . . From the facts recited, gathered from the testimony of reliable witnesses, there can be no doubt that the *Commodore* was lost by reason of her manifest unfitness to withstand a gale of any severity in the waters which she was employed in navigating, arising partly from her age and subsequent weakness, partly from her light draught of water, and partly from the indiscretion of her Captain—first in taking her to sea, and then, when at sea, in not making a harbor. She was also lacking in equipments, and therefore unseaworthy, and being navigated without a certificate, her owners are liable to penalty for a violation of law."

Elaborating on the saving of life, another account stated, "None of the passengers, fortunately, were lost. If the vessel had gone ashore at any other point, east or west, for five miles, all on board must have perished, as rocks are on each side of her that distance, with precipitous and frozen banks, and no houses within a mile of the beach. As it was, they were all safely landed through the aid of the residents along shore, and sent to New York by the first trains. . . . she went ashore a complete wreck. Her engine and boilers will probably be recovered." It also stated that the Commodore's destination was Stonington, Connecticut.

The *Commodore* incident provides valuable insight and historical background to jurisprudence and to the cultural philosophy of a government's obligations to its citizens. As the Treasury Department so wisely noted, "The loss of this vessel affords another commentary on the necessity for additional and effective legislation. The law, as it now stands, is totally inadequate to the enforcement of the moral obligation of owners and others toward those who place their lives in their hands. Happily there are exceptions to this necessity, for there are many honorable and high-minded owners of vessels whose constant desire is to obey the law in all its provisions, and provide their passengers and crews with adequate protection to the best of their ability, and regardless of expense. But, on the other hand, there is a class of owners (far too numerous for the public welfare) who can be reached at once by the most stringent enactments, and made to fear the consequences of defying the laws and regulations by the certainty of a swift and appropriate penalty; and such enactment's must be made as soon as practicable, and such rigorous enforcement thereof prevail, embracing in their scope every obligation which a shipowner owes to the people whom he serves, and providing a punishment for reckless offenders inaccessible to higher motives, which shall be severe enough to deter them from periling human life and property."

Courtesy of the Suffolk County Historical Society.

CULLODEN

Built: 1776
Previous names: None
Gross tonnage: 1,659
Type of vessel: 74-gun ship of war
Builder and owner: British navy
Cause of sinking: Ran aground
Location: Off Culloden Point, near Montauk

Sunk: January 23, 1781
Depth: 20 feet
Dimensions: 170' x 47' x 19'
Power: Sail

In 1770, Great Britain was engaged in a bitter struggle to maintain dominion over her colonies in the New World. Political unrest ran rampant, and talk of revolution was being whispered throughout North America. The Declaration of Independence lay six years in the future, when the Founding Fathers met in Philadelphia to write the document that changed the course of history, and although England did not know what events were about to unfold, she knew that she had to prepare herself for what might occur. In that year she authorized the construction of the HMS *Culloden*.

Ships are not built overnight. They are complex structures which require the same imaginative design, precise measurements, and painstaking workmanship that go into a gothic cathedral, in addition to which the final product must float and be stable in the water. Thus from concept to commissioning the *Culloden* was six years in the making. She officially entered service on May 18, 1776. By that time hostilities in America had reached a fever pitch; the starting date of the American Revolution lay only six weeks away. One might think that the newly commissioned *Culloden*, her three decks bristling with seventy-four guns, and manned by a crew of more than 600 officers and men, would be sent at once to defend British property and possessions. But the Admiralty took a broad view of the growing insurrection. Since military uprisings require arms and ammunition to prosecute, stopping the flow of imported materiel could achieve the goal of quelling a revolt better, and more bloodlessly, than direct confrontation with soldiers.

So the *Culloden* left the British Isles to serve as part of Robert Digby's Squadron, which was then operating off the coast of Spain, from which point the American upstarts were being supplied with weapons of war. She was then and to the day of her loss under the command of Captain George Balfour. Since France and Spain were lending aid to the British colonies, all vessels of those nations were subject to attack by British forces. For two years the *Culloden* conducted operations against Great Britain's European enemies, returning several times to the home waters surrounding the British Isles.

The *Culloden* made her first foray against American shores commencing on June 9, 1778, when she sailed for North American with a dozen other ships of a squadron under the command of Admiral John Byron. After enduring a month of mid-Atlantic storms, the squadron arrived piecemeal on American shores. The *Culloden* was so damaged during the crossing that Captain Balfour veered away from Long Island, where the French fleet lay waiting for action, because neither his ship nor his men were in fighting trim. He steered instead for Halifax, and there met up with Admiral Byron and other elements of the squadron which were also battered by the continuous storms. By this time it was the middle of August.

In September the *Culloden* accompanied two ships of Byron's Squadron to Sandy Hook, New Jersey, and met up with half a dozen other ships of the squadron, all of which were the worse for wear. Anticlimactically, although the *Culloden* captured a French tender, there were no fierce battles or confrontations with the enemy fleet. In October the squadron sailed for Boston. On the way they encountered such a fierce gale that the *Somerset* was lost off Cape Cod, along with twenty men. The *Culloden's* masts were splintered and broken by the high winds and, after being blown far off the coast, she labored her way across the Atlantic and returned to England for repairs.

Late in 1779, the *Culloden* joined the Western Squadron, and was dispatched to the West Indies to engage whatever French and Spanish forces could be found. On the way to the Caribbean, on January 8, 1880, while passing along the western coast of Spain, the British fleet encountered a large fleet of Spanish merchantmen and escorts consisting of nearly two dozen vessels. The Spaniards were severely beaten in the fierce battle that ensued, and the entire fleet was captured; nearly 1,300 men were taken prisoner. With the British fighting on three fronts (France, Spain, and the newly created United States of America) her resources were severely strained, so the capture of the Spanish fleet was a gift of which she immediately took advantage. The prizes of war were taken to Gibraltar for the relief of the men occupying the besieged base.

In the spring of 1880 the *Culloden* returned to England and was put into dry dock so her bottom could be coppered; that is, thin sheets of copper were nailed to the wooden hull below the waterline as a means of preventing marine fouling organisms such as barnacles and shipworms from attaching themselves to the wood. Thick clusters of barnacles slow a vessel's speed, while shipworms (actually wood boring mollusks called teredoes) ate into the wood much the way termites eat into a house's foundation. On June 3, the newly sheathed ship sailed for the Leeward Islands, in the Caribbean, where she operated, somewhat unsuccessfully, during the hot summer months. In September she sailed for New York.

Here the *Culloden* met her untimely end—not as a result of naval action, but from the overpowering forces of nature. For months she lay at anchor in Gardiner's Bay, the safe and protected refuge occupied by many British vessels which were waiting to engage the French fleet should it break out of Newport, Rhode Island, across Block Island Sound. This stalemate persisted until January 1781. Intelligence reports indicated that a French departure was imminent. On January 20, the *Bedford*, and the *America* set sail in order to be in position to engage the French when they broke out of their harbor; the *Culloden* followed a day later.

The day after that, as the three British warships patrolled the area, a winter storm struck the coast in all its fury. None of the British vessels caught in the open fared well. Sails were torn, masts were split, and anchors dragged. On the night of the twenty-third the *Culloden* found herself in a bad way, with topsails shredded and masts splintering. Captain Balfour was unable to maintain control of the ship, and in the rain-swept darkness he was unsure of his position.

The leadsman tossed the lead line every half hour, according to British custom, and each time sang out a comfortable twenty fathoms; he had to sing loud in order to be heard above the raging wind of the tempest. Then, between squalls and through the stygian darkness, a lookout spotted land and shouted that breakers lay ahead. Captain Balfour screamed for the anchors to be let go, but so quickly was the *Culloden* being blown toward the shallows that she touched bottom before his order could be carried out.

According to the *Culloden's* deck log, the order to drop the anchors was at once countermanded "as the ship was then fast aground." The crew scampered into the rigging and did what they could with the remains of the canvas which was beating in the wind. "We backed her head offshore, then filled and endeavored to run her off, but her bow came round to the westward and lay fast."

At dawn Captain Balfour saw that his ship was in a precarious position. Verbatim, with antique spelling and constructions: "At 10 the gale increased, also the sea, she labored and strained much. At 1/2 past 10 cutt a way the topmasts to ease the Ship. People employed in clearing the wreck and pumping the ship."

All day long the wind howled furiously and without surcease. The temperature was fearfully cold, especially for the "tars" who had to work the deck and rigging. Down below, the men pumped the holds by hand and fought to keep back the sea; but water seeped in through opened joints and sprung planks faster than it could be ejected. The crew struggled all day long and late into the night in a vain attempt to save their ship. Not until the next afternoon, on the 24th, did the storm abate. By that time the forward holds were filled with water to a depth of fifteen feet.

The last chance to save the ship was to warp her off the bar at high tide. The sailors manned the boats and carried the *Culloden's* anchors into deep water. Others took their places at the capstan bars and put on a strain, hoping to haul in the hawsers and pull the ship toward the anchors. The ship did not move. The hull appeared to have settled into the sandy bottom as much as nine feet, and was gripped by a powerful suction which proved impossible to break. The *Culloden* was there to stay.

The wreck lay in shallow enough water that its upper deck was exposed to the sun. At low tide the *Culloden* appeared to be moored near shore; but when the tide came up, the ship did not rise with it. Then it was apparent that the vessel was not afloat, but was sitting on the bottom with its holds flooded. The men rowed ashore in the ship's boats, and it must have taken quite a few trips to transfer more than 600 sailors to the beach. There they lived while the wreck was being salvaged for everything of value. They must have suffered miserably from the winter cold.

The wreck was picked apart like a beached whale. Everything of value was

removed, including the anchors, hawsers, tackle, sails, rigging, powder, shot, even the masts. The crew managed to recover some of their belonging from the flooded lower decks. Two brigs moored alongside and offloaded nearly fifty cannons, more than likely those which were the most accessible. This did not happen overnight, but took more than a month of hard, backbreaking labor under the worst of conditions. When the British salvaged as much as they thought they could, they burned the hull to the waterline to prevent the enemy from making use of what remained.

Nevertheless, one enterprising patriot, Joseph Woodbridge, salvaged a further sixteen guns and made them available to George Washington's army—at a price, of course, since even then Americans had a penchant for opportunism.

Captain Balfour was exonerated from blame. He went on to serve aboard other ships in the British navy and was eventually promoted to admiral.

What was left of the hull slowly rotted away. A war was being waged, and there were more important items on England's agenda than a sunken hull whose charred ribs protruded from the water during successive low tides. The *Culloden* rated barely a footnote in the history of the American Revolution. Ironically, the loss of the ship of war was remembered more as a result of a geological reference than as a casualty, for the name of the headland where the vessel was blown ashore was changed from Will's Point to Culloden Point.

The wreck can be accessed from the beach. Drive north through Montauk Harbor on West Lake Drive, turn left onto Soundview Road and continue for three-quarters of a mile until the macadam gives way to a sand trail, which is hard-packed and navigable by car. Go about 1.5 miles and turn right onto another sand trail, then go to the end and park in the turnaround, a distance of less than one tenth of a mile. Climb down the sand cliff face about fifteen feet, then, facing the water, walk diagonally and to the left along the beach to a rounded boulder about three feet across and half that in height and width. Swim straight out a couple of hundred feet to the wreck site.

Hardly anything remains of the wreck today except for a few timbers and iron cannons, which protrude occasionally from the bottom when the sand is washed away by a storm. You may be disappointed to find that nothing is exposed and that no wreckage of any kind is visible.

A cannon and a pair of gudgeons which were recovered from the site are on display at the East Hampton Town Marine Museum. The gun carriage in the accompanying photos is a restoration.

DRUMELZIER

Built: 1895
Previous names: None
Gross tonnage: 3,625
Type of vessel: Freighter
Builder: J. Laing, Sunderland, England
Owner: Astral Shipping Company, Ltd. (Gillison & Chadwick, Managers)
Port of registry: Liverpool, England
Cause of sinking: Ran aground
Location: 26674.1

Sunk: December 25, 1904
Depth: 15 feet
Dimensions: 340' x 44' x 18'
Power: Coal-fired steam

43754.3

The *Drumelzier* was only eight hours out of New York, bound for Havre, France, with a general cargo valued at $344,000, when she ran aground irrevocably and ended her career. "At about 3 a.m., during a blinding snowstorm, with strong NE. wind and sea running high, the *Drumelzier*, a large freight steamer carrying a crew of 30 men, stranded upon Fire Island Bar, 2 1/2 miles from Oak Island station, 4 miles from Fire Island station, and 2 1/2 miles from shore."

If Captain William Nicholson, master of the *Drumelzier*, and his crew managed to have a merry Christmas in New York City, they were not slated to have a happy New Year. The ship was stuck fast amidships with the bow and stern free; no amount of engine power could propel the vessel off the shoal, either forward or backward. She was impaled like a bug on a collector's pin.

"At 5.30 a.m. an Oak Island patrolman sighted a distress signal burning on board the vessel and promptly reported to Keeper Doxsee, who telephoned the news to Keeper Front, of Fire Island station. Both life-saving crews manned their surfboats and boarded the steamer, the Oak Island crew reaching her at 7.30 a.m., and the Fire Island crew an hour later. At the suggestion of Keeper Frost the master set the ship's numbers, in order that the telegraph operator on shore might report the vessel, and later in the day the wrecking tug *I.J. Merritt* arrived upon the scene and lay to near the steamer. As the *Drumelzier's* crew did not wish to abandon the ship, the life-savers arranged for the master to telephone them in case of need, then returned to their duties on shore."

There were hopes that at high tide the tug could pull the stranded steamer off the shoal with very little damage, and that she could then continue on her way. However, early confidence eroded to doubt when the tug proved incapable of the task. A dense fog settled in as the temperature rose above the freezing point. By noontime the wind shifted to the south and rose in velocity. The sea that had been calm now became violent, especially on the shoal. Rain mixed with snow continued unabated, and under these trying conditions salvage proved impossible. Not helping the situation was the *Drumelzier's* heavy cargo of steel, copper, pigs

of lead, and oil. Better conditions were needed in order to bring in lighters and offload enough weight to make the steamer buoyant. Nor was the additional hauling power of the tug *William E. Chapman* sufficient to drag the ship off the shoal.

For the next two days the *Drumelzier* lay hard aground. Much to everyone's chagrin, she appeared to have been driven in closer to shore by the pounding of the waves. Conditions on board became so perilous that the Revenue Cutter *Mohawk* was dispatched in the morning of the twenty-ninth to take off the captain and crew. "The *Mohawk* stood by the stranded steamer for two hours, but the officers of the revenue vessel declare that the tremendous seas that swept the *Drumelzier* for and aft rendered any attempt at rescuing the crew impossible."

Lieutenant Lauriat, the *Mohawk's* second officer, said, "We found the vessel lying broadside to the Fire Island shore, about three-quarters of a mile from the inlet and a similar distance from Bell Buoy No. 8, which had been placed there as a warning signal for the sand bar further in. The steamer had her port side turned to the land and her bow pointed in a southeasterly direction. She had a list to starboard, and pounded heavily, as one tremendous sea after the other struck her.

"We stopped near the bell buoy, about three-quarters of a mile off the stranded vessel. Further in, and just outside the breakers, lay the Merritt & Chapman wrecking tug *William E. Chapman*. As we drew near and observed the size of the seas that were sweeping her deck we saw at a glance that it would be impossible for us to render any assistance. The great breakers were rolling along, veritable mountains of water, and as they struck the side of the stranded steamship she would tremble and pound in the sand. Most of the time she was lost to us behind a solid wall of spray. The seas swept clear over her decks and deckhouses, and great frenzied sheets of water were constantly playing about her funnel top and her masts.

"It seemed impossible that any of her crew could venture out on her decks under the conditions that prevailed. We could see no living soul aboard the *Drumelzier* while we were standing by her. The men must be cooped up below decks or in the deck houses, and it seems difficult to understand how they can escape from the seas even there. Their sufferings during the days the steamer has been aground must have been awful."

Captain Ross, master of the *Mohawk*, reluctantly admitted defeat in his attempted rescue of the *Drumelzier's* crew, "as no boat could live long enough among the breakers to reach the lee of the stranded steamer. So, after standing by the *Drumelzier* for two hours and exchanging signals with the wrecking tug to make sure that she would remain on guard during the night, the *Mohawk* returned to port."

Chief Engineer Wood described the situation on the ship at the time: "Fearing that the main steam pipe would break I maintained a full pressure of steam and kept the engines running alternately ahead and astern, hoping to get clear. . . . Then she began to be ruptured, and fearing that all hands in the engine and boiler rooms would be killed, I drew the fires, and we gave up all hopes of getting the ship off. From that time matters grew worse, and as she rolled and pounded the ship strained so that it seemed that she would certainly go to pieces. . . . As the straining continued rivets were sheared off in hundred from the bulkheads and flew in volleys like rifle bullets, making it dangerous below decks. All that kept her from going to pieces was the fact that the longer she lay there the more firmly she became anchored in the sand. We owe our lives to that."

That the wreck lay in dire straits was confirmed when the *Drumelzier* transmitted that one of her boilers had broken loose. From this it was surmised that she could not long sustain the pounding of the seas, and that she might already be succumbing to the powerful forces of nature.

During this time the men of the Oak Island and Fire Island Life-Saving Stations were not sitting idle. Time and again during the daylight hours of the twenty-eighth they tried to launch their boats through the surf, and time and again the boats were driven back by the waves. So the Life-Saving Service decided upon a different tack.

"Directions were sent through the inspector's office at New York for the keeper of Sandy Hook station to endeavor to reach the wreck. Keeper Patterson received the order at 9.30 p.m. of the 28th, and at once telegraphed for a tug, and finally succeeded in employing the *Catherine Moran*. At 2.45 a.m. of the 29th the surfmen launched the lifeboat, boarded the tug, and with the lifeboat in tow started for the wreck, 42 miles distant. At 8 a.m. the tug lay to off the stranded ship, about which a turbulent sea was breaking high, and the surfmen manned the lifeboat for their perilous undertaking. After beating off the ice that had encased the boat and her fittings, they reefed and set her sails, then with a leading wind sailed through the breakers, rounded to under the lee of the *Drumelzier*, took off all of the crew who wished to leave the ship, 16 men, made sail again, and at 11.30 a.m. reached the tug without mishap. Considering the fact that the lifeboat carried 25 men on the return trip, and that the feat was performed in a gale and a very rough sea, this deed reflects great credit upon the skill and courage of the keeper and crew of Sandy Hook life-saving station. The return trip to Sandy Hook was safely accomplished, the shipwrecked crew being taken to New York by the tug, while the life-savers returned to their station, which they reached at 5 p.m."

A newspaper reporter described the plight of the *Drumelzier* at the time of the rescue: "Although the sea had gone down some during the night, giant breakers were still sweeping clear across the stranded vessel. Her list to starboard— toward the open sea—was so heavy that the starboard rail was only two feet above the water. When the seas broke against the steamer's side, the rail was submerged from fore to aft. The crest of the waves reached clear above the bridge and deck houses, and the spray was tossed as high as the mastheads of the *Drumelzier*. Her stern and bow were solid masses of ice and huge stalactites of fantastic shape hung from her rigging everywhere. Only the starboard side, where the breakers smote the ship, was free from a coating of ice."

Despite these awful conditions, Captain Nicholson and thirteen men entertained hopes of saving the ship as soon as the weather moderated. However, the situation worsened and the end, when it came, occurred suddenly. "While laboring heavily among the breakers that ran mountain high and pounded the bed of sand under her hull, the crew heard a cannon-like report, way down in the depths. The next moment there was a sudden bulging up of her decks amidships, as though a volcanic eruption had occurred in her hold. The engine was torn from its fastenings and slid six feet aft. The boiler slid forward a like distance. The stern buried itself deep in the sand, with the result that rudder and propeller were both ground to pieces. Capt. Nicholson needed no further evidence to tell him that the *Drumelzier* had broken her back and that his fight with the ocean had been lost."

Now there was no further reason to stay aboard, but there was every likelihood that no rescue could be effected. "There were six feet of water in the forward hold of the vessel and eight feet aft. The storeroom, where the ship's provisions were kept, had been flooded, and there was hardly anything on board for the crew to eat."

Captain Nicholson gave the signal to be taken off: the Union Jack flying upside down. "Both the Oak Island and Fire Island crews promptly responded to the call. The keeper of the latter station, having 2 1/4 miles overland to transport his boat, called upon the Point of Woods crew, which came to his assistance, helped to transport the lifeboat, and also to man it during the four-mile pull to the wreck. Just as the Oak Island crew were about to launch, they saw a lifeboat from the tug *I.J. Merritt* pulling for the shore, it having been alongside the *Drumelzier*, and then failed in an attempt to return to the tug. The surfmen hastened to the aid of the incoming boat, assisted the crew to land through the surf and to secure their boat, then launched their lifeboat and pulled to the *Drumelzier* and brought to shore seven men, while the Fire Island boat rescued the remainder."

In the true tradition of the sea, Captain Nicholson was the last man to leave his ship; he departed with the final lifeboat and did not arrive on shore until 9:30 that night. Left on board to their fates were one parrot, two cats, and a goat.

Much of the cargo was subsequently recovered, but the hull was too broken up to be worth the effort of salvage.

Today the wreck is known to local fishermen as the Fire Island Wreck, or the Quadrant Wreck; the latter name is applied because the steering quadrant is exposed at low tide. For this reason, caution must be taken if approaching the wreck by boat, or else those on board may find themselves swimming to the beach at Robert Moses State Park. Storm and wave action have done a good job of demolishing the wreck until very little remains other than scattered, low-lying debris. If there are any hidden treasures they lie buried in the sand—until the next big blow uncovers them.

Upper left and lower right: sea ravens in different color phases. Upper right: a bergall, also known as a cunner. Lower left: a black sea bass (upper left corner) and a tautog.

Courtesy of Bill Quinn.

FINANCE

Built: 1883
Previous names: None
Gross tonnage: 2,603
Type of vessel: Passenger-freighter
Builder: John Roach & Son, Chester, Pennsylvania
Owner: Panama Railroad Company
Port of registry: New York, NY
Cause of sinking: Collision with SS *Georgic*
Location: Three miles east of *Sandy Hook* lightship

Sunk: November 26, 1908
Depth: Unknown
Dimensions: 295' x 38' x 23'
Power: Coal-fired steam

    For three days a thick fog lay like a pall over the approaches to New York harbor. Inbound and outbound traffic was temporarily suspended due to the unprecedented long-term lack of visibility. Bells clanged mournfully and fog horns bleated warnings to small boats proceeding cautiously among anchored steamships waiting for the clinging mist to clear. Finally, around 8 o'clock in the morning of November 26, 1908—Thanksgiving Day—the haze began to burn off and traffic started to move.

    The *Finance* got up steam, weighed anchor, and moved down the shipping lane past the *Sandy Hook* lightship, which guarded the harbor approaches with bells, whistles, and searchlights. On board the *Finance* were, in addition to the officers and crew, seventy-five passengers, including nineteen women and fifteen children; most of the passengers were employees of the Canal Zone, or the employees' families, bound for Colon or Cristobal. The *Finance* proceeded at quarter speed, sounding her whistle continuously.

The *Finance* had actually begun her voyage three days earlier, but got no further than Quarantine when Captain Norman Mowbray, master, ordered her to anchor because of the pea-soup fog that all but closed off the harbor to steamship travel. Three times in subsequent days the *Finance* attempted to proceed on her way, as the fog lifted teasingly, but each time she was forced to stop when further safe progress was barred by coalescing fog.

Said passenger M.C. Azima, "We had been anchored in such a confusion of whistles that we were getting used to it."

Inbound crawled the White Star Line's *Georgic*, nearing completion of her passage from Liverpool heavily loaded with freight. She had been held up outside the harbor and had waited impatiently for the opportunity to enter. Stated Captain W.H.M.B. Clarke, master of the *Georgic*, "The fog was very thick. It lifted and I started ahead. Suddenly there loomed up in front of me—not more than a few hundred feet away—the form of a vessel. I whistled sharply one blast. The other vessel responded, and then started astern. Had she kept ahead she would have passed us. When I saw the situation I rang to stop. But we drifted ahead and the collision occurred. Under the circumstances it could not be helped."

Captain Mowbray had a different perspective from the bridge of the *Finance*. He was feeling his way through fog so thick that at times nothing could be seen beyond the bowsprit. When he saw with horror the huge bow taking shape in the mist, he shouted, "You are going to strike us," whereupon he leaped for the engine order telegraph and yanked the handle for reverse, then swung the helm to port.

Great ships respond slowly because of their incredible mass and momentum. The *Finance* had hardly begun to slow and to swing when the bow of the much larger *Georgic* cleaved the *Finance's* port side "like a knife into cheese. . . . For a few seconds the *Finance* seemed to lie on her beam ends, and then, as the *Georgic* swerved, her bow pulled out from the hole it had made in the other ship, and the *Finance* righted. A moment later the rattle of her anchor chains told the officers on the *Finance* that the *Georgic* had anchored." Although disputed, a claim was made that the *Georgic's* anchor had been let go too soon, and that it had fallen into the hole in the *Finance's* hull, where one of the flukes caught in the wreckage and tore out several hull plates.

Nevertheless, the sea poured into the gaping wound as if a flood gate had suddenly been opened. The mass of water caused the ship to list uncomfortably. Captain Mowbray knew right away that his ship was doomed, so he ordered the lifeboats prepared for launching. The deck crew swung the lifeboats over the side as water gushed into the holds and machinery spaces, "when from the hold came oilers, engineers, firemen, and stokers, climbing pell-mell up every ladder and companionway from the interior of the vessel." Among them was one William Todd, the third engineer, who "was partly overcome by ammonia fumes from a flask that had exploded in the forward hold. He staggered to the rail, steadied himself there for a second and then jumped overboard. He was not seen again."

Due to the early hour and the previous days of boredom, only a few of the passengers had arisen and dressed for breakfast in the dining saloon; most were still in their berths and wearing their nightclothes. The shock of the collision aroused immediate panic among those below deck, many of them women, who now, scantily clad, clambered topside, some carrying children in their arms.

Pandemonium reigned aboard the *Finance*. It was reported that, "When the first rush to the deck began Capt. Mowbray disappeared for a second, and when he came into view again he had a revolver in his hand. 'Now, men,' he shouted, meeting the rush from below, 'there is going to be no crowding, and the women and children are going to take the boats first.' The gun was not put to use, for the men for the most part behaved well."

J.E. Goldman added detail to the incident. "I saw half a dozen coal passers jump into one of the boats. I think it was the second. Then I saw the Captain draw his revolver and point it at the men. I didn't hear what he said, but one of the other passengers told me later that he had heard the Captain yell, 'Get out of there; women and children first.' As a matter of fact the women and children, I believe, had all got off in the first boat, but any way, those coal passers jumped back to the *Finance* and went off again later after the passengers."

Most of the panic was displayed by fear-stricken passengers. Mrs. S.F. Talbot threw her baby overboard then jumped in after it. Mrs. Minnie Strothotte had her seven-year-old son with her: "I took up my boy and ran to the side, intending to jump into the water, when some one grabbed me and pulled me back. I cannot describe my feelings while the life raft was being lowered. I could feel the vessel settling under us. Finally the raft was ready, and I got on it. There were other passengers clinging on it, one a women with her thirteen months' old child in her arms."

S.E. Blackhorn, a district judge in the Canal Zone, recalled, "I was in the cabin with my wife. Following the listing of the steamer I ran on deck with the baby in my arms and my wife following me. We found the passengers gathering there and the men getting the boats over the side. I worked my way forward along the deck, clinging with one hand to the rail, and with my wife holding to me. I got pretty well forward, and was waiting with one arm about some rigging, for the boats to come. The *Finance* had sunk low in the water and where we stood the deck was almost awash. A wave broke against the side of the deckhouse and the wash nearly carried me overboard. 'Go to the stern,' some one shouted, and I worked my way aft again. In that wash of water along the deck I saw children knocked down, and two were washed across my feet. I cannot understand how they were saved. When we got to the stern I found a boat there, and we were taken on board."

John Steward shuddered when he said, "I shall not soon forget this day." He jumped overboard with a life preserver, and witnessed a less fortunate passenger drown right before his very eyes. Henry Muller "appeared to me to be in distress, though he could evidently swim. I shouted to him to grab a chair that was drifting near him. He did so, but for some reason let it go a minute after."

Mrs. Thomas Halligan was in her cabin with one of her five children when the *Finance* listed so drastically. "Getting up as the vessel settled, she saw that a small boat was alongside. As she held her baby before the porthole in her cabin one of the men in the boat shouted to her to throw the infant to him. This she succeeded in doing, not believing that she would be able to reach the deck herself. She managed, however, to struggle up the companionway, just as Miss Minnie Mahoney, her sister, who occupied an adjoining cabin with some of the children, got them to the deck. Fear of suction as the ship sank caused the women to drop the children overboard near boats, which picked them up. Then they both jumped themselves and were saved."

Mrs. Hattie Schwartzbergh leaped for her life. "As she was drifting away and making frantic efforts to keep afloat she grabbed George H. Simmons of Detroit. Simmons was holding up Miss Bertha Gebhart. In her excitement, Mrs. Schwartzbergh caught him about the neck, and the three were in danger of sinking, when Simmons cried out for her to cling to him by his life belt. This she did, and the man kept both women afloat until one was rescued by C.B. Jennings, a freight clerk."

Mrs. M.J. Cody was traveling with four children. "I was dressing in the cabin with Annie, who is 8 years old. We heard a whistle, then came a crash and the boat listed. I saw a small boat come along side, and I pushed Annie through the porthole. My brother-in-law helped me rescue the other children, putting life preservers on them before they jumped."

Many people who jumped into the water during the *Finance's* final moments were saved by lifeboats from the *Georgic*, for Captain Clarke wasted no time in mustering his crew to go to the other ship's aid. This quick action resulted in the saving of all lives but four: the two already mentioned, and Irene Campbell and Charles Schweinler.

In the tradition of the sea, Captain Mowbray remained on the bridge as his ship sank beneath him, refusing to relinquish command until it was forcibly taken from him. As it turned out, he never even got his feet wet; the water was so shallow that when the keel came to rest on the bottom, the wheel house rose up above the surface.

This predicament was noticed by Captain C.P. Langmaid from the bridge of the Royal Mail Steam Packet *Orinoco*, inbound from Panama. "He sang out to Chief Officer Exleston, who was standing in the bows of the *Orinoco*, to hail the officers in the pilot house of the wrecked liner, to see if they needed any more boats. As the *Orinoco* neared the *Finance* it was seen that the majority of the passengers had left the ship, and there were three more lifeboats alongside her ready to take off those who were gathered in the pilot house. Capt. Langmaid's offer of aid was not accepted.

"When the *Orinoco* arrived at her pier Capt. Langmaid said that the gathering of the great merchant fleet of twenty-two ocean liners at anchor off Sandy Hook yesterday morning was the finest sight he had ever seen. The steamships steamed up the harbor toward New York in single column, and they were met by another column of vessels going out that had also been detained by the fog, with the Cunarder *Lusitania* bringing up the rear."

Captain Mowbray was taken off his steel island and placed aboard the *Georgic*, which returned the *Finance's* entire crew and all her passengers to New York. The smashed in bow posed no threat to the *Georgic's* immediate ability to float.

At least one person was fortunate that the collision occurred when it did, and was likely in later days to give thanks for the events of that Thanksgiving Day. "Nine-year-old Pepita Etommomou had been given to the immigration authorities by the Sisters of Mercy who have charge of the Roman Catholic Asylum at Sedgwick Avenue and Kingsbridge Road, in place of Blanche Matara, the eight-year-old child of Tony Matara, who was adjudged insane and unfit for citizenship. He was shipped out of the country together with his six-year-old son and the little girl who was supposed to be his daughter. Had the *Finance* not been wrecked, Pepita would now be en route to the Canal Zone in the care of an insane man."

One would think that, if the blessed sisters could not distinguish one dark-eyed, dark-haired girl from another, the family could. And the family did, but Blanche was not reunited with her father and brother until the *Finance* left port. Communications evolved, and the wireless operator relayed the situation to authorities in New York. An immigration inspector and an asylum officer went aboard the tug *Eugene F. Moran* to search for the *Finance*, then at anchor in the harbor, but could not locate the ship in the fog. When the survivors were brought back by the *Georgic*, the officers were waiting to take charge of little Pepita and exchange her for Blanche—who then got sent to the Canal Zone in the care of an insane man. Apparently, the authorities believed that it was appropriate for a little girl to be in the care of an insane man as long as that man was her father.

Most of the survivors were lodged aboard the *Finance's* running mate, the *Allianca*, which was docked in New York. Two days later, forty-five of them were given passage on the *Orinoco* for transport to the Canal Zone, wearing "no other clothing than those they stood in." Clothing had been ordered for them, but had not arrived at the time of the *Orinoco's* planned departure. "The side-wheel tug *George B. Starr* came up to the end of the pier and landed the passengers from the *Finance* who were to go on the ship. Dock Superintendent Phillips sent half a dozen longshoremen to the tug to carry the baggage, but the men were not needed. The rescued passengers carried their own effects in paper parcels and bundles. Two men carried new suitcases. Some of the passengers had nothing at all. As they walked along the pier to the gangway of the *Orinoco* some of the women and children were without hats or coats, others were wearing men's shoes, and some of the men were without hats or coats. It looked like the landing of people who had been marooned for months away from civilization."

A representative from the Panama Railroad Company pleaded for the ship to delay departure, a plea to which Captain Clarke acceded. An hour later, "taxicabs hurried up to the Royal Mail pier loaded almost up to the chauffeurs' neck with packages of all sizes. The articles for each person were packed separately and addressed to the passenger they were intended for. In all, large and small, there were 225 packages."

"The rest of the passengers from the *Finance* stayed behind in New York to get new outfits, as some of them had taken supplies for two years. Their temporary outfits ordered by the Panama Railroad Company were sent to the houses of friends they were staying with or to hotels."

Recriminations began immediately, with each shipping line blaming the other's vessel for responsibility for the collision. An oddity in this instance was the ownership of the *Finance*. The Panama Railroad Company was 65% owned by the U.S. government, which had dropped insurance on company vessels the previous July and assumed the risk itself. Therefore, the government was accountable for reimbursing the Panama Railroad Company, which it could do by taking funds from the Canal Commission. (This was at the time when the Panama Canal was under construction.)

Alternatively, the government could try to recover damages from the White Star Line, should the *Georgic* be found liable for the accident. Captain Clarke perhaps spoke out of turn while describing the collision, for he "was heard to say that his vessel refused to answer her helm, and that she was too light to be easily handled." In response to this statement, on February 17, 1909, when the *Georgic* steamed into New York after returning to service, two U.S. Naval officers boarded her at Quarantine and requested Captain Clarke to return to sea and come in again "through the channel in order to see how the vessel steered and how the channel was negotiated. . . . The naval officers wanted to study conditions under which the two vessels collided with a view of giving expert testimony." Captain Clarke refused to grant their request.

The circumstances of the accident were examined by the local board of the U.S. Steamboat Inspectors, in New York. After careful deliberation, the inspectors exonerated the *Finance's* Captain Mowbray and declared that "he had taken all necessary steps for the protection of his passengers." Mowbray was also commended for "compelling some of his crew at pistol's point to give up a lifeboat to the women and children when the *Finance* was sinking." At the same time, the board "did not attempt to pass upon either the conduct of Capt. Clark of the *Georgic* or to fix the blame for the collision that cost four lives. As the White Star liner is under the British flag, that side of the case will be investigated by the British Board of Trade."

Salvage of the *Finance* began the day following the collision and was an ongoing project for the next seven months. The vessel was worth a quarter of a million dollars and her cargo an equal amount. A large part of that cargo was $100,000 in gold, locked in the ship's safe, and was needed in Panama to pay company employees. "As soon as the wrecking boat went alongside the *Finance* yesterday morning the divers began the work of recovering the treasure. The strong room was on the main deck aft, and was easily reached. Two keys open the safe. The diver had but little trouble. Entering the room, the diver brought out the nine or ten boxes containing the gold, and it was hoisted to the lighter." It was reported that the purser's safe, containing the passengers' valuables, broke through the deck and into the hold. Nevertheless, also recovered were a number of mail bags containing registered letters, packages of jewelry and other valuables, and $7,200 belonging to the U.S. Navy.

Because the lighter arrived at the Panama Line's pier after the banks had closed on Friday, company officials were stuck with the task of guarding the gold until Monday. After a hasty meeting and discussion, they let it be known that the gold had been placed aboard the *Advance* and was already on its way to the Canal Zone. As one company official noted wryly, "We don't want to take any chances. In these days when thieves travel in squads we want to be on the safe side. These days have nothing on the days of Capt. Kidd."

However, the statement was pure misinformation intended to deceive would-be robbers. The gold and other valuables were simply kept in the company offices under guard, until it could all be transferred to the Treasury Department when its doors opened on Monday.

Salvage operations proceeded haltingly throughout the winter months, frequently hampered by storms and bouts of bad weather, to say nothing of working in the middle of the main shipping channel. One day in March was called "Grocery Day" by beachcombers from Seabright to Asbury Park. "Hundred-pound sacks of Gold Metal flour, their contents well preserved by the burlap bags and the inch coating of paste which formed outside, were gathered. Cans of castor oil, boxes of butter, bottled hair oil, tins of lard, packages of raisins and dried beef, codfish and parboiled codfish roes, candy and corned been, all in a good state of preservation, were also picked up."

Not until June could the Postmaster General breathe a sigh of relief. "After some six months of heavy work under the surface of the water in the lower channel, divers employed by the War Department yesterday rescued six bags of first-class mail, some of it containing registered letters, from the wreckage of the steamer *Finance* of the Panama Railroad Company. The bags themselves, sealed and locked, were in good condition, though the mail within was thoroughly soaked with water. It is now drying out in the engine room of the General Post Office. . . .The War Department gave the contract of removing the wreckage and recovering the mail to a wrecking company, whose divers have been at work ever since. Some second-class mail was recovered months ago, dried out with good results, and sent on to its destination, but the first-class mail, in bags weighing from 30 to 40 pounds, was so enmeshed in wreckage that the divers could not work their way to it until yesterday."

Eventually, most of what remained of the *Finance* was demolished with explosives as a menace to navigation, a rather ignominious end for a vessel which, when new, was one of the most advanced refrigeration vessels afloat, equipped with a sophisticated brine cooler for the transportation of beef, fruit, and vegetables through tropical climates without spoilage.

FRANKLIN

Built: 1850
Previous names: None
Gross tonnage: 2,183
Type of vessel: Side-wheel steamer
Builder: Westervelt & McKay, New York, NY
Owner: New York & Havre Steam Navigation Company
Port of registry: New York, NY
Cause of sinking: Ran aground
Location: Opposite Moriches Village, 20 yards from shore inside the outer bar

Sunk: July 17, 1854
Depth: 8 feet
Dimensions: 263' x 41' x 13'
Power: Coal-fired steam

In 1849, Edward Mills conceived a plan to operate a steam packet line between New York and Havre, France, with two ships assigned as running mates to cross the Atlantic at the same time but in opposite directions. In part, this inspiration came from the U.S. government, which offered him a mail contract and an annual subsidy of $150,000 a year for ten years, if he could guarantee regular service between the two ports.

So Mills had the shipyard of Westervelt & McKay construct the paddle wheel steamers *Humboldt* and *Franklin*, at a cost of more than half a million dollars each. Although the *Franklin* was twenty-nine feet shorter than the *Humboldt*, she had a broader beam and consequently was slightly larger in tonnage. Her side-lever engine was built by the Novelty Iron Works, in New York City—the

Courtesy of the Suffolk County Historical Society.

Leaving Havre for New York. (Circa 1852, from a woodcut in the author's collection.)

same company that built the machinery for John Ericsson's ironclad *Monitor* a dozen years later. The *Franklin's* paddle wheels were 32 feet in diameter, could churn the water at thirteen revolutions per minute, and could propel the ship at a respectable ten knots, although faster speeds were possible. The ship also bore three masts and was rigged as a bark.

Management of the two ships was given to Fox & Livingston. The vessels entered service in 1850, and maintained a stately pace between ports. Their advertised running time between Cowes (in southern England) and New York was just under thirteen days, and while that may not seem very fast compared to the flight time of the French Concorde, it was a significant improvement over the speed of a sailing vessel which had to rely on the vagaries of the wind for propulsion.

Disaster came to both running mates. First to go was the *Humboldt*, which ran aground off Halifax, Nova Scotia on December 5, 1853, with the loss of one life. Seven months later, on July 17, 1854, the *Franklin* met a similar fate off Moriches. She was westbound in a thick fog which masked her approach to land. Unbeknownst to Captain Wotton, master, a stiff northeasterly current had pushed the ship off course. Thinking that he was well clear of Long Island's south shore, he proceeded at slow speed with the steam whistle bleating rhythmically in time with the throbbing engine.

The end, when it came, came softly. At 8 o'clock in the morning the *Franklin* lightly touched a sand bar about one hundred yards from shore, and ground to a halt. The fog was so thick that Captain Wotton could not see the beach from the wheel house. He reversed the engine and starboarded the helm, but the ship was stuck fast. The sea was so calm that there was no danger to life and limb, and there was every expectation that the ship could be pulled off the bar with the rising tide. In order to ascertain their situation, a lifeboat was lowered and soundings were taken "and they commenced firing for a pilot, which was heard for an hour and a half before a sight could be obtained of the village from the ship, on account of the thick fog."

All the heavy stores were thrown overboard, as was the starboard anchor and fifteen fathoms of chain. Then the kedging anchor was run out in the boat and dropped offshore; with the hawser wrapped around the windlass, Captain Wotton was hoping to warp the *Franklin* into deeper water. But she was solidly embedded in the sandy bottom; the hawser parted, and nothing was gained by this effort.

"Finding all attempts useless, about 10 o'clock Monday morning the landing of the passengers was commenced in boats, and when landed they were met upon the beach by the inhabitants. Mr. J.H. Bishop, who keeps a boarding house near by, took several of the passengers to his house, and other proprietors of houses sheltered the remainder. They were all landed by 2 o'clock. The number of passengers landed was about 150, Captain Wotton remaining on board."

As the wind upon the canvas combined with the increasing surge was making the ship roll violently, the sails were reefed. For the rest of the day and all that night the pumps were kept working in order to keep the water out of the holds, where the precious cargo was stowed: some $800,000 worth of silk and miscellaneous dry goods.

During the night, the surge beat against the hull and gradually worked the ship closer to shore. The wooden hull creaked and groaned as the timbers were sorely strained. Seams opened up, the caulking leaked, and cracks developed in the hull. Then the water came in faster than the pumps could eject it, and rose at a rate of six and a half inches an hour. By the next morning the depth of water in the hold was eight feet.

Soon lighters and salvage tugs arrived from New York. In the northeast sea that had picked up during the night, the lighters could not get close enough to the *Franklin* to discharge any cargo. Nor could the steam tugs *Hector* and *Achilles* get hawsers aboard.

"Tuesday morning commenced sending ashore baggage, which was landed dry, and also one hundred packages of freight, which was stored at Mr. Bishop's under charge of Custom-House officers. The mails were sent on to New York on Monday night, at 10 o'clock. The surf at high water yesterday afternoon was so rough that no freight could be landed with facility, and the idea was abandoned. The ship was careened outward from the beach, which makes it unfortunate for her, the sand causing her to fall over, and the surf to work with more mischievous results upon her exposed side. During high water yesterday the spare spars and sails were got ashore, in order to make tents for the ship's company, and baggage and cargo which was left. These tents, in the evening were occupied by the ship's company and many visitors, who retreated from the rays of the sun. The ship's crew got their luggage yesterday afternoon, and all left the ship with the exception of the captain, the fourth mate, and one or two more, the ship working so heavily that it was deemed necessary to send all the crew ashore who were not absolutely wanted on board."

As a precaution, a hawser was run from ship to shore in case Captain Wotton and the others required rescue. The *Franklin* carried a life-saving car which could be pulled to the beach with its occupants dry inside.

By nighttime the *Franklin* was in desperate straits. She lay broadside against the beach with the bow pointing westward, "the sea making a clean breach over her." By then the depth of water in the holds was twelve feet. Since she lay in only eight feet of water, that meant that her hull had already dug itself four feet into the sand. The *Hector* and the *Achilles* left for New York; they were soon replaced by the *Leviathan*, but she was powerless to help in any way.

Five lighters waited nearby to take off the cargo, but although they were shallow draft vessels they could not approach the stranded steamer due to the shoals of the outer bar, even though the heavy seas had subsided. By the next day, so much sand had built up on the shoreward side of the *Franklin* that it was possible, at low tide, to offload the freight directly onto the beach without anyone getting his feet wet. An agent for the New York Board of Underwriters, which insured the *Franklin's* hull and cargo, employed more than a hundred men to help remove the 800 tons of freight before it was damaged by the sea. Horses were used to back carts up against the hull, so that eventually most of the cargo was saved.

All hopes of saving the *Franklin*, however, were abandoned, and soon the hull was broken apart by the breakers. There were plans to salvage the machinery, but this seems not to have been accomplished. As late as 1895 it was reported in the *New York Times*, "The remains of the boilers and engines of the steamship *Franklin* . . . are still there." That was 41 years after the event. There might not be much left after another century of battering by storm-driven waves.

GATE CITY

Built: 1878
Previous names: None
Gross tonnage: 1,997
Type of vessel: Passenger-freighter
Builder: John Roach & Son, Chester, Pennsylvania
Owner: Ocean Steam Ship Company
Port of registry: Savannah, Georgia
Cause of sinking: Ran aground
Location: 1-1/4 miles west of Moriches Life-Saving Station, 200 yards offshore

Sunk: February 8, 1900
Depth: 20 feet
Dimensions: 254' x 38' x 15'
Power: Coal-fired steam

The *Gate City* ran regular service for freight and passengers between Savannah, Georgia and Boston, Massachusetts, and did so monotonously year in and year out, earning money for her owners and providing reliable service for her customers. She could carry as much as 3,700 bales of cotton in her capacious holds, and she could berth 114 passengers in staterooms, plus an additional thirty in steerage. According to one account, "The main saloon is 80 feet long by 30 feet wide, and is finished in French walnut, birdseye maple, rosewood, and mahogany, and elegantly upholstered in red plush. The saloons are furnished with revolving chairs and other modern conveniences. She carries six metal lifeboats, two rafts, and 200 life preservers." She cost $375,000 to build.

However, the years of monotony came to an end on July 19, 1886, near the end of a northbound passage. At the time she had on board fifty-two passengers and 53,000 watermelons. As the *Gate City* entered Vineyard Sound she encountered a fog so dense that her master, Captain Hodge, ordered the engine stopped.

For four hours the ship drifted with the current. When the fog finally thinned, the captain decided to go ahead at the ship's slowest speed. The *Gate City* barely had way on when a seaman, ordered to cast the sounding lead, sang out, "We have no water," and the ship ground to a halt on a shallow rock off Naushon.

More than a few hackles rose when the passengers discovered that they were off Devil's Bridge, where only two years before the *City of Columbus* ran aground and sank with great loss of life. The *Gate City's* middle compartment began taking on water, but not so fast that the pumps could not reduce the flooding. Otherwise the ship was sound and in no immediate danger of sinking or breaking up; the sea was calm. The first mate put off in one of the ship's boats and managed to flag down a passing tug, the *W.O. Brown*, which returned with him to the stranded steamer and offloaded thirty-seven passengers and their luggage, then conveyed them to Boston. The other fifteen passengers chose to remain on board until transportation could be arranged to take them to their destination, Wood's Hole. They were accommodated the next day by the steamer *Monohansett*.

At the same time, salvage tugs of the F.W. Nickerson & Company were dispatched to the scene, and divers were put in the water to ascertain the extent of damage to the hull. By this time another compartment was flooding; three were still dry. Nevertheless, the vessel had grounded so lightly that no one expected much difficulty in pulling the ship off at high tide. But the report from the divers was not good, for the underwater survey revealed that "the bottom of the vessel was in a bad condition, and even if it were possible to haul her off the expense of repairing her would be very heavy." Subsequently, the *Gate City* was abandoned and turned over to the underwriters.

Salvage of the cargo was commenced, as it still had a substantial value. On July 21 it was reported in New Bedford that "ten thousand watermelons of the cargo of the steamship *Gate City*, ashore at Naushon, were forwarded to Boston to-day. Forty-three thousand were thrown overboard, and many small craft are picking them up. Vineyard Sound is a green sea." Much of the miscellaneous cargo, such as cotton, did not fare well, either.

The vessel's insurers were in a quandary about how to mitigate their losses. As everyone knows, insurance companies show profits by collecting premiums, not by paying claims. The vessel was insured for $200,000, which was spread among more than a dozen companies, most of which were based overseas. It was estimated that her machinery was worth some $40,000, but that it might cost as much as $100,000 to float the hull. The underwriters debated for several days. As one reporter quipped, "If much more time is lost a heavy sea will settle the matter for both owners and insurance companies beyond any question."

Finally, the underwriters bit the bullet and decided to go for broke. They hired the Boston Towboat Company to attempt to salvage the vessel in its entirety, with the typical provision of "no cure, no pay." It was the right decision. In less than a week the salvage outfit pulled the wreck off the rock and placed a canvas patch on her hull. Under her own steam, and assisted by the tugs *Steam King* and *Confidence*, the *Gate City* proceeded to Boston where she was docked so that permanent repairs could be effected. "The principal damage appears to be direct-ly under the fire room, where a great boulder forced its way through the plates. The rush of water through this lead was stopped by sewing a dozen blankets together, and wedging them down. The starboard strake is badly torn, and her fore foot is twisted, about 26 feet of her keel forward being gone." The Boston Towboat Company received a substantial reward for its efforts, since salvage awards are based upon the value of the wreck, not upon the amount of work expended. As one reporter put it, "The towboat company had an extremely soft snap, and will be entitled to a nice little plum when the matter is settled." But I thought the ship was carrying watermelons?

Monotony again assailed the *Gate City*, until February 8, 1900, when she was under the command of Captain Googan. Even ships can experience deja vu. She was again on the northbound passage when she encountered dense fog while attempting to round Long Island, and before land was sighted she ran aground off Moriches, at nine o'clock at night. Gun signals from the stranded steamer alerted members of the Moriches Life-Saving Station of her predicament. The

Courtesy of Sharon Reese.

Courtesy of Sharon Reese.

vessel could not be seen from shore, and when the life-savers burned Coston flares in response, those aboard the steamer could not see the signal lights.

The life-savers launched a surfboat and, guided by the sound of waves splashing against the *Gate City's* hull, located her in the darkness and fog. She was lying easy and appeared to be in good condition, so there was every hope that she could be pulled off the next day by wrecking tugs. The life-savers took off the three women (two passengers and the stewardess), but left on board the forty-five men. As a precaution, they established a line from ship to shore in case further rescue became necessary.

High tide came early in the morning, before the wrecking tugs could arrive. Instead of being pulled to the offshore side of the shoal, the waves from an increasing sea shoved the *Gate City* completely over the bar until she grounded some 200 yards off the beach. "The keeper set up the beach apparatus, and, with the aid of the Potunk and Forge River crews, landed twenty men safely in the breeches buoy and succored them at the station." Among the men landed were the rest of the passengers and some of the crew, all of whom were put up at the station and served meals.

All day of the ninth the stranded steamer waited for assistance, meanwhile embedding herself deeper in the sand. The next morning, the tenth, the wrecking tug *William F. Chapman* arrived. "The surfmen put part of the crew back on board, and wreckers took charge of the steamer." All did not go as planned, and despite the best efforts of the wrecking tug, the *Gate City* remained immobile. In order to lighten her load and to recover some of the cargo, the two crews worked hard for the next two days to begin offloading the cargo of 2,173 bales of cotton. Meanwhile, the passengers and some of the crew were sent to New York City by rail.

Then came the rain and the fog, accompanied by a high surf which rocked the wreck miserably and began to break the hull apart. The pleasant mid-winter temperature plummeted suddenly to below freezing, so that ice formed where the waves washed across the exposed deck.

"On the 13th signals of distress were sounded from the wreck, and surfmen again hauled off the hawser and breeches buoy. With the aid of the Potunk and Forge River crews once more, they landed four wreckers and the remainder of the steamer's crew, who were succored at the station until they were sent to New York by the agent of the vessel."

Despite the cold, the Moriches life-savers spent February 14 recovering the crew's baggage from the wreck.

Wreckers continued salvage operations for the next three months, always hopeful that when enough of the cargo was removed the hull could be refloated. As time passed, however, the prospects of successful salvage became more dismal. "On Feb 20 had twelve feet of water in her. Wreckers were still engaged taking out cargo. On the 21st there was no change in the situation of the steamer. Wreckers were still taking out cargo. The gale and high sea of the 22d washed the stranded steamer further in shore, where she settled in the sand, with remaining part of cargo wet and hold full of water. The port side of the cabin was stove in and flooded out. The Wrecking Co were working on her and thought they would float her on the night of the 27th."

The *Gate City* did not come loose as planned. She remained mired in the sand despite the powerful pull of the tugs. All hopes were finally dashed at 2 a.m. on March 2, when the hull split in two. Total hull salvage was then given up, but operations continued with removing the cargo. "March 8—The sea became sufficiently smooth to resume work on the *Gate City* this morning. The ship is filling up with sand to such an extent that it is almost impossible to free her with sand pumps used by the wreckers, and it is a tedious process removing the cargo under such conditions. There are yet about 700 bales of cotton in the ship and some other freight."

It was reported on March 28 that "The Merritt-Chapman Wrecking Co is still engaged in taking cotton out of the steamer *Gate City*." Work finally ceased some time in April. The last official shipping notice was published on May 2, proclaiming that the *Gate City*, "together with what cargo remains in her, was sold by auction at New York on May 1 by Messrs Burdett & Dennis. Mr. L.E. Lunt was the purchaser. Price $1950." Before she ran aground, the *Gate City* was appraised at more than $100,000.

Salvors then dismantled the wreck rivet by rivet, hull plate by hull plate, extracting everything of value and in the process reducing the wreck to a hulk, until very little remained other than a bare metal skeleton, appearing like some giant, flensed whale which had beached itself in the agony of its death throes. Much of the metal was sold for scrap.

What was left of the wreck was abandoned where it lay. Part of it went to pieces as it was pounded relentlessly by the waves, part of it was entrenched in a shallow, sandy grave. For half a century some of the steel structural components resisted complete breakdown and immersion, serving as a constant reminder that the beams and plates of a ship lay barely submerged beneath the watery foam and spray. As late as the 1960's, the top of the machinery could be seen in the troughs at low tide. Today, no part of the wreck reaches above the surface, and very little of its remains can be recognized for what they are by even the most observant diver. Nevertheless, the *Gate City* provides a habitat for a wide variety of marine life, and has much to offer the diver who likes to poke around shallow ruins and see what there is to see. Who know what treasures might reappear after a fierce winter storm sloughs off some of the embracing sandy shroud?

Courtesy of Sharon Reese.

GLEN ISLAND

Built: 1880   Sunk: December 17, 1904
Previous names: *William C. Egerton, City of Richmond*   Depth: 40 feet
Gross tonnage: 615   Dimensions: 238' x 35' x 12'
Type of vessel: Side wheel excursion steamer   Power: Coal-fired steam
Builder: Birely, Hillman & Strecker, Philadelphia, Pennsylvania
Owner: J.H. Starin
Port of registry: New York, NY
Cause of sinking: Burned
Location: 26893.6   43937.6

Undoubtedly the best known and most tragic ship casualty in New York's maritime history was the burning of the *General Slocum*, which occurred on June 15, 1904. Nearly 1,500 people, mostly women and children on a daytime outing, died in the conflagration or drowned after leaping into the water as the burning side wheel steamer drifted past Hell's Gate. The hulk was subsequently raised and converted to a barge, which foundered in 1911 off Ludlam Beach, New Jersey. Several books have been written about the burning of the *General Slocum*, and an account of her final loss can be found in this author's book, *Shipwrecks of New Jersey*.

The burning of the *Glen Island*, which occurred six months after the *General Slocum* was gutted by fire, seems to have been overshadowed by the immensity of the *General Slocum* disaster and the recriminations which followed. Although the *Glen Island* has not been completely lost in history, she has suffered comparative anonymity, probably because the number of fatalities was not as many.

At the time of her loss, the *Glen Island* was running excursion service between New York City and New Haven, Connecticut. The paddle wheeler was twenty-four years old, but her wooden hull was in good condition, and she had undergone considerable renovation during her career, having been practically rebuilt in 1893. Extensive remodeling included the installation of "an electric lighting apparatus in place of the old system." (The electric light bulb was a recent invention.) For ten years the *Glen Island* was a popular sight on Long Island Sound.

The *Glen Island's* first brush with misfortune occurred on the night of July 15, 1900, when she ran aground in the Sound. She was stuck solid, so all her passengers had to be transferred to another vessel which landed them at New York. The steamer was subsequently floated off and taken to Staten Island for repairs. Her final demise was not destined to transpire for another four years.

It was just after midnight on December 17, 1904 when fire was detected below decks amidship. At the time, the *Glen Island* was passing Greenwich east bound, and was two or three miles from the Connecticut shore. In her holds was stowed $20,000 worth of Christmasware in boxes. Captain Charles MacAllister was in bed; in the wheel house were Pilot Thomas McMullin and Quartermaster John O'Brien. "Suddenly the electric lights went out. O'Brien, who was steering, kept at the wheel, but two minutes later it blocked. The pilot and the quartermaster both were working frantically at the wheel when a moment later the fire alarm bell in the pilothouse began to ring. McMullin dashed out to see what the trouble was and he was met by a cloud of smoke rolling through the upper saloon. There he met Capt. Charles E. MacAllister and Mate Larsen, who had been in their rooms, calling the crew to quarters for fire drill. The Captain was clad only in trousers and overcoat."

Courtesy of the Steamship Historical Society of America.

As one reporter wrote rather melodramatically, the flames quickly "spread through an inflammable cargo and the flimsy, tinder double-deck superstructure."

It took only five minutes to turn the *Glen Island* into a raging inferno. Six crew men were trapped below and incinerated at their duty stations in the engine room. One passenger was overcome by the heat and suffocating smoke. "The captain saw at once that there was no chance to save his boat, and little time to save the passengers, so under his orders gongs everywhere were set a-ringing to wake the passengers, and lifeboats were unshipped with all dispatch."

The passengers emerged from their staterooms in various states of dress, some with little more than "coats over their night robes." A deck hand "led them through the smoke up to the deck. The boats had just been launched. 'Women first' had been Capt. MacAllister's order, and the crew had formed in line to pass one of the girls down, when a terror-stricken man rushed up and tried to get down first. One of the crew struck him a blow in the face that sent him reeling backward, and the women were handed down rapidly into the first boat.

"Mrs. Silken had come out of her stateroom and Stewardess Sarah Smoot was showing her the way to the deck when Mrs. Silken remembered that she had left her money in the room, and she dashed back after it. When the second lifeboat was filling up and the woman had not reappeared, Fireman Newman Miller went below to look for her. The whole boat was a roaring furnace by that time, and both fireman and passenger perished. O'Brien remained at the wheel until the flames began to lick up around the pilot house. Assistant Engineer Hendrickson was burned at his post in the engine room.

"When the two boats at last pushed off the *Glen Island* was a blazing mass. Those members of the Larchmont Yacht Club who happened to be at the club-house had an unobstructed view of the brilliant spectacle, and in the clear night the lurid sight was easily seen at Bayside across the Sound. Both on the Connecticut and Long Island shores hundreds gathered to watch the burning steamboat and wonder which of the Sound's night fleet it might be." The abandoned ship drifted south toward New York. People in Rye said that she "burned like a torch and made such a brilliant light that it was possible to read a newspaper."

Passenger Frederick Street estimated that "the boat, with the exception of a small spot at the bow, was ablaze from stem to stern in eight minutes."

The lifeboats stayed within a few hundred feet of the burning steamboat "in the hope that passing vessels would be attracted by the flames. . . . In the first of the *Glen Island's* lifeboats were seven persons and in the second fifteen. Hardly had the first boat got under way when it was noticed that one of the plugs in the bottom was out, and that the water was pouring in. Men used their hats to bail out, but the water kept gaining." Passenger Nathan Dubin tore the collar out of his companion's coat "and tried to cork up the hole, and still the water gained. Dubin took his handkerchief and with that succeeded in stopping up the plug hole. Then it was possible to bail out the boat."

Soon thereafter a tug and tow hove into view. The tug *Bully* cast off her tow and drove in to the rescue. In short order all of the *Glen Island's* survivors were taken off the lifeboats and were "carried down in the engine room to get warm." The *Bully* then drifted about "in the hope of meeting the *Erastus Corning*, another Starin Line steamboat, which was on her way from New Haven to New York." The *Erastus Corning* appeared right on schedule, and the people from the *Glen Island* were transferred to more commodious quarters.

The burning hulk went aground on Captain's Island, "where she burned to the water's edge. The wreck later drifted ashore off Glen Cove, L.I., near the Dana estate." This caused no little misunderstanding, for the Rye volunteer firemen, upon seeing the flames from the station, thought that "the large mansion of William L. Crowe at Pine Island was on fire. They rang in an alarm and dragged their fire engine through the snow to Rye Beach at 2 o'clock in the morning. After their three-mile run they discovered that the boat had been beached on the Long Island shore of the Sound near a small island on the estate of the late Charles A. Dana, just below Mattinacock Point. . . . When the Rye firemen reached the beach they could plainly hear the cries of the passengers and crew.

Although the burning steamer was several miles off shore, those who gathered at Rye Beach say they heard women scream 'Save me!' as distinctly as if the women were only a few feet away."

Even though the passengers lost all their possessions except what they were wearing, they had nothing but praise for the conduct of those in whose charge they had been placed. Said Mrs. Samuel Duke, "All of us, I am sure, appreciate the heroic conduct of the Captain and crew of the *Glen Island*, who did all in their power for us." Arthur Wallace declared, "The crew behaved splendidly through it all."

By morning, at high tide, all that could be seen of the *Glen Island's* remains were the smokestack and the steam whistle. The vessel was valued at $125,000, but against fire she was insured only for $23,750—a serious oversight on the part of her owners. A tug and a derrick were dispatched to the site, "and a diver made three descents to the hulk. No bodies were found. He reported that if any bodies were found they would be badly burned. Those at the wreck said that the hull would hardly be worth raising, and that some of the parts of the engine were warped."

Of greater moment were concerns about the laxity of safety procedures by the *Glen Island's* owners in particular and steamboat traffic in general, especially considering the recent controversy over the burning of the *General Slocum*. According to the records, "the *Glen Island* carried 2,017 life preservers, three metal lifeboats, three wooden lifeboats, and three life rafts. She had two fire pumps, 100 feet each of 2-1/2 and 1-1/2 inch hose. She also was equipped with an antiquated fire-fighting apparatus, which included thirty-five fire buckets, six water barrels, three water tanks, and eight axes." She had last been examined on May 25, 1904—less than seven months prior to her loss—by two inspectors from the Steamboat Inspection Service, and was pronounced fit for service.

A complaint was made by one of the passengers about the lifeboat's missing plug, but the steamboat inspectors waived this point as inconsequential since it was common practice for the plugs to be removed so the lifeboats did not fill up with rain water which leaked under the tarpaulins. No one addressed the issue of carrying extra plugs, or of having the plugs secured with a lanyard so they did not get lost.

The primary matter for investigation was the cause of the fire. This was found to be either crossed wires or defective insulation in the dynamo, an examination of which had never made by government officials. In this regard, Supervising Inspector Capt. Harris stated in no uncertain terms, "The local boards of Inspectors in the steamboat service do not inspect electrical equipment on any vessels. There has been no occasion to do so, and the Government has had no electricians members of the boards capable of doing it. We do not even make a record whether a boat is wired for incandescent electric lights, whether it has a dynamo or whether there is a motor aboard, and in fact the electrical plant of a ship is entirely ignored by the Government."

Thus the Steamboat Inspection Service was absolved from blame, and the question "How long is a short circuit?" was left for someone else to answer.

An official inquiry revealed a few other salient facts. After the burning of the *General Slocum*, every vessel in the harbor was supposed to be reinspected with an eye toward preventing a similar disaster. The *Glen Island* was "reported to the Steamboat Inspectors to be out of commission at the time" that edict was issued, as was her running mate, the *Erastus Corning*, so that both escaped reinspection. This may seem rather picayune in light of two facts already mentioned and acknowledged at the time: that the *Glen Island* had been inspected less than three weeks prior to the burning of the *General Slocum*, and that in any case the inspectors would not have examined the most probable cause of the *Glen Island's* fire—the faulty wiring of the dynamo. But this was not a time for cool-headed review.

Mate Ivon Larsen admitted at the inquiry that he had no license, and that he "did not know what freight was barred by law from passenger steamers," although he had charge of the loading of the vessel. He also stated that there was whiskey in the cargo and that the ship carried "a few barrels of oil." How damning or pertinent any of this was to the events that occurred was overlooked. Of tangential importance was his declaration that the *Glen Island* had on board at the time of her loss sixty-five fire buckets (thirty more than were reported officially) but that "of these sixty-one were empty or frozen." This begs the question of how valuable a bucket of ice may be under the circumstances, in the middle of winter.

To cast doubt on the theory of the electrical nature of ignition, Chief Engineer Vernon Layman believed that the fire started in the cargo.

Pilot Thomas McMullin testified that "fire drills had been held every week on the *Glen Island*; that on these occasions the boats were lifted and swung clear and water pumped into the fire hose, all of which . . . was regularly accomplished in ninety seconds."

After hearing much testimony and examining the incident from every angle, the Steamboat Inspectors issued a report that was 120 pages in length. Instead of castigating everyone within reach, it was highly commendatory. Not only did it not seek scapegoats to blame, it exonerated the *Glen Island's* officers and crew, and went so far as to applaud Chief Engineer Layman. "His duty technically was to start the fire pump and stop the engine when he got the signals from the pilot-house. He fortunately reversed the order: stopped the engine in the dark—an operation of a fraction of a minute—then started the pump, another minute or fraction of one. By that time the flames were roaring about the very place he had left, and to which he must have returned in order to have stopped the engine, if he had not already done so. It is clear that if he had not done exactly as he did the engine would have not been stopped, and, with the vessel speeding along through the sound, the flames would have had complete possession in a very much less time than the exceedingly brief period in which they did, and every soul on board would have been confronted with the necessity of trusting to the icy waters, with a life preserver, as it would have been impossible to launch and man the boats, especially in the wake of the swiftly revolving paddle wheels. It is certain that under those conditions very few would have been saved."

One reporter noted with great insight, "This is the first time that the Supervising Inspector's office has gone on record as praising a man for the violation of any rules, as promulgated by the steamboat inspection service. In this case, however, Capt. Harris wishes to impress licensees of steamers and sailing craft that human life stands above all rules that may be enacted."

The double tragedy of the *General Slocum* and the *Glen Island*, coming so close together, did not fall upon deaf ears. At a special conference held in Washington, DC, between Secretary of Commerce and Labor Metcalf and steamship people from all over the country, suggestions were made concerning steamboat safety. One high official of the department said:

"Neither the *General Slocum* nor the *Glen Island* would be permitted to house a single human being if they were brought ashore and an attempt made to use them for that purpose. Yet they are permitted to carry upon the waters thousands of people every day when every minute there is danger of just such a catastrophe as that of the *Slocum*. It was only because the *Glen Island* had a small passenger list that the loss of life was so small, and yet in proportion to the number carried it was nearly as large as that of the *Slocum*. The *Glen Island* burned as fast as the *Slocum*, and there was just as small an opportunity for the passengers and crew to escape. The people need protection against these things, and I thoroughly believe in a great change in every detail of the Steamboat Inspection Service."

Buried in this much-needed rhetoric, no doubt, were memories of the *Lexington* and the *Atlantic* (both of which are covered elsewhere in this volume). The wake-up calls rung in 1840 and 1846 were finally being heard.

The wreck of the *Glen Island* is marked on the chart. Very little remains that is recognizable as the majestic paddle wheeler she once was: charred timbers now full of holes bored by wood boring mollusks, and bits and pieces of machinery left behind by salvors. But somewhere, buried under the debris, lies the jewelry which Captain MacAllister says he left in a drawer when he dashed out of his room with such haste.

Courtesy of the Smithsonian Institution.

GLUCKAUF

Built: 1886
Previous names: None
Gross tonnage: 2,307
Type of vessel: Tanker

Sunk: March 24, 1893
Depth: 20 feet
Dimensions: 300' x 37' x 23'
Power: Coal-fired steam

Builder: Armstrong Mitchell & Company, Newcastle on Tyne, England
Owner: Deutsche Amerikanische Petroleum-Gesellschaft, Hamburg, Germany
Port of registry: Geestemunde, Germany
Cause of sinking: Ran aground
Location: 26546.9

43765.3

    Ship owner Wilhelm Anton Riedemann had a dream to build the first ocean-going steamship specifically designed to carry oil in bulk, rather than in barrels. He experimented with the idea by installing seventy-two steel tanks in the sailing vessel *Andromeda*. The ship was such a success that he quickly capitalized on the principle by designing the *Gluckauf* (German for "Good luck"). In his concept of the "tank ship" he incorporated such innovations as fore and aft expansion tanks, a centerline bulkhead that ran full length through the cargo section, and tank compartments which were interconnected by a sophisticated piping system so that oil could be pumped quickly and efficiently throughout the ship. The combination iron and steel hull was propelled by a triple expansion reciprocating steam engine. The *Gluckauf* carried three masts and was barkentine rigged, but it is doubtful that she ever bore canvas.

    The initial difficulty which Riedemann had to overcome in the construction of a tank ship built to his specifications was that Lloyd's, the world's largest classification society, refused to accept his plans due to the lack of a double hull. It was a well accepted principle in marine engineering that the installation of one hull inside another greatly increased the chances of a ship remaining afloat in the event of an accident in which the outer hull was pierced, as flooding was usually confined to the small compartments between the two hulls. Riedemann's reasoning for single hulled tank ships developed from the explosion of the experimental tank steamer *Ferguson* in 1880. The *Ferguson* was partially converted from a double-hulled cargo vessel to carry some oil in bulk by the simple expedient of installing an inner shell to be used as a tank compartment. Oil leaked from the compartment into the double hull, which was sealed and inaccessible, and created fumes which were subject to spontaneous combustion. A certain amount of leakage around the rivets was unavoidable, so Riedemann figured on carrying the oil in direct contact with the hull; in such a manner, explosive concentrations of oil and fumes could not build up within the vessel, and the small amount of leakage would be washed away by the sea.

Eventually, the French classification society Bureau Veritas approved design. When Riedemann could not find a shipyard in Germany to build his dream boat, he searched the British yards until he found one willing to construct the tank ship under Bureau Veritas supervision. Thus the job fell to Armstrong Mitchell & Company at Newcastle on Tyne. The *Gluckauf* slid down the ways in September 1885 and was fitted out that winter.

As noted in *Shipbuilding and Shipping Record*, "It is not surprising that Riedemann found it hard to collect a crew to man the ship; on the other hand, the first successful voyage, with scarcely any leakage, was accompanied with the greatest success, and aroused considerable interest. The first cargo brought to Geestemunde, in 1886, consisted of refined petroleum from the Ocean Oil Company. This cargo in barrels would have taken three average sailing vessels to carry, and as many weeks to load as it took the tank-steamer days. A barrel of American petroleum weighed 400 lb. gross. The empty barrel weighed 64 lb., so that there were in each barrel 336 lb. net of oil, or in all 2,700 tons, or 18,000 barrels of petroleum, plus 360 barrels, which may be considered for the average leakage. Estimating the average price of the new barrel in 1886 at 5s., and the empty barrel at 3s. 6d., the saving in barrels amounts to nearly £1,400. To this must be added the wages for filling the barrels, transport of barrels to the ship, stowing on ship, as well as discharging of barrels on arrival. Finally, there is the important factor of room necessary for 18,000 barrels, equal to freight for three average sailing vessels."

Riedemann had great hopes for the success of his new venture. As it turned out, the *Gluckauf* was almost *too* successful. On her maiden voyage she steamed into New York harbor with empty tanks and thirsty pumps, eager to tap the abundant reserves of American oil refineries. (This was in 1886, not 1973.) In practice, with her pumps working to their fullest capacity, she was able to take on or discharge her full capacity of 3,000 tons in twelve hours, less than one tenth the time it would take to handle the equivalent amount of oil in barrels, rolled along the wharf and across the gangplanks by means of exhausting manual labor. This great savings in time caused contention among dock workers who would rather have spent the longer amount of time performing the task. (Far be it for good union people to condone efficiency. We have seen the same hindrance toward progress in the twentieth century with the advent of the container ship.)

So rankled were the longshoremen that when it came time for the *Gluckauf* to depart, she was refused coal with which to fire her boilers for the return passage to Germany. She went all the way to Newfoundland before filling her bunkers. (Which was not too far out of her way along the great circle route.)

Despite the auspicious American labor problems, the prototype tanker operated profitably and continuously for the next seven years, and paved the way for tankers of the future and the supertankers of today. It is interesting to note that the reliance on single-hulled tankers has continued far past the time of necessity. Modern welded seams are not prone to leakage, and the spaces between hulls are now interconnected with piping and used as ballast tanks, which are filled with sea water, so that a dangerous build-up of oil and fumes can no longer occur. The reason that oil is carried in single hulled ships today is one of economy: they are much cheaper to build. And by some inexplicable arrangement, the classification societies and the governments of the world permit such ships to be built and to steam the seven seas, to incur the ecological disaster which eventuates when such a ship meets with ultimate misadventure.

Such misadventure occurred to the *Gluckauf* on March 24, 1893. She was on a routine voyage from Stettin, Germany to New York when she ran aground nearly abreast the Blue Point Life-Saving Station on Long Island's south shore. A dense fog shrouded the coast at the time.

The *Gluckauf* was periodically sounding her whistle as was customary under such conditions, and succeeded in attracting the attention of the men within the station. The life-savers could not see the ship through the fog, but as each succeeding whistle blast sounded louder, they quickly concluded that the vessel was approaching shore. The life-savers fired the shot gun four times in warning, to no avail. The *Gluckauf* grounded some 600 feet east of the station.

Earlier that day the life-savers had been drilling with the beach apparatus. Now they had the opportunity to conduct the operation for real. At the moment one man of the eight man crew had gone to the mainland to get a doctor for his sick child, and two others were out on patrol, leaving only five men to drag the cart. Fortunately, they did not have to drag it far. Within twenty minutes they had fired the first shot from the Lyle gun. Wrote station keeper Rourke, "The shot was successful landing the line on the steamers deck just forward of the foremast."

The *Gluckauf's* crew secured the line. The life-savers tied a thicker line to the messenger line, which was pulled aboard the tanker; then came the whip line and finally the hawser for the breeches buoy. "The fog had in the mean time shut down so thick that we had lost sight of the str she being in sight only about long enough to range the gun and place the line." By this time the two surfmen returned from patrol and added their hands in hauling off the line, and shortly thereafter came the keeper and a surfman from the Bellport station. With all this manpower the fall blocks were quickly established and the breeches buoy was hauled out to the stranded steamer.

Upon hearing a boatswain's whistle from the *Gluckauf*, the breeches buoy was hauled back. It contained a message from Captain Borger, master of the tanker, requesting that a telegram be sent to his agent and that tugs be dispatched for assistance. This was done immediately.

With the arrival of the keeper and three men from the Lone Hill station there were more than enough hands available to begin bringing the *Gluckauf*'s crew ashore. When the breeches buoy was hauled in again it contained only another message, this one stating that the line should be slackened as the engine was being put in reverse in hopes of pulling the ship off the bar, "but the tide was falling and the sea large and I knew she could never get afloat unaided.

"We waited some time until the tide had fallen so there was no possibility of her floating. I then had the hawser set up good and taut she having come in some and caused the hawser to slack. I then sent a message on board asking him if he wanted to be landed. He at once answered asking if he could come on shore dry. I replied telling him he could land without wetting his feet. We had the lines nice and taut and high from the water and the vessel hard aground had stopped rolling leaving the gear in good shape. He replied in a short time saying his vessel was lying easy and not leaking and he did not want to leave her thanking us for our attentions and asking us to watch him and if he needed our assistance he would sound his whistle."

The life-savers then returned to their respective stations to await developments.

About 10:30 that night came several blasts of the *Gluckauf*'s lonesome whistle. The men of the Blue Point Station hastened to the beach thinking that the tanker's crew had decided to come ashore. The life-savers tightened the hawser, which had slackened, and "were about to send the buoy on board when some one aboard cut our hawser and let the stud come ashore. He also fouled our whip line so we could not send it off again. It was now nearing midnight, also near high tide and the steamer rolling and lying 300 yds from the shore. I thought it would be safer to wait until daylight and low water. We kept down on the beach all night watching the vessel and waiting for daylight."

At 1:30 they found one of the tanker's boats bottom up on the beach. "We went about 2 miles thinking she might have been used to come on shore with some of the crew, although I had cautioned the Capt not to try to land with his boats as the sea was rough and the current strong. Finding no trace of bodies, concluded she had broken adrift, as afterward proved the case. They now began to fire rockets on the str. which I thought was to indicate her position to the tugs for which we had telegraphed. We answered her at intervals with a red Coston light to let her know she was being watched. We also built a large bon fire on the shore."

Then came the laborious task of re-establishing the breeches buoy. Once again the men from the Bellport and Lone Hill stations were called to assist, and again the life-savers accomplished the job in the dark. At daylight surfman James

Reynolds was hauled out to the ship in the breeches buoy in order to get a situation report and "to find out what they would like us to do." Reynolds returned with several written messages and instructions for procedure. "The Capt was profuse in his thanks for the services rendered but did not want to leave his vessel. She being his first command he said he would stick to her if she broke in pieces and had to float ashore on an oar."

During the day a fresh breeze blew away the fog so the *Gluckauf* was visible for miles around. The wind also kicked up the surf. All day on the 25th the tanker was buffeted by the waves. The rising tide buoyed up the helpless ship, and inch by inch she was driven further toward shore. Gradually she "worked over the outer bar and came well up on the beach."

The Merritt wrecking tugs arrived on the 26th and took charge of the *Gluckauf.* Hawsers were secured to the tanker's stern bitts, and the powerful engines of the salvage vessels strained to pull the ship out to sea. The life-savers lent whatever assistance they could provide. Day after day the salvors labored at their task, but all efforts to tow the *Gluckauf* back over the bar proved fruitless. After a week there was no change in the tanker's position, but at least the salvors were not losing ground as they had the ship secured to an anchor which was stretched far out to sea.

On April 1 the Bell Point Life-Saving Station log noted dryly that the *Gluckauf* "came further up on the beach." That night a gale struck Long Island with disastrous results for the stranded steamer, for not only was she driven higher than ever up on the beach, but she was swung around nearly broadside to the waves. Furthermore, she was now leaking through loosened rivets and strained hull plates. Throughout the storm the *Gluckauf's* stalwart captain and crew remained aboard their vessel. The pumps were started and began the task of ejecting sea water from the bilges.

Divers examined the hull on April 3 and found no immediate cause for alarm. The Merritt Wrecking Company remained hopeful that the ship could be floated off in a few days. The life-savers were more realistic in their assessment of the situation, writing in the station log that the ship now lay in a "bad position" with a "very bad list to port with sea washing decks."

By the next day all hope of salvaging the *Gluckauf* was abandoned. Because she had been in ballast there was very little weight which could be removed to help lighten the load. The wrecking steamer *I.J. Merritt* then began the onerous task of offloading everything of value from the tanker. The Blue Point life-savers started removing baggage and the personal belongings of the crew. They also put up for the night six wreckers who were unable to return to their ship due to the running surf.

On April 5 it was noted in the station log that during the night the *Gluckauf* had been "damaged by the sea." Still the captain and crew held to their posts aboard the tanker. For two weeks they had worked and prayed that their ship could be saved; now their very lives were at stake. Only through the great energies of the wreckers and life-savers were they gotten off their ship. All thirty-two men were sheltered at the Bell Point station. The next day twenty-two of them were put on a train for New York. For the next few days Captain Borger, his engineer, and the remaining crew men returned to the *Gluckauf* daily and helped the wreckers to further strip the ship.

Another gale struck on April 21 and "badly injured" the tanker: "port side smashed and cabin flooded." On the 22nd the insurance underwriters visited the wreck and "pronounced her in bad condition, will probably be condemned." And so she was. For another week the stripping continued. Finally, after taking everything loose or which could be dismantled, the wreckers abandoned the *Gluckauf* to her fate. The date was April 30.

On May 3, what was left of the *Gluckauf* was sold at public auction in Stapleton, Staten Island. Although at the time of her loss she was valued at $125,000, the highest bid received was the lowly sum of $350.

For years afterward the *Gluckauf* was a much talked about spectacle seen by untold thousands of gawkers, beachcombers, and vacationers. Her lofty metal hull dominated the landscape. As one newspaper reporter noted in 1895, "On a clear day she can easily be distinguished from the train on the Long Island Railway, if you know where to look for her. On the ocean beach she is visible for ten miles either way, if there is not too much mist from the surf. Watching her from the bay, on the sail across from the mainland, it looks exactly as if she was trying to get across the Fire Island beach into the quiet waters of the Great South Bay."

The writer also described her condition: "The sea has dug a pit at the stern, with the result that the bow is steadily rising. She is also canted over at a sharper angle. From the land, or port, side, a wire cable hangs over the side, enabling visitors with any ambition to climb the twenty feet to the deck. Until last year there was a rope ladder provided, but the privilege was abused by relic hunters, the last one carrying off the ladder with him, and now the wire cable has to suffice, and it does suffice for most men and for lots of women. From the deck the view is a fine one, especially if the tide is high and a good surf crashes against the other side. Each incoming wave or breaker meets the iron sides of the ship with a tremendous crash that sends the spray forty feet into the air. The ship shakes from stem to stern, and the wonder is that, if a July surf can produce this effect, how anything is left after a January pounding.

"Having recovered breath from your climb, you make the tour of the ship, holding on to the rail most of the way; the deck is almost at an angle of 45 degrees. . . . Everywhere are evidence of the marvelous power of the waves--iron bars an inch thick twisted as if made of wax; bits of machinery weighing tons tossed 40 feet out of place; bolts too heavy for a man to lift torn out and hanging in the rigging. It is a common thing for people who visit great steamships to exclaim as they examine the massive fittings, that it is incredible that seething water could create havoc and make playthings of such ponderous things. Let them climb aboard the *Gluckauf*, where everything bears the mark of the ocean's fury—where nothing is quite erect, or straight, or whole, where everything is bent, twisted or broken.

"Down in the main cabin, by means of the now crazy steel stairs, the impact of the surf reverberates like thunder, driving the more timid visitors to the deck. Bits of seaweed and sand fill what once was a comfortable cabin. Everything that man or the elements could carry away is gone. In the cook's galley souvenir hunters have even pried up the encaustic tiles; every bolt or nut that could be unscrewed has been taken. Made bold by familiarity and the absence of any caretaker, people have brought axes, saws, and hatchets with them with which to hack away trophies. What they cannot carry away they disfigure. Some wretched vandals even succeeded this summer in tearing away two of the brass letters of the name, *Gluckauf*, on the port side. The letters K and F are gone. Those who carried off the K and the F must have had a cold chisel with them. A recent visitor managed to chop off a copper bolt from one of the hatches. Later he had the name of the *Gluckauf*, with the date, engraved upon it for a young woman who wanted a paper weight.

"Where people have failed to get a piece of the *Gluckauf*, they have vented their spite in scribbling their insignificant names in conspicuous places, upon the masts especially. Worse than that, some pillmaker has scrawled the name of his nostrum in letters 3 feet high on the sides of the ship. It appears to be only a question of time when every available square foot will be covered by these signs which deface our trees, fences, and big rocks. It was here on this beach last year that a Long Island genius plastered the advertisement of his cough syrup upon the broad back of a dead whale that drifted ashore."

Today none of the *Gluckauf* remains visible above the sand or surf.

Courtesy of the Long Island Maritime Museum.

GREAT WESTERN

Built: 1872
Previous names: None
Gross tonnage: 979
Type of vessel: Iron-hulled screw steamer
Builder: Whitwell & Company, Sunderland, England
Owner: Great Western Steamship Company (Whitwell & Son)
Port of registry: Bristol, England
Cause of sinking: Ran aground
Location: Two miles west of Life-Saving Station No. 21

Sunk: March 26, 1876
Depth: Unknown
Dimensions: 276' x 32' x 15'
Power: Coal-fired steam

The *Great Western* described herein should not be confused with an earlier vessel of the same name, a wooden hulled sidewheel steamer which, in 1838, lost by a few hours her entry in the history books as the first vessel to cross the Atlantic completely under steam. She was beaten by the *Sirius*.

This chapter is about the screw steamer *Great Western* which was a tramp freighter that spent much of her time traveling between New York and Bristol, England, in the early 1870's. On her final voyage, she was on a passage to New York from the Mediterranean with a miscellaneous cargo consisting of "400 tons of sulphur, 80 tons of sumac, 100 tons of white linen rags, and a large quantity of oranges in boxes." The cargo, which was consigned to E.D. Morgan & Company and Phelps Brothers & Company, was valued at $75,000.

Under the command of Captain Windham, the *Great Western* left Messina on February 26, 1876, stopped at Palermo on March 1, touched at Gibraltar on March 7, than passed through the Pillars of Hercules (the Straits of Gibraltar) and steered a course for New York. No difficulties were encountered across the broad Atlantic, but upon approaching the American coast a dense fog obliterated the sun for three days, so that no sextant sightings could be taken. The steamer was being navigated by dead reckoning, but apparently there was more of a northerly set to the current than Captain Windham counted on.

According to statements made by the ship's officers, "they were thirty miles out of their course when they struck. Their last soundings indicated sixteen fathoms of water. The steamer struck the outer bar at 7 o'clock, and finding that they were on the coast, rockets and blue lights were fired by the crew. The signals of distress attracted Capt. Baker, of Life-saving Station No. 21, and his men to the spot, where they arrived just as the crew were landing. The last boat left the vessel at 12:30 o'clock Sunday morning. No lives were lost, although the sea was very high and the spray dashed in volumes over the forearm of the steamer." All thirty men were graciously accommodated at the station for three days. Captain Windham, described as having a "bilious attack," was confined to bed the entire time.

"The Coast Wrecking Company dispatched their steamer, the *Relief*, to the scene of disaster on Sunday morning, where she arrived at 4 o'clock the same afternoon. The waves were so high that it was impossible for the boat to venture very near the wreck, but as the weather was less tempestuous yesterday afternoon the wreckers commenced the work of saving the cargo. At that time the steamer lay broadside toward the shore, about ten rods from high-water mark. When the tide runs out it will be possible to walk out to her. Her keel is embedded to the depth of twelve feet in the sand."

By the time the crew left for New York City on the South Side Railroad, the *Great Western's* holds were filled to a depth of fifteen feet. On April 11, Lloyd's reported that "the vessel is high and dry at low water, but has broken in two; the cargo saved will be carted across the beach. . . . the steamer is being stripped of sails and rigging." Later reports indicated that much of her cargo was salvaged and that the wreck was sold where it lay, on Fire Island beach, on April 26, for $1,067. This represented quite a financial loss to her underwriters, since the iron-hulled ship, newly built only four years previous, was worth $300,000.

Presumably, the wreck was sold for salvage, but no mention is made as to whether the compound engine was recovered, so it might still be there on or under the sand.

HUSSAR

Built: 1763

Previous names: None

Gross tonnage: 627

Type of vessel: 6th Rate full-rigged ship

Builder: Robert Inwood, at Brotherhith, on the Thames

Owner: British Navy

Cause of sinking: Struck a rock

Location: Hell's Gate in the East River, between 131st and 135th Streets, Bronx

Sunk: November 23, 1780

Depth: 70-90 feet

Dimensions: 124' x 33' x 11'

Power: Sail

Armament: 28 guns

The *Hussar* is a ship whose name evokes images of sunken gold, undiscovered treasure, overnight wealth, and everlasting fame. Yet there is more legend to New York's famous underwater El Dorado than there ever was to that imaginary city of riches sought for centuries by Spanish conquistadors. Nevertheless, modern day salvors and crafty publicity seekers continue to spend the fortunes of goggle-eyed venture capitalists in the fruitless search for a submerged chimera, promoting claims of an unfound trove of precious bullion lying within easy reach of common scuba, despite documentation to the contrary. Alas, with this chapter another myth joins the realm of such fables as the legendary canals of Mars, the pantheon of Greek and Roman gods, and the fabulous roc of the Arabian nights.

Built in 1763 as a commonplace sixth rate warship of small tonnage, the size of the HMS *Hussar* can better be visualized by a few statistics and an appropriate comparison. The length of her keel was 102 feet, the length of her gun deck was 114 feet, and her overall length was 124 feet; her beam was 33 feet 11 inches; the depth of her hold was 11 feet. Thus the *Hussar's* dimensions are approximately equivalent to those of today's commercial fishing trawler. Her hull was pierced along its single deck for twenty-six guns, in addition to which she carried a bow and a stern chaser. Her three masts were square rigged. Packed aboard to handle the sails and guns was a complement of 200 men.

The *Hussar's* early career was rather undistinguished. For five years she cruised the Cape Clear area off the south coast of Ireland, under the consecutive commands of James Smith and Hyde Parker. In 1768 she sailed for North America, then a British colony, where she was commanded by J. Corner, then T. Bishop, and finally H. Bellew, who sailed her home to be decommissioned, in March 1771. After being laid up for six years she was recommissioned. This was July 1777, when the American Revolution was in full swing. (For a description of contemporary events, see *Culloden.*) With a newly coppered bottom, the *Hussar* was adequately prepared to operate in tropical seas, whose marine fouling organisms were repelled by the toxicity of copper oxide. During a two-year stint off the coast of Portugal she engaged in fleet naval actions in which she had a hand in the capture of several enemy warships. On November 19, 1779, under the command of Elliott Salter, she took part in the taking of the 64-gun *Nuestra Senora Del Buen Consejo*. In 1780, under the command of Charles Maurice Pole (sometimes mistakenly spelled Poole), she overwhelmed two 12-gun privateers: the *Jeune Leon* and the *Renard*. Then she sailed for America, only this time as a belligerent instead of as an envoy.

"On the 15th of August, 1780, his Majesty's ships *Bienfaisant*, Capt. McBride; *Charon*, Capt. Simms; *Hussar*, Capt. Poole, and *Licorne*, Capt. Cardigan, with ninety-eight sail of merchant ships and transports for New-York and one of the Leeward Islands, sailed from Cork. New-York was then in the occupation of the British, and the central point of Army and Navy operations for the subjugation of the revolted colonies. The patriotism of the population in driving the supplies of cattle beyond the reach of army foragers forced the commanders to depend almost wholly for their supplies upon Great Britain, while the enterprise of the American privateers and gunboats which patrol the coast made it indispensable to protect the convoys by a strong escort."

The huge fleet landed at Charleston, South Carolina in early October. After nearly a month in port, the ships, except for twenty merchant sail which remained behind, set sail for New York, which was made on November 16. One week later, while attempting to pass Hell's Gate in the East River, the *Hussar* struck a rock and sank within a stone's throw of shore. Persistent rumor has it that at the time she carried in her holds seventy prisoners of war who were manacled to the bulkheads, and 960,000 pounds sterling, equivalent to 4,800,000 American dollars, to pay the British troops. Yet the letter which Captain Pole submitted to the Admiralty makes no such mention. Nor does it make sense for a lightly armed and manned sixth rate warship to be carrying such a cargo, in flesh or in gold.

Captain Pole: "It is with great regret I acquaint their Lordships, that on the 23d. ult. His Majesty Ship the *Hussar*, being on her way with Dispatches of consequence from the Commander in Chief at New York, to the Squadron in Gardiners Bay, most unfortunately struck on a rock in Hell Gate, and received so considerable a Damage that in a few minutes she sunk and is totally lost. The Captain, Officers and Company (Eight or ten Seamen excepted, which perished in the wreck) are all saved, and distributed among other Ships now here, such of the Officers excepted as prefer a return to England."

No mention of gold, no mention of prisoners. Only dispatches, which a vessel of her size, armament, and speed *would* be entrusted to carry. A court-martial was held on November 29, the minutes of which also make no mention of gold or prisoners. After hearing testimony from the *Hussar's* officers and some of her crew, Captain Pole and his men were exonerated from blame: "The Court are of the opinion that the said ship was lost by its falling calm as she was entering the passage of Hell Gates, by which circumstance she became ungovernable and was drove by the tide on a rock called the Pot, where she bulged, and was from thence carried by the tide over to the Morrissend Shore, where she was unavoidably lost." (By "bulged" the Court meant "bilged," which means that her hull was pierced below the waterline.) It seems to me that the Court might have shown more concern over the loss of a sizable quantity of gold.

A graphic and imaginative account of the *Hussar's* final moments was published a century later, when salvage operations were proceeding, and undoubtedly did much to preserve, or possibly to create, the mythic proportions of the treasure hunt in progress. Read it with caution, believe it with abandon.

"She struck heavily when her passage was almost completed, and when a few rods of farther progress would have carried her into open water. . . . She drifted off, and, ponderous as she was, she was hustled onward by the powerful currents. She made water with great rapidity, and all attempts to stop the large leak were unavailing. The only chance for salvation was in beaching her. There was a promising place three-quarters of a mile farther on. It looked as though there might be a mud-flat there, or, at least, a gradually-shelving shore, and toward this the sinking vessel was urged with all possible haste.

"She again struck, and hawsers were sent ashore and secured to some trees, in order to keep her from slipping back into deep water. This was futile, for the rent in the ship's side admitted the flood too rapidly. She began to settle, and the crew began to leave her as best they could. Some men who were at work on Randall's Island hastened up to help them ashore, and the officers fled as the huge craft keeled over and dragged the trees up by the roots.

"No man has told, or can tell, of what fearful scenes then took place in the deep hold of the ship. The seventy shackled wretches must have known of the disaster from the first, and they must have been rushed from the lowest degree of fright to the highest degree of terror in the twinkling of an eye. How they must have strained and writhed at their manacles, and how loud must they have shrieked as the foaming water boiled up about them in the terrible darkness, and bounding hither and thither, and always jerked back by their iron tethers, what bitter curses must they have cast upon the heads of those who deserted them! Even emaciated and weakened as they were by their long tortures in the dreadful prison-ships, how powerful must have become their languid muscles, and how loud and fierce their weakened voices! Half-dressed, unshaven, gaunt; chained together, tugging desperately at their manacles, and shrieking aloud; now with their terrible faces turned upward, and now downward, and with their uncertain feet forever slipping on the inclining deck—what a spectacle was there! As the savage flood reached their waists, then their armpits, then their necks, and, as the spurts of spray and foam covered their heads, how must they have strained to stand upon their tiptoes to eke out the last few seconds of precious life, even then not hopeless of it! And what a Hadesian picture must have been that last, when the ghastly row of faces striving to blow off the waters with the quick breaths of their mouths and nostrils, and emitting horrid shrieks and prayers, gradually sank while glaring upon each other! And how the water must have boiled from other causes than its own powerful rush and flow, and how many bubbles must have struggled to its surface which were not gathered in the open air! So seventy men, brave and true, went down in the *Hussar*, and there is no record of their names or homes. . . .

"The ship sank with great speed, and slid from the rocks upon which she struck into a submarine valley nearly ninety feet in depth." Another account gives the depth as 72 feet.

If the British made any attempts to salvage the *Hussar* soon afterward, Admiralty accounts of such operations are buried at the bottom of more important reports of the prosecution of the war against the rebellious Americans. But later chroniclers seemed to believe that more than a few outfits ventured to recover from the wreck whatever remained of value. The first recorded salvage of the *Hussar* did not occur until fourteen years after the event: a long time to idle if the worm-eaten hull truly contained a king's ransom in specie. In 1794 the place where the wreck came to rest was known as Port Morris. A pair of brigs supposedly spent two summer seasons trying to raise the intact hull with grapples, without success.

In 1819 a diving bell was brought into use by one Major Baird, of the U.S. Navy. If this is true, Baird must have been the only major ever to have served in any navy in the world, as "major" is an army rank. Keeping this preface in mind, he is supposed to have formed a company which worked the wreck for two years, during which time several cannons were recovered. However, the diving bell ultimately proved a failure due to the current.

A Samuel Davis formed another company in 1825, by selling shares of stock, and worked the wreck that summer, again from a diving bell. He reputedly raised several more cannons, but no treasure.

In 1852 a Captain Taylor (service unspecified) spent two months exploring the wreck—not first hand, but by sending down divers in "submarine armor," as the deep-sea diving rig was then called. The rig was one of his own invention. He had previously employed it quite successfully on other wrecks, but not so on the *Hussar*. He was called away on another job "to raise the U.S. frigate *Missouri*, which had just sunk in the Straits of Gibraltar." He was in such a poor state of health upon his return that he was "unable to resume his enterprise of attempting to secure the treasure on board the *Hussar*."

In 1856, a group of businessmen formed a partnership which sold shares of stock in order to generate the revenues necessary to fund an enterprise which must get the award for endurance. At first called the New England Submarine Company, then the Worcester *Hussar* Company, the venture was later incorporated as the Frigate *Hussar* Company. Under these various names the company

Opposite page: The salvage vessel moored over the site of the *Hussar*, as seen from shore. Above: a view of the shore as seen from the salvage vessel. It is a bit more built up today. (All woodcuts in this chapter are from a contemporary magazine article in the author's collection.)

worked the wreck for more than twenty years. The head of the board of trustees was Charles B. Pratt, of Worcester, Massachusetts (and later the mayor of that town); he himself made several descents in Captain Taylor's submarine armor, but recovered nothing of note.

The company moored a partially dismantled sloop over the well-known site and used the vessel as a work barge for extended operations. Divers made daily descents during slack tide, alternating so that one went down at high tide and another went down at low tide. The men were lowered over the side of the sloop by block and tackle secured to a ringbolt on top of a copper helmet. Ninety pounds of lead helped them maintain position on a bottom which was then described as sandy. Air was forced through the hose and into the helmet by a coal-fired engine which was connected by a belt to a pump. The divers were lowered without the use of a stage; rather, they looked like sides of beef hanging from a hook in a butcher shop. Their only means of communication with the surface was a thin hand-held line, used as a messenger through which the divers made known their wants by tugging a number of times in conformance to a pre-arranged code.

According to a contemporary account, the diver's work "consists in picking and shoveling the hard conglomerate, formed of sand and gravel, hardened into a compact mass by the dissolved iron and by the almost constant rush of water. When the present searchers first struck the wreck, they found themselves about midship directly over the keel, and they immediately began to push aft, where it was reasonable to suppose the treasure lay. At a certain period in the operation lanterns were used, so constructed as to illuminate scenes under the water, but in this particular instance they were found to be useless, in consequence of the turbid state of the currents. There the divers labor wholly by feeling, it being as dark as Erebus below."

In this manner the divers struggled to "attack and drag apart the huge and water-sodden beams and ribs of this enormous ship. . . . All that remained of her after eighty years of decay was thick with greenish weed and slippery to the touch; her open ports yawned like the half-remaining windows of an ancient castle, and the sand had piled up about her as the sands of the desert pile up about the bones of camels and stifled men. Her masts had disappeared, save the jagged and spongy stumps, and the gnawing currents and eating tides had stripped away

the planking, so that even in the solemn gloom of the depths where she lay she seemed a deserted and broken skeleton. Her threatening guns, which had done hard and frequent service against the French, had long since slipped down one after another and been lost through the decks among the bones and rubbish below, and slowly but surely was she losing all resemblance to her former powerful and shapely self when these two leather-clad figures, with brazen heads, descended upon her, and with pick and powder began to drag her to pieces. And they worked well, for now there is little of her but a platter-shaped mass of worm-eaten and water-logged beams and knees which formed her bottom."

Quite a few items of interest and value were recovered. "In various parts of this country, in different museums here and there, are numbers of water-worn relics which the divers have brought up from this tragic wreck. In the museum at Central Park are some cannon, rusty and misshapen, which once did duty aboard the *Hussar*, and people gaze at them with stimulated remembrances of the curious story of the ship. At the British Museum there is a bronze gun for which the English Government paid fifteen hundred dollars. One day a diver brought up a brass box, all green and mouldy, and it was opened with curious hands amid a group of men. It contained necklaces, crosses, rings, bits of coin, ear-drops and jewels, and pearls of great value. For a moment it was laid down upon the deck, and some secret hand was put upon it, and it flew away, none knew whither, and has not been seen again to this day.

"There has also come to the surface, dripping wet, and all green and slippery, many bushels of gun-flints. Also tons of rotten cordage, twisted as yet in regular and symmetrical shapes, still as fragile as so much paper, with all the fibres dissolved to pulp, and with all its ancient strength departed. Numberless huge platters of pewter, dented here and there where falling timbers have crushed into them, have also come to the light of day and passed from hand to hand, distributing a savor of antiquity which begets a deep regard for even their battered and tarnished sides. Upon some, one may discern various initials and names, scratched perhaps by idle stewards, and again rude pictures of flags and beasts, done with a nail or the point of a knife-blade. There are pots and jars of anti-quated shapes, used in their day for preserves, but from which all perfume has departed and given place to the smell of salt-water. Upon their sides are the stamps of the vessel and the royal monogram, enclosed in a circle, and com-memorative of Georgius Rex. Slender beer-pots, of curious construction, also swell the odd collection, and also leathern buckets, with the name 'Hussar,' in broad letters, still legible upon them. Thousands of cannon-balls, as brown as sienna, and as rough and unpolished as lumps of garden-mould, and as tender to the pressure of the fingers, have been laboriously brought into the air, besides many twisted lengths of chain and heaps of glass and earthenware.

"There are many pieces of silver table-service belonging to the mess-chests now half obliterated, and there is a little hand-stamp of the French *fleur-de-lis*, which may have been private property. Then there is the ship's bell, twenty inch-es high and nearly as many across its mouth. This also has the monogram of the king and the seal upon its greenish sides. Its tongue has long since rotted out, and there is a crack that makes the ring of its metal disconsonant.

"There are plenty of manacles, huge bands of rusty iron connected with sev-eral mighty links, and strong enough in their day to bind a Samson. In a little out-house, not far from the ship, there is a champagne-basket filled with human bones and skulls, all thrown in haphazard, just as they were lifted out of the mason's bucket from the wreck. One cannot help a feeling of vexation that these remains are forever done with the vanities of talk and recollection, and must henceforth be silent."

But of actual treasure there was little. Despite years of prodigious effort very little gold glinted in the noonday sun, and certainly no more than could be

After dressing, the diver is lowered over the side and tended with lines until he is hauled up from the depths.

accounted for by pocket change. Gold guineas, dated between 1711 and 1776, "were all of them in perfect condition. A piece was shown of three guineas, a crown and a half crown, found in one solid lump. The silver was in the centre, and by coming in contact with the gold a sort of galvanic battery action had taken place, making the whole a compact mass."

According to another writer, "There has been a constant yet a fitful turning up of gold-pieces among the loads of mud and sand. Perhaps they were about the clothing of some of the officers, and through the wash of the tides became embedded in some substance which subsequently hardened and thus preserved them. I have seen a precious lump, consisting of several silver-pieces, which the action of the water has welded together, at the same time washing away the glow and totally destroying the stamps of the coins. and upon this little mass of silver are half a dozen true English guineas perched as delicately yet as firmly as garnets in a bit of quartz."

One reporter wrote that the profusion of "human bones found have been principally disjointed sections of the human skeleton. Connected with the lower bones of a large number of arms, have been found manacles, and showing, evidently, that a part, if not all the American prisoners on board, were manacled and chained. A few days since an entire skeleton, the first whole one discovered, was found. Singular as it may appear, the head of this skeleton still contained a portion of brains. A chain was connected with a manacle on the right wrist-bone of this skeleton."

Perhaps the talk of American prisoners who drowned in irons was not all hearsay. Or was there skullduggery in the reporting?

The lure of gold dies hard. In 1869 there surfaced a rumor of the progress of the Frigate *Hussar* Company to the effect that "several boxes of guineas of the coinage of George III have been raised," which charge was emphatically denied by the company.

The year 1880 saw a development of a new kind in the search for sunken treasure: government intervention. If the world knew what this official meddling portended it would have revolted immediately and let anarchy reign supreme. But foresight is not hindsight, so now we are saddled with endless laws, rules, regulations, statutes, ordinances, mandates, and acts of Congress which make free enterprise so difficult to perceive that one wonders if the United States is a democracy any more or just a bureaucratic artifice which, like a stage performing magician and prestidigitator, presents merely an illusion of the concept. Ever since then, it seems, each act of Congress regarding sunken treasure has been a vaudeville performance of poor song and dance. Nor is there a hook in the wings to drag the august body off stage. No longer can a person take it upon himself to achieve his goals, he must plead with the government to let him make the attempt—at a cost, of course, to the would-be achiever. In those pre-inflation days the Treasury Department demanded its tithe, and compelled the receipt of its unearned share by executing a contract replete with stipulated clauses before it sanctioned the proposed salvage by issuing a permit.

George W. Thomas made such unwise application to the government after wresting from the Frigate *Hussar* Company 75% of its vested interest in the vessel and, by inference, its treasure—if any—on the promise of establishing an outfit to locate and work the wreck. (How the *Hussar* became lost after almost continuous salvage has never been explained.) He then proceeded to mortgage his newfound title to wealthy investors. Over a period of years he managed to rake in tens of thousands of dollars from hopeful if gullible would-be entrepreneurs whose eyes widened at the prospect of multiplying their capital investments many-fold, but whose vision was limited by ample folds of wool. If all this sounds like a confidence game, before you hurl accusations at Thomas and make aspersions against his character, know that prior to his arrangements with the Frigate *Hussar* Company and subsequent investors he worked hard on the streets of New York as a merchandiser of patent medicines: he peddled catarrh snuff to people with sinus congestion and post nasal drip. Moreover, before swinging the salvage racket he contemplated assuming vestments of a different kind and becoming a street preacher, undoubtedly with the intention of gathering a large flock to fleece.

Thus, it would seem, Thomas was an old hand at monetary manipulation and creative if cunning financial maneuvers. He borrowed from numerous people, pledging repayment at the rate of 750%; thus a $1,000 loan secured a promissory note of $7,500 payable—and here is the catch phrase—upon recovery of the treasure. This high rate of return was enough to whet the pecuniary appetites of penny pinchers of the likes of Ebenezer Scrooge, who driveled over their gruel while dreaming of riches beyond excogitation.

The wrecking schooner *Georgiana Belle* was subsequently moored over the newly located site and the crew aboard were engaged in boring and blasting through the solidified sediment which now encapsulated the *Hussar's* treasure compartment. Work proceeded apace. Thomas visited the diggings every few weeks, stayed long enough to hand out wages, then retired to other business. But the investors who stopped by to see how the job was coming along thought the pace was more of a walk than a trot, or perhaps, giving the devil his due, an exhibition canter at most.

Matters came to a head on December 12, 1883, when the investors held a meeting which Thomas was invited to attend under the pretense, promulgated by Joseph Hartshorne, the investor who asked for his audience, that the two were to have nothing more than a private tete-a-tete. When Thomas saw that he had been duped into doing what he would have preferred to duck, he became indignant. He refused to account for expenditures, or to harken to ideas for facilitating operations, both of which he claimed were his business and not theirs.

In January 1884, Thomas's house of cards, so to speak, collapsed. He was accused of purchasing an estate in Hackensack, New Jersey, and of making improvements upon the property, with funds advanced for salvage purposes. Not only did the twenty-three investors file charges in court, but the government followed suit as well since it was likely to lose a tidy sum in misappropriated revenues, the latter being somewhat ironically a case of the thief remonstrating against being swindled out of ill-gotten gains.

Foreclosure proceedings were subsequently initiated against the *Georgiana Belle*, the company's only real property, everything else having been leased. Thomas managed to secure a temporary restraining order against the schooner's sale, and filed a counterclaim against the investors and their attorney, the purpose of which seemed to be to muddy already silty waters in order to stall for time. The stall worked only for that summer. In October the Secretary of the Treasury directed that the contract with Thomas be annulled, and that "a new contract to raise the vessel be made with Messrs. Bean & Hartwell, of Providence, R. I., on the same terms. The contract with Mr. Thomas was terminated on the ground that he did not use due diligence in the prosecution of the work. The new contractors represent the persons who have already advanced money to carry on the work, and who are willing to push it to completion." The actual contract spelled out the names of the benefactors as Eben J. Beane and Mortimer H. Hartwell; the name they worked under was Treasure Trove Associates.

Not to be done out of what he considered to be his due, Thomas again stirred the mud in the pool by changing bureaucratic horses in midstream, symptomatic of the child who asks his doting father to give him what his mother will not. Within three days he requested that "no immediate action be taken by the department toward making a new contract for that work. He gives it as his opinion that the property in question is wholly within the jurisdiction of the state of New York, and there the Government has no authority to act in the premises. He says further, that the Governor of the State coincides with this view, and will have the question of jurisdiction referred to the Attorney-General of the State. He asks that action be postponed until the question is settled."

Three years later the case came to an unsatisfactory conclusion for all concerned. Joseph Hartshorne was still suing to have his investment capital returned, but, although Thomas's contract with the Government was annulled, his property attached, and his equipment sold, Vice Chancellor Bird, after hearing the facts in contention, said, "I can discover nothing which tends to the conclusion that the defendant, Thomas, attempted in any sense to mislead. That the accomplishment of the undertaking was certain in his mind is very plain. He undoubtedly believed that he would be successful, and he made every reasonable effort to convey this conviction to the minds of those from whom he sought pecuniary aid. It would not perhaps be departing from the truth to say that his expressions were over-confident, and that cautious men—men not given to speculation or fond of pursuing chimeras—would not have entertained his propositions. Most probably such men would have spurned them, and would have found his convictions utterly baseless in the immense regard that was offered for the loan; that is, $37,500 for the advance of only $5,000. But it is not the first time that a shining hook has been grasped to be followed by mortification and loss."

Despite this strong admonition to the unwary, and his finding that Thomas was not guilty of intentional wrongdoing, Bird pressed Thomas to account for expenditures. Nothing ever came of it, however, and Thomas's victims did not continue to press their lawsuit, deciding instead to forget the whole matter after so many years of legal adversity. Then, as now, the court system was designed to wear down the litigants rather than to dispense justice.

The furor over the treasure of the *Hussar* faded gradually from public view. But, like a dormant volcano lying in wait to erupt with the next noxious movement of the earth, barely half a decade passed before, "in October, 1892, the Chapman Wrecking Company tried their hand at the game without success, and later came Capt. Thomas Merrill, who claimed to be in possession of information that his predecessors did not possess; but he did not find even so much as a pewter spoon." If these latest two contenders did indeed conduct salvage operations they did so without Treasury Department approval.

In 1894, the Treasury Department received another contractual request, this from one Francis Eppley, an attorney. Eppley was first approached by stingmaster George Thomas, who tried to perpetrate another fraud by selling to Eppley his original 1880 contract, which was of course null and void. When Eppley queried the Treasury Department about the validity of the contract, it created quite a stir. Vice-Chancellor Bird's comments notwithstanding, Treasury had not the slightest doubt about Thomas's inherent dishonesty, and this latest scam added fuel to an already blazing fire. Thomas had made repeated applications throughout the years—all of which were summarily denied—and now went so far as to try to thwart Eppley's access to the site by hiring a scow which he anchored over the wreck, and posting a notice which read "No Admittance—Government Work." Thomas had to be thrown off the site.

Eppley was duly granted a contract, in which the *Hussar* had been upgraded to the classification of a frigate. The split from the proceeds of the treasure was 90-10, with Eppley to receive the larger portion with the very considerable exception that "all guns, military arms, implements and equipment, munitions of war, naval store and apparatus, or other like articles, shall be held to be relics and shall be the exclusive property of the United States, and upon the discovery and securing of any such relics the same shall be deposited by said Francis M. Eppley in some safe place and without expense to the United States." Far be it for the government to share any of the work or cost; it wanted only profits without investments. Furthermore, Eppley had to put up a $10,000 bond "conditioned for the faithful performance of this contract." In a rare exhibition of governmental generosity, Eppley was granted three working seasons commencing in July 1895 to salvage the site, with a provision to extend his exclusivity should it prove necessary in order to complete the recovery of the gold.

In a Treasury Department document which castigated Thomas and gave a brief account of applications concerning the *Hussar*, it was written, "The application of Mr. Eppley for a contract under section 3755 has, upon requirement, been accompanied with satisfactory evidence of his integrity, financial ability, and scientific and mechanical skill, he having heretofore been engaged in the Coast and Geodetic Survey, and having engaged the services of the renowned and successful firm engaged in submarine exploits, it is believed that he will make an honest and faithful effort to accomplish success, or at least demonstrate for all time the hopelessness of this undertaking, and by so doing confer a great benefit of many who in after years might yet seek this phantom of riches."

Eppley did not let the Treasury Department down, particularly with respect to the last sentence printed above. He proved smarter than all his predecessors, for instead of promptly plunging into the water with both leaded feet in cumbersome diving rig, he dived into the vast archival repositories in Great Britain—not pesonally, of course, for lawyers seldom do their own leg work. He hired private researchers to comb Admiralty files and other primary sources available in London. In March 1885 he received a wealth of historical information and original documentation about the wealthless wreck on which he was about to spend so much easily-earned income in salvaging, and for the next three months he continued to receive follow-up elaborations. It will come as no surprise to the reader that Eppley, without strong preconceived notions, and having taken the proper course of action to establish or demolish the claim that the *Hussar* indeed had on board a cargo of gold at the time of her loss, was not unwilling to be convinced that there never had been any treasure other than in the imaginations of his delusory forerunners.

His researchers delved thoroughly into the *Hussar's* logs, her captain's letters, the admiral's dispatches, correspondence of the Lords of the Admiralty and their orders and instructions, war correspondence, purser's reports, accounts of the Paymaster General, Exchequer records, audits of declared accounts, ledgers of the Treasurer of the Navy, Treasury letters, and half a dozen official war histories, and found no mention of gold *ever* having been placed aboard the *Hussar*. "The Log of the *Hussar* further shows that she captured two prizes near New York and took 53 prisoners on board, that she anchored in New York Harbour on November 13th. and on the 15th. sent the prisoners on board the prison ship." So much for the seventy anguished Americans who drowned in their manacles, a story which more likely was anti-British propaganda.

Thereafter, Eppley wisely asked to have his contract canceled.

Eppley's revelations should have put a permanent cessation to future notions of salvaging the *Hussar* for profit. Yet, human nature being what it is, the truth did not deter later blind visionaries from having a try at the gold at the end of

New York's underwater rainbow. The old adage, "Those who do not study history are bound to repeat it" proved prescient. A generation passed. Then history repeated itself.

In 1930, Simon Lake, the famous submarine inventor, applied to the Treasury Department for a contract on the *Hussar*. At first, the Department wanted no part of it because wiser heads knew that the treasure was a will-of-the-wisp. But Lake persisted, got his congressman involved, and was given the contract he sought. The project proved more difficult than he predicted, so he was forced to make several applications for extensions. Ultimately, he spent some eight years seeking the golden mirage off Port Morris, which was now called Stony Point. Much of that time was consumed building a submarine, the *Laksco*. which was fitted with a downward looking window. Then, he had to relocate the wreck: not an easy task considering that the wooded island had changed considerably throughout the years, from a deserted and idyllic beach to the crowded cityscape of the Bronx.

Lake concentrated his search efforts in the area between 131st Street and 135th Street. He thought he located submerged wreckage at a depth of 70 feet, and moored a buoy on the site, "but I cannot be sure it is her or that there is any treasure on board until I get my submarine salvager down on the bottom and remove sufficient of the silt and debris with which the hulk is filled, to get down to the bottom ceiling of the ship." He drilled more than one hundred holes through the silt and mud, sometimes as close as fifty feet from the piers, but always struck bedrock instead of timber.

To make a long story short, Lake never found any treasure, but he did make some interesting observations about conditions in the East River, particularly with respect to tide, current, visibility, and ecology. Raw sewage swept back and forth with tidal regularity, limiting visibility to near zero except at the very bottom, where, with powerful lights, his divers could see as far as three feet. This was because most of the effluent was buoyed along in the fresh river water, which, being less dense than salt water, rode above the salt water which hugged the very bottom of the channel. Today we call this interface zone a halocline.

From studying old maps, Lake formed the belief that a shallow bay that once extended off Stony Point had been filled in and that docks were built over it. He wrote, "It is even possible that the dock itself might have been built over a portion of the hulk."

And there the matter rested until two generations later, when another visionary forgot the lessons of history. Enter treasure salvor Barry Clifford, the *Whydah* maker from Massachusetts. He had succeeded against all odds in locating the wreck of the pirate ship *Whydah* off Cape Cod, and wrested from her sunken hull—which was buried beneath the submerged sand—a buccaneer's will-o'-the-wisp. In 1985, he thought he would gamble on relocating the lost *Hussar* and recovering a treasure he claimed now to be worth five *hundred* million dollars. (Inflation, I suppose; or does the value of gold grow with the telling?)

By this time treasure hunters no longer went around drilling holes haphazardly. Technology had come a long way since the sharpened augur. Treasure salvage had become a business, a science, and a sophisticated art, and the tools of the trade consisted of electronic sensing devices such as side-scanning sonar, proton magnetometers, and sub-bottom profilers. It was with this kind of equipment that Clifford surveyed the bottom of the East River—and claimed to have found the hull—completely intact—under five feet of mud.

At that point the project became a commercial diving operation. No longer relying upon the hook and helmet used a century earlier, modern divers wear longjohns, drysuits, and full face masks, not only as insulation against the cold, but against infection from the bacteria in the water, for today the East River is more of a biological hazard than an industrial waste dumping site. Or are they the same thing?

In any case, I will not belabor the point since, predictably, no treasure was found. My good friend Billy Campbell was one of the divers hired to work the "wreck." He told me that once he was submerged he could not see his hand in front of his face, even near the surface, because from top to bottom the water was as black as pitch. He spent several days groping through the mud at the bottom of the river without making any significant finds. Eventually, the project was abandoned.

We are more than two centuries removed from the loss of the *Hussar*. Much has changed since the time when an unimportant British warship struck a rock and sank near the banks of a deserted beach. A great metropolis has arisen from the primeval forest which was once occupied only by natural flora and fauna and a few scattered tribes of Native Americans. Pot Rock and all the other shallow reefs at Hell's Gate have been blasted down to a least depth which is safe for passing ships, a job which required many tons of gunpowder and which took several decades to complete. The river is now free from obstruction and is negotiated with relative ease. But one thing that has not changed is the persistent belief among wistful speculators that a fortune in British gold lies at the bottom of the East River, within arm's reach and just waiting to be retrieved by the right person with the right idea for its location and recovery. The quest for treasure, it seems, no matter how evanescent, is as deeply embedded in the human psyche as the quest for eternal peace. It is likely that in this case, however, salvage is more fanciful than salvation.

The epitaph written by the author who chronicled contemporary operations on the *Hussar* in 1872 are as pertinent today as it was when the words were penned: "But it is with what still remains that grasping man has yet to do. The stories and romantic scenes suggested to his imagination by what he has already recovered do not begin to satisfy him, and so with the skill of the divers, the force of powder, the strength of machinery, and the ingenuity of his own brain, he is still fighting the current and wrestling with decay."

Logic and common sense notwithstanding, dream-driven treasure hunters of tomorrow will undoubtedly make excuses for the failure of previous salvors, will ignore the truth of history, and will rationalize the existence of gold where none is known to exist. Fancy rather than fact will endure, and the legend of the *Hussar* will live on forever.

Courtesy of the San Francisco Maritime National Historical Park.

HYLTON CASTLE

Built: 1871
Previous names: None
Gross tonnage: 1,258
Type of vessel: Freighter
Builder: T.R. Oswald & Company, Sunderland, England
Owner: Laws, Surtees & Company, North Shields, England
Port of registry: North Shields, England
Cause of sinking: Foundered
Location: 26569.4

Sunk: January 11, 1886
Depth: 100 feet
Dimensions: 251' x 32' x 19'
Power: Coal-fired steam

43695.3

When the *Hylton Castle* left New York City for Rouen, France, the seas were mild and the weather did not portend anything for the passage worse than cold temperatures, which hovered around zero. The iron-hulled, single-screw steamer was laden with 57,880 bushels of corn worth $30,000. In command was Captain Colvin; the crew of twenty stalwart men were usually occupied tending the engine and the fires under the boilers, but could also rig sails on the ship's three masts.

A few hours from port found the *Hylton Castle* off Fire Island, laboring under a fresh breeze. "Before midnight the moderate day breeze had become a northeast gale. Within a few minutes the sea was lashed into billows. The air grew thick with snow. In less than an hour a gale was howling across the steamer's deck and big seas were drenching her. Capt. Colvin's barometer, which had fallen rapidly in the morning, was still going down. By midnight the wind suddenly veered about to southwest, making an ugly chop sea of rapidly growing fury."

The vessel's stern appeared to be heavy and rode lower than it should. That coupled with the worsening weather and broaching seas decided the captain upon a new course of action: to reverse direction and head into the wind. As the wind shifted, the *Hylton Castle* followed suit, until she was steaming back toward her port of departure. "At every dip the vessel buried her nose, and the waves swept her from stem to stern. Everything movable was carried away except two of the boats. At one time, it seemed as if these would be torn from their davits. It was impossible to remain on deck. Capt. Colvin was on the bridge together with the helmsman, both lashed fast. Navigation was a hopeless task. The only aim was to keep the vessel's bow to the wind and above water. The storm kept growing and the cold was intense. The rigging and the decks were covered with snow and ice. Men half froze at the wheel. The heavy cargo and the engines astern gave the vessel the appearance of making a futile effort to climb up hill. As a result she had a dreadful sag to the stern, which, when she was put about for the run back, was almost entirely submerged.

"Saturday broke upon a wild sky and a wilder sea. The vessel became unmanageable. The rudder was the first part to give way. Then the discovery was made that water was oozing into the hold. It was not from the deck, for the hatches were battened down, and a trial of the steam pumps showed that a leak had sprung. The clank of the pumps then arose above the howl of the storm, and for a while foamy water gushed out of the nozzles in streams. Suddenly a few grains of corn came up with the water. Then came a few more, and presently there was a tiny stream of corn, almost choking the pumps. None of the crew had a moment's rest that day or night. By Sunday morning the furnaces were flooded. Nothing remained but to try to work the pumps and pray for mercy from the wind and waves. That was the way the day passed, and the long night. Nearly all of the men were frost-bitten. At daybreak on Monday morning Fire Island Light was sighted, and orders were given to prepare to leave the ship, which was settling rapidly. At best she could not keep afloat many hours. The captain called the ship's crew together and divided them into two boats' crews, one under his own command and the other commanded by Mate Marshall. Nine men were in the mate's boat and 13 in the Captain's. Capt. Colvin was the last man to leave the ship. The two boats lay near for half an hour waiting for the ship to sink. A huge wave lifted her stern high up in the air, and she went down bow first. The plunge did not last a minute. The Captain's boat was so close to the sinking ship that it barely escaped being swamped. In the spurt to get away one of his oars broke and another was disabled by cracking. The mate could not turn back in such a sea, but waited for the Captain to come up. It was more than an hour before the boats could be brought together. Then the Captain transferred two of his men to the mate's boat.

"There was a 12-mile pull ahead in the face of the wind and in a dangerous sea to Fire Island Light. Both crews went heartily at this task. The mate forged ahead because he had the lighter boat. In a few minutes the boats were out of sight of each other. Only once in a while did the lighthouse come into view. The waves were all that could be seen. It was intensely cold. Bailers had been put into the boats. There was no use for them, for the water froze as fast as it washed in, coating the boat heavily and incasing the clothing of the men in crystal."

At 4 o'clock in the afternoon a lookout from the Point of Woods Life-Saving Station spotted a boat approaching the beach. It was the one in charge of the mate, John Marshall. "The boat was thickly coated with ice, and it could be plainly seen by the movements of the people that they were nearly exhausted." Despite the frigid cold and a "high and dangerous sea," the life-savers launched a surfboat and rowed through breakers toward the beleaguered survivors who were nearly frozen at their oars. "Three of the surfmen were transferred to the boat to bring it in over the bar, while the castaways, who were nearly all more or less frost-bitten, were taken into the surf-boat and conveyed ashore to the station and comfortably provided for. A watch was also set and word sent to the adjacent stations to be on the lookout for the other boat in case it should attempt to land."

Meanwhile, Captain Colvin and the ten sailors with him were struggling in the freezing sea to stay afloat. "The second mate held the tiller under his arm until the spray had formed a mass of ice which fastened his sleeve securely to his coat. Still the brave man held his post for hours. Others offered to take the tiller, but he refused to part with it. At length, the ice completely covered him, and he showed signs of exhaustion. He then had to be dragged away from the tiller. His boots had frozen to the bottom of the boat, and he was frozen fast to his seat. After another man had taken his place as much of the ice as possible was knocked and scraped from his clothing. The spray froze on the Captain's whiskers until the latter were joined fast together over his mouth. Others who caught the spray became covered with ice. All suffered intensely from the cold.

"The men looked around in vain for passing vessels. Some looked forward hoping to see the mate's boat, but the later was miles nearer to the shore than the little ice-clad shell in which they floated. Occasionally the vapor, which frequently spread in clouds over the horizon, hid the tall tower of the Fire Island Lighthouse, but this was still miles away."

All afternoon the half-frozen men struggled. "Twilight fell and soon deepened into darkness. . . . Soon after dark the Fire Island light seemed to loom up close at hand. The men were surprised to find it apparently so near them. After rowing for a while they fancied themselves close to the Fire Island shore and almost within hailing distance of the lighthouse. They yelled themselves hoarse, but received no answer. Then they thought that the inmates of the lighthouse were asleep and that no one was on the lookout. It did not occur to them at first that the vapor on the water had produced something similar to a mirage, and that they had been deceived about their distance from the Fire Island light. At length they stopped crying for help, and with a feeling akin to hopelessness, drifted aimlessly for some time.

"Shortly before 9 o'clock in the evening the men were fast becoming exhausted. Several had been frostbitten. Suddenly they observed a small light, toward which they headed. As they made toward it they shouted lustily. They thought for a time that it was a lighthouse. Their shouts were unanswered, however, and they feared a repetition of their recent experience. They did not dare to row any nearer the light for fear that they might be caught in the surf and swamped. Soon they discovered that their boat was drifting directly toward the light, and in a few minutes they discerned the outlines of a vessel to which the light belonged. The stranger proved to be the fishing smack *Woolsey*. She grew larger and larger until they could make out that she was at anchor."

All aboard the *Stephen Woolsey* were ensconced below deck, and none heard Captain Colvin's first cry to his frozen crew, "Throw your painter around her cable!" Numbed fingers were unable to comply with the captain's command. As the lifeboat drifted past the fishing smack, the crew shouted for help, this time loud enough in chorus to arouse the fishermen, one of whom "sprang to the side of the smack and threw a line to the men in the boat. They caught it and in a moment found themselves alongside the smack. The latter's crew were now on deck, and they assisted the exhausted men out of their boat. Three were so badly frostbitten that they had to be lifted on deck.

"The half-frozen survivors of the *Hylton Castle* were taken down into the cabin, where they found a hot stove. A warm supper was immediately prepared for them by their rescuers, who took off their own clothes and offered them to the half-frozen seamen." The next morning, Captain N.S. Keeney, master of the *Stephen Woolsey*, raised anchor and set sail for port, even though the fishing smack's holds were not yet full. But as several survivors required hospitalization for frostbite, he cut short his cruise to accommodate them. On the way, the *Stephen Woolsey* encountered the tug *Rambler*, which, apprised of the desperate situation, took the fishing smack in tow at greater speed than the *Stephen Woolsey* could make under sail. "The fishing vessel was afterward hailed by the tug *Millard*, Capt. Phil Dick, which took off the rescued men and landed them at Castle Garden, shortly before noon. They at once proceeded to the British Consulate, where they were told to go to the Sailor's Home, in Cherry-street." Three of the most severely frostbitten men were treated at the hospital for their injuries.

While at this point in the narrative all members of the *Hylton Castle* have been saved from the sea, the ordeal of those ashore at Point of Woods was far from over, for at that time there were no bridges connecting Fire Island to the mainland, and boat traffic was impossible due to the ice in Great South Bay. At first, John Marshall and his men did not even think of making the crossing, because they were concerned about the rescue of their captain and the rest of the crew aboard the boat with the broken oars. As soon as they warmed up, they joined the life-savers who were prowling the beach in search of the remaining survivors. Not until the boat was spotted in tow of the *Stephen Woolsey* did they haul back to the station and begin the trek to the city.

"They had nine miles to walk along the wild and icy beach, and then four miles across the Great South Bay on the thin ice. It was a blustering walk of 13 miles to the Patchogue station." They then boarded a train for New York, and arrived there at 5 o'clock in the afternoon, only to find that the British Consul's office was closed for the day and the doors were locked. "Some one came along and said there was a Sailor's Home boarding house about two blocks off. For that point the battered procession headed, only to find that the 'Home' was bolted and barred, having evidently gone out of business.

"Then a policeman recommended the Twenty-seventh Precinct Station House, into which haven the mariners steered at about 6 o'clock. The Sergeant in charge sent them to the common lodging room where the tramps go. It was cold and dark down there, and the men didn't like it. They crept out into the hall, and lay on the floor gazing at the fire that blazed in the lodging room for women. When Capt. Berghold found them there most of them had struck up a chatting acquaintance with the women lodgers, and were smoothing their troubles as sociably as could be expected of men who were desperately hungry and only half thawed out. The Captain invited them up stairs to the warm, bright room in which the police lounge, and in a little while they were enjoying, as the Captain's guests, steaming bowls of soup and coffee, with bread."

Then began John Marshall's odyssey and indefatigable efforts to find British hospitality for his crew. In the freezing cold he set out upon the streets of New York. Since the Consul's office was closed, he went to the house of J. Pierpont Edwards, the British Consulate. There he learned that Edwards was in Europe. Next he went to the house of Gilbert Fraser, who was in charge of the consulate offices during Edwards' absence. "From him he obtained an order on Superintendent Alexander, of the Sailors' Home, in Cherry-street, for food and lodging for the party. It was nearly 9 o'clock when the mate, with this paper in his pocket, joined his associates at the station house, and about 9:30 o'clock they shuffled into the Sailors' Home. The mate by this time was ravenously hungry and the others had only had their appetites sharpened by the station house lunch, so they lost no time, after handing in their names and getting their lodging room keys, in making for the dining-room, where a hasty table was prepared for them," after which they immediately repaired to bed for a well deserved sleep.

It was here that they were reunited the next day with Captain Colvin and the rest of the men from the *Hylton Castle*.

There followed allegations that the steamer was overloaded. According to one so-called authority, "Vessels usually carry 50 per cent more than their net tonnage. The net tonnage of the *Hylton Castle* was a little short of 800 tons. At the outside she should not have carried more than 1,200 tons, but she left this port with over 1,400 tons of corn on board. She could not have left an English port with such a large cargo." Captain Colvin disagreed, claiming that the ship's load lines were not under water, and there the matter rested.

Today the *Hylton Castle* is one of New York's more interesting wrecks to explore. The hull, what is left of it, is contiguous from bow to stern, and is not so large that it cannot all be seen, albeit briefly, during the course of a single dive. There is a well defined waist nearly all around except at the ends.

The depth to the sea bed is 100 feet. The compound engine is the highest point of relief, rising 18 feet off the bottom. Immediately forward of the engine are a pair of boilers which are slightly lower in height. Forward of the boilers is a vertical metal cylinder, and off its after port (placing it just forward to the outboard edge of the port boiler) is a condenser, whose top is rusted away so that the tubes are visible. This constitutes the largest concentration of wreckage.

Aft of the engine, the starboard hull is disjointed as if it broke apart when the ship slammed against the bottom. Debris covers the propeller shaft so that it cannot be seen; this debris extends all the way to the propeller and rudder. Two blades of the iron propeller are exposed, each blade being about five feet in length. The rudder fell to port with the tiller arm on the outboard side. Just forward of the tiller arm is a ten-spoked wooden wheel with two spokes missing, secured to an iron stand some of whose parts are brass. At first glance this wheel appears to be an auxiliary steering station, but as it faces outboard and is firmly affixed to the top of the port hull, I rather suspect that it was used for hoisting lifeboats on the davits.

This machinery area comprises about one-third of the length of the wreck. The forward two-thirds is far less interesting, although the scattered wreckage here offers more hiding places for lobsters and game fish; also, along the perimeter of the wreck, both at the waist and farther off in the sand, there is the potential of finding the remains of the ship's rigging, such as the masts, belaying pins, and deadeyes.

Forward of the vertical cylinder which lies in front of the boilers, the wreck consists of little more than low lying debris with less than five feet of relief. About 75 feet away, a windlass lies in the sand on the port side, but so far back from the bow that it seems out of place. Forward of the windlass, the wreckage for the most part disappears beneath the sand, and it is difficult to navigate further because so few beams are exposed. However, by continuing in a straight line along the keelson, which is about the only reliable reference point, the capstan will be found about 75 feet farther along. The wreck just peters out after that, with no stem visible to denote the termination of the hull.

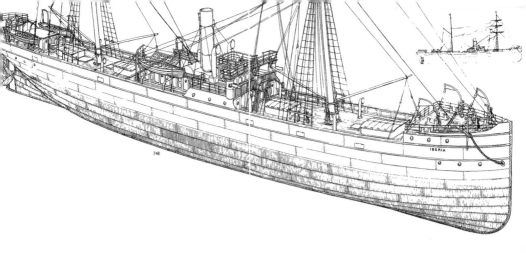

IBERIA

Built: 1881
Previous names: None
Gross tonnage: 1,388
Type of vessel: Iron-hulled freighter
Builder: S & H Morton & Company, Leith, Scotland
Owner: Cyprien Fabre & Company, France
Port of registry: Marseilles, France
Cause of sinking: Collision with SS *Umbria*
Location: 26855.5

Sunk: November 10, 1888
Depth: 60 feet
Dimensions: 254' x 36' x 19'
Power: Coal-fired steam

43736.2

On the morning of November 10, 1888, New York harbor was shrouded in fog so thick that visibility was reduced to less than 1,000 feet. The two vessels fated to meet under lamentable circumstances were under way at precautionary speeds.

Inbound came the *Iberia*, a French ship under the command of Captain Sagois, with a crew of twenty-nine, nearing the end of a long passage from the Persian Gulf. She was carrying coffee, hides, and dates consigned to Arnold & Cheney of New York. The *Iberia* had cleared the Iraqi port of Bussorah (today called Basra) on September 21, passed through the Suez Canal and transited the Mediterranean Sea, steamed by Gibraltar on October 17, crossed the Atlantic without incident, then, despite a complete overhaul the previous year, experienced engine trouble shortly prior to arrival in port. The ship anchored outside the harbor for thirty hours while the crew effected repairs. Then she proceeded at slow speed (3-1/2 to 4 knots) toward her date with destiny.

Outbound came the *Umbria*, a Cunard liner commanded by Captain William McMickan, on her way to Liverpool with more than seven hundred passengers and a crew of nearly three hundred. Her gross tonnage was 7,798. She slipped her mooring lines at 10:45 a.m., passed Sandy Hook shortly after noon, and, with open ocean ahead, discharged the pilot at 12:30. Traveling at 16 knots, the *Umbria* passed the SS *Normandie* and soon was so far ahead of her that the latter's whistle could no longer be heard by the officers on the bridge of the *Umbria*. For a short time, silence prevailed off the fog-shrouded coast.

By 1 o'clock the situation was such that the *Iberia* was heading west northwest, while the *Umbria* was crossing her intended track heading east. Neither vessel could see the other. As the distance between the two ships closed, the discordant notes of steam whistles spoke the approach.

Iberia: "The whistle of the *Umbria* was heard a little on the port bow . . . The course of the *Iberia* was thereupon changed to N.W., and she kept on blowing her whistle, in response to the *Umbria's* whistle, till the *Umbria* was seen through the fog near at hand, and heading for the *Iberia's* beam. The latter's engines were at once put full speed ahead."

Umbria: "A faint whistle was heard ahead on the starboard bow of the *Umbria*, and then another whistle on the same bow, but more ahead than the first. The engine of the *Umbria* was slowed. Again the whistle was heard, and then the engine of the *Umbria* was put full speed ahead, her master supposing by the sound that the approaching vessel was clear of his course; or, as the official log stated, thinking that the approaching vessel would port for the *Normandie*, he ordered full speed ahead, to pass her. Shortly afterwards, nearly dead ahead, and on a course crossing that of the *Umbria*, appeared the steam-ship *Iberia*. The *Umbria's* wheel was put hard a-port, and her engines reversed, notwithstanding which she struck the *Iberia* on her port quarter, cutting her in two."

From *Harper's Weekly*.

It is somewhat of an exaggeration to state that the *Iberia* was "cut in two." Such a description leaves a mistaken impression about the amount of damage done to the hull and about the present condition of the wreck on the bottom. In actuality, the *Umbria's* bow sliced off fourteen feet of the *Iberia's* counter: that part of the upper deck which overhangs and extends beyond the rudder. "This section, holding the flagstaff with colors flying, drifted away on one side of the *Umbria*, and the bulk of the disabled steamer floated away in an opposite direction. There was very little resistance to the blow, and the shock was so slight that few persons aboard the *Umbria* were conscious of the accident until later."

The *Umbria* stopped engines. "The fog thickened so quickly that the *Umbria* was soon lost in it, and it was 20 minutes before she could find the steamer that had collided with her." A quick inspection of the bow proved that the "big steamer had been wounded, but not seriously enough to endanger any lives. . . . Two plates were broken on the starboard side above the water line. The opening was pear shaped and it could be covered by a soft patch of 3 feet by 6 feet. The plate opposite, on the port side, was bulged out and split in a ragged way. The steam [stem] piece was intact. The wounds were in the narrowest part of the *Umbria*. They were too high up to let in more than dashes of water, and what was shipped in this way was confined to the 10 feet of space between the opening and the first water-tight bulkhead."

On the *Iberia* the situation was not quite as good. She had "six feet of water in the engine room, and she was well down by the stern." Captain Sagois ordered a flag of distress to be flown. Then, when the *Umbria* hove into view out of the clinging fog, Captain Sagois sent an officer in a small boat to report his ship's condition to the captain of the Cunard liner. Captain McMickan sent his chief engineer to the *Iberia* to provide what assistance he could. After a thorough inspection, the engineer was of the opinion that, "with her six water-tight compartments, she could float long enough to be towed into port, but advised that the crew abandon her and go aboard the *Umbria*. Capt. Sagois refused to desert his vessel, and, the weather continuing nasty, with considerable sea on, the two steamers anchored not far apart and remained outside all night."

By dawn "there was no change in the situation, except that the *Iberia* had settled a little, and Capt. McMickan did not consider it practicable to attempt any towing. He was anxious to get back to port, and finally persuaded the crew of the *Iberia* to come aboard the *Umbria*." No sooner did the large liner reach port than repairs were begun on her damaged bow.

The pilot boat No. 13, the *Caldwell H. Colt*, tied up alongside the *Iberia* at her temporary anchorage and put a salvage crew aboard to watch over her until tugs could arrive, but the steamer soon slipped gracefully beneath the waves. There was no loss of life.

The *Iberia* was valued at $125,000, exclusive of cargo. She sank in shallow water in a location approximately known. Within forty-eight hours a salvage scheme was put into effect. Two tugs from the Merritt Wrecking Company employed the method of wire-dragging in order to locate the sunken hull. "A long cable three and a half inches in diameter was swung from one tug to the other, and swept along the bottom of the sea till the *Iberia* was found. Having found her, the wreckers first began the serious work of extracting her cargo. Packed in her hold were some 28,000 boxes of dried fruits, a few bales of skins, and seven or eight hundred bales of wool."

Four divers, working in teams of two, began the process of recovery. They found the hull intact except for the truncated stern, and lying so far over on its starboard side that the tips of the masts stuck in the bottom. It was reported, "They cannot work in bad weather, nor can they remain under water at such a depth for very long without serious inconvenience from the great pressure of the water. As a matter of fact the men in this work are working on shifts of from two to three hours. The consequent delay, and the storms that are to be expected at this season of the year, are likely to prolong the work, so that it will be spring, or perhaps summer, before the hull is either raised or abandoned."

From *Harper's Weekly.*

The hull was abandoned, for it rests there today. How much of the cargo was recovered before salvage operations were discontinued went unrecorded. This did not mean, however, that all was lost. Even in the nineteenth century, Americans were learning that it was easier and less costly to recover their losses from the courts than from beneath the sea. A lawsuit was filed in federal court of the Eastern District of New York. Against the Cunard Steam Ship Company, owner of the *Umbria*, were seven litigants, all underwriters which had insured the hull of the *Iberia* and the various cargoes in her holds at the time of her loss, and which had paid off against claims.

After hearing extensive testimony from four of the *Umbria's* officers (the captain, the chief officer, the second officer, and the extra third officer) and two expert witnesses, all of whom defended the captain's order to increase engine revolutions to full speed, the court rendered a decision which held that "the cause of the collision was the erroneous order of the master of the *Umbria* to put that vessel at full speed in a fog, before the position and course of the vessel whose whistle had been heard were known."

Defense attorneys attempted to muddy the waters by claiming that the *Iberia* was partially responsible for the collision by approaching New York from the south instead of along the east-west shipping lane, and that by porting her helm she had turned toward the *Umbria* instead of away from her. The court concluded otherwise: "It is not proved here, and of course cannot be proved, that in the locality of this collision no course is proper except an east or west course. No statute nor rule nor custom proved forbids a vessel to cross the track of vessels leaving New York bound to the eastward. . . . She was sounding with her lead, and she had not yet reached 10 fathoms of water. Pilots called in this case declare such a course to be proper." As to the other charge, the court found that "the porting of the *Iberia* was not a fault, and did not contribute to the collision."

As is their wont, defense attorneys tried other obfuscatory tactics, all of which were rebuffed by the court. "Another charge against the *Iberia* is that she kept no proper lookout. But the *Umbria's* whistle was heard in due time, and the *Umbria* herself was seen as soon as possible. Want of a lookout was no cause of this collision. Again, it is charged on the *Iberia* that her whistle was insufficient. As to this, all that is necessary to be said is that the proof shows that her whistle was sufficient to warn the *Umbria* at the distance of a mile, and to indicate to the officers on the *Umbria* that she was distant a mile and on a course crossing the course of the *Umbria*. . . . So far as I am able to discover from a laborious examination of the testimony, the *Iberia* was guilty of no fault which conduced to the collision. My conclusion, therefore, is that the *Umbria* alone is liable for the damages caused by the collision in question. Let decrees to that effect be entered in the several causes."

It is ironic to note that the shipping channels were not as safe for navigation as the *Umbria's* attorney's would have made the court believe. On June 27, 1896, the *Umbria* left the Cunard pier at the foot of Clarkson Street and proceeded outbound from New York harbor to Queenstown and Liverpool. She had on board some seven hundred passengers. About two miles off Sandy Hook, near the turn into Gedney Channel, the liner was traveling at full speed when she came to such a sudden screeching halt that some of the passengers were thrown sprawling onto the floor of the saloon. As it was barely 10 o'clock in the morning, it was too early for most people to have consumed enough alcohol to render themselves unfit to stand. And as the ship was in mid-channel it was impossible that she had run aground. In fact, the *Umbria* had struck "the coal-laden wreck of the barge *Andrew Jackson*, once a swift American clipper, which was sunk on May 22 in collision with the steamship *Vedra*."

Wreckers had already removed the masts of the schooner barge and were in the process of demolishing the hull as a hazard to navigation, when they were chased off the wreck by bad weather. The marker buoys left behind were spotted by lookouts on the *Umbria*, and the great liner swerved aside with intention to pass the wreck to starboard, when the steering mechanism unpredictably took temporary charge and forced the vessel's bow to veer straight across the submerged hull. The engines were hastily reversed and helped the ship to lose way; nevertheless, three-quarters of the great liner's length drove over the *Andrew Jackson* before forward motion stopped, leaving her trapped like a moth on a pin.

Ten hours passed before the *Umbria* was pulled free on the flood tide, with the assistance of five tugs and her own engines straining in reverse. She then anchored while a diver made an inspection of the outer hull. "Save a scratch on her bow made by one of the spar buoys that marked the location of the hulk, the *Umbria* came out of her predicament unscathed." To the great joy of the passengers, the vessel was pronounced fit to proceed on her way.

Due to its shallow depth, the wreck of the *Iberia* is an ideal dive site for beginners who have as much to learn about the wreck diving as they do about their equipment. For more experienced divers, extended bottom times permit more opportunities to dig in the debris in search of lobsters, game fish, sea shells, and souvenirs.

Judging by the present condition of the wreck, the hull was probably demolished by explosives as a hazard to navigation. Low-lying debris dominates the site, although there are several areas of high relief. The bow, which lies on its starboard side, is separated from the main hull and lies off the starboard side at somewhat of an angle to the longitudinal line of the hull. The bowsprit lies low and is recognizable. A capstan is still firmly secured to the deck.

The two boilers lie side by side, nearly touching. The compound engine, which rises some twenty-five feet off the bottom, is clearly distinguishable despite thick encrustation. The shaft is exposed and extends all the way aft to the four-bladed iron propeller, one of whose blades is broken off.

Portholes and deadeyes are occasionally found when the sand shifts and exposes the deeper lying portions of the wreck, but the most prominent souvenirs to be collected are square wooden crate ends from the cargo of golden dates. The top, bottom, and side slats of the boxes were thin and have broken up throughout the years, but the ends were constructed of thicker boards; the name and address of the manufacturer are stenciled in black and in most cases are still legible: Arnold Cheney & Co., 148 Water St., New York. The largest concentration of crate ends is found aft of the engine on the starboard side of the wreck. Elsewhere, the astute diver will be able to distinguish machinery parts despite the thick organic growth.

Courtesy of the Institute for Great Lakes Research.

JOHN C. FITZPATRICK

Built: 1892
Previous names: None
Gross tonnage: 1,270
Type of vessel: Wooden-hulled schooner barge
Builder: F.W. Wheeler & Company, West Bay City, Michigan
Owner: J. Mitchell (Boutelle Transportation Company)
Port of registry: Cleveland, Ohio
Cause of sinking: Boiler explosion
Location: 26135.6

Sunk: April 3, 1903
Depth: 135 feet
Dimensions: 242' x 39' x 16'
Power: None

43770.4

When the *John C. Fitzpatrick* was launched, on May 31, 1892, she was a sleek wooden-hulled schooner sporting four tall masts. She was built at the prestigious yard of F.W. Wheeler & Company, which had been in operation in West Bay City, Michigan, for fifteen years, and which had turned out quite a few other schooners for the inland sea trade. The twilight of sail had not yet arrived, so once the wind billowed the canvas of the *John C. Fitzpatrick*, she went to work carrying freight throughout the Great Lakes.

In 1898 she was chartered for ocean service. This was at the time when the era of sailing ships was on the wane. Replacing the schooner fleet was a new generation of water transport: the steamship. Although steamers had been around for decades, they were costly to build, maintain, and operate. When labor was cheap and the world moved at a slower pace than it does today, it was affordable to hire a large crew to man the sails and take months to complete a voyage. The wind was free, and fuel to fire the boilers that provided steam for an engine was expensive. But as labor costs increased, as marine engines became more reliable, as iron- and steel-hulled steamships grew in size and speed, and were able to carry many times the cargo of the majestic but sluggish sailing ships (always at the whim of heaven's breath), the gap between construction and operational expenses narrowed.

Finally, sailing ships became a liability. Steam powered vessels took over the merchant marine, and "sailors" became stokers, oilers, and engineers. In an attempt to save manpower, sailing ships converted to steam and were fitted with boilers and engines—not to turn a paddle wheel or to turn a screw propeller, but to operate winches and windlasses. These small boilers became known as "donkey boilers." Now a winch by each mast could raise or lower the sails at the flick of a lever. Instead of a schooner requiring a work force in the dozens, a handful of men could take the ship completely around the world.

Eventually, even such labor saving devices became cost prohibitive, because a single steamship could haul much more freight than the comparatively small windjammers, and do it reliably despite adverse weather conditions such as head winds and doldrums. But what to do with the hundreds, perhaps thousands, of schooners leftover from the heyday of sail? If they could not be used as sailing vessels, it was reasoned, then do away with the sails and utilize the hulls. Thus was born the schooner barge. A schooner barge is an ex-schooner whose masts have been cut completely away, or perhaps only cut down so that her lower masts could be used to support cargo booms. These dismasted "hulls" were towed by a tug much like a locomotive tows freight cars. Often a tug towed two or three or possibly four schooner barges along the coastal routes, forming an ocean-going train, and more often than not the cargo was the very coal that fired the boilers of the steamships that had put the schooners out of business.

It was an ignominious end to a form of water-borne transport that stretched thousands of years into man's maritime past. Such was the fate of the *John C. Fitzpatrick*.

So it was that in April of 1903, the ex-schooner found herself at the end of a hawser secured to the towing bitt of the steam tug *Sweepstakes*. Aboard the barge were 2,400 tons of bituminous coal and a crew of five. The responsibilities of the crew were to steer the rudder, pump the water from leaky holds, and keep steam on the boiler which ran the pumps. Captain George Davis was in command of the barge and the four able-bodied seamen.

Tug and tow left Philadelphia bound for New Bedford, Massachusetts. They slipped down the Delaware River into the broad reaches of the Delaware Bay, then shaped a course north along the coast. They veered eastward along the south shore of Long Island to the vicinity of the Hamptons, which they reached on April 3. Those on the *Sweepstakes* heard a tremendous explosion on the *John C. Fitzpatrick*, which they later attributed to the boiler blowing up, although it is not known for sure because the schooner barge sank almost immediately, taking with her the entire crew. All five men drowned.

The precise resting place of the *John C. Fitzpatrick* would be unknown were it not for Ronald Barnes, who recovered the brass capstan cover engraved with the ship's name. Until that time the popular dive site was called the Jug. Very little remains of the graceful lines that once cleaved the waves under sail. Today the wreck consists of low lying debris and a few wooden timbers protruding from the sandy bottom: a "snag" whose main attractions are lobsters and game fish.

As the *Madagascar*. (Courtesy of the Milwaukee Public Library.)

KENOSHA

Built: 1894
Previous names: *Madagascar*
Gross tonnage: 1,677
Type of vessel: Wooden-hulled steamship
Builder: James Davidson, West Bay City, Michigan
Owner: F.B. Cheseborough
Port of registry: Marquette, Michigan
Cause of sinking: Foundered
Location: 26599.0

Sunk: July 24, 1909
Depth: 105 feet
Dimensions: 243' x 37' x 21'
Power: Coal-fired steam

43644.7

The *Kenosha* is one of those wrecks which was "discovered" in reverse order. That is, the wreck site was well-known and was fished and dived for years before it was properly identified. For some unknown reason the site was popularly called the Fire Island Lightship, despite the facts that no such lightship ever sank in the area and that the actual *Fire Island* lightship was constructed of steel, whereas the submerged hull which was called the lightship was made of thick wooden timbers. Local legend notwithstanding, the wreck could not be that of a lightship which never sank. So what wreck was it?

Marc Weiss can be thanked for providing the penultimate clue which led to the wreck's true identity. The site has always been highly regarded for its consistent yield of that clawed culinary delight, Homarus americanus: the American lobster. August 23, 1986 found Weiss diving the wreck for "bugs." In a letter which he wrote to me after his find, he wrote, "As I got approximately 30 feet away from the anchor I spotted a fairly decent bug (5-6 pounds). I extracted it from its home between the ships ribs and placed it into my bug bag. Looking to the right of the wreck I noticed a large green bowl shaped object about 20 feet out into the sand. As I approached it I thought this must be a storm cover to a porthole. When I further examined it I realized it had writing on it. It was then that I knew I had more than a storm cover, it was a capstan cover." Other divers later claimed to have seen the "bowl," but all had passed it by unrecognized.

"I could not find any way to attach my lift bag to it, and my bug bag was too small at the-opening to fit the capstan cover inside. . . . Being very close to a decompression dive and over 200 feet from the anchor line with no way to send the capstan cover to the surface, I made a free ascent with my find." Then he swam it back to the boat: no easy feat considering the size and weight of the brass.

The capstan cover was stamped with the ship's name, *Madagascar*, the date of construction, the name of the builder, and the manufacturer of the capstan: the "American Ship Windlass Co., Providence, R.I." The *Madagascar* was renamed *Kenosha* in 1907, and it was under the latter name that she docked at her final port of call, on July 24, 1909.

Not much was recorded about the sinking of the *Kenosha*, seemingly as if the loss of a major vessel was of little consequence in the world of merchant shipping. This cryptic note was dispatched from Boston on July 25, 1909: "Str *Kenosha*, from Baltimore for Boston with coal, sprung a leak and sank 6 miles off Fire Island lightship yesterday morning. The *Kenosha* sank rapidly and the crew of 18 were forced into small boats, from which they were picked up by str *Howard* and brought here." Thus the *Kenosha* slipped silently beneath the waves with little or no fanfare, and entered the pages of history and present day wreck diving.

Most of the wreck's wooden hull has rotted away. The timbers have little more than a foot or two of relief, and it is between these structural members that lobsters hide from their natural predators. The largest intact section is the bow, which rises eight to ten feet off the bottom. Elsewhere deep sand has drifted across the wreck, effectively burying the bottom of the hull and making it appear that the wreck is broken into two distinct pieces. The four-bladed iron propeller is exposed, as is the encrusted machinery lying close to the stern. Despite moderate diver activity at the site, the *Kenosha* still yields a fair share of lobsters and game fish, and is worth a visit if only to see the sights.

Who knows what other treasures lie inches beneath the sand?

Courtesy of the Institute for Great Lakes Research.

LEXINGTON

Built: 1835
Previous names: None
Gross tonnage: 488
Type of vessel: Wooden-hulled side wheeler
Builder: Bishop & Simonson, New York, NY
Owner: New Jersey Steam Navigation Company
Port of registry: New York, NY
Cause of sinking: Fire
Location: Eaton's Neck, in Long Island Sound

Sunk: January 13, 1840
Depth: 150 feet
Dimensions: 207' x 21' x 11'
Power: Coal-fired steam

The number of people aboard the *Lexington* at the time of her loss is in dispute: figures range between 126 and 165. But there is no doubt that only four people survived the conflagration which engulfed the paddle wheel steamer and sent so many mortal souls to everlasting peace. It is only through the testimony of those four survivors that the story of the *Lexington's* last moments can be told.

The *Lexington* provided freight and passenger service between New York City and New England at a time when steamboats were in their infancy and railroads had a monopoly on the movement of goods and people. She began her career in 1835, and for five years steamed reliably and at reasonable rates between ports in Long Island Sound. As the passage took about twelve hours, the *Lexington* steamed during the day and laid over each night at her port of call, then returned the following day.

The vessel was constructed under the personal supervision of shipping and railroad magnate Cornelius Vanderbilt, who later said, "she was built of the first rate materials, or what we considered so at the time,—of locust, chestnut, cedar, oak and white and yellow pine. She was fastened in what we thought was the best manner, and had thirty per cent. more fastening than any other boat that ever navigated Long Island Sound. As an evidence of this, she is the only boat that, during four years navigating the Sound, never lost a trip."

In order to get more use out of the vessel, and so she could accommodate passengers at night, cabins and berths were added during the winter of 1836-1837. The following year Vanderbilt sold the *Lexington* to the New Jersey Steam Navigation Company, which converted her boilers to burn coal instead of wood, and installed fans which blew air across the fires. Coal burns hotter than wood and contains more latent heat per unit volume, and forced draft makes combustible materials burn hotter yet (the way a bellows works on a camp fire or fireplace); the combination of these physical principals produced more steam for the vertical beam engine, and made it run faster, thus increasing the rotational speed of the paddle wheels and, consequently, the speed of the vessel through water.

Captain William Comstock, company agent, described the alterations. "The grate-bars were raised up eighteen inches, the flues contracted, and the insides of the furnaces were filled up with fire brick and iron pans that always had water in them, and the whole width of the boiler at the after end was filled up with brick and iron."

At 3 o'clock in the afternoon of January 13, 1840, the *Lexington* left New York for Stonington, Connecticut. In command was Captain George Child. In addition to the passengers and crew she carried "a large freight consisting principally of cotton," which was carried on deck. "At 7 o'clock, when about three or four miles from Eaton's Neck, Long Island, some bales of cotton, and the casings around the smoke-pipe, were discovered to be on fire. The wind at the time was blowing fresh from the north."

Captain Stephen Manchester was the *Lexington's* pilot. "When I first heard the alarm of fire, about half past 7 o'clock, some one came to the wheel-house door and told me that the boat was on fire; my first movement was to step out of the wheel-house and look aft; saw the upper deck burning all round the smoke pipe, the flames coming up through the promenade deck. I returned into the wheel-house and put the wheel hard-a-port to steer the boat for the land. I then thought it very doubtful whether the fire could be extinguished. We were about four miles from Long Island shore, and at the rate we were then going, it would take about twenty minutes to reach it.

"We had not yet headed to the land, when something gave way, which I believe was the tiller rope; thinks she was heading about south-east, and Long Island bore about south, when the tiller rope gave way; the engine was then working; and the boat fell ahead more to the eastward. Captain Child then came into the wheel-house and put his hand to the spoke of the wheel, and, as he did so, the rope gave way; presumes it was the rope attached to the wheel; it was the larboard rope gave way; and at the same time the smoke came into the wheel-house, and we were obliged to go out. I suspect he went aft, but I never saw him afterwards; when he went out he went down on the forward deck; I do not recollect whether he expressed any alarm. I then called to them on the forecastle to get out the fire engine and buckets; the engine was got out, but they could not get at the buckets, or at least I only saw a few. I am of opinion the wheel-ropes burnt off, but I could not have stood it longer even if there had been chains round the wheel.—I think there was then an opportunity to go from the wheel-house aft, where there was another steering apparatus, a good tiller, with chains which ran through blocks; all boats are so rigged, in order that if any thing happens to the rudder, this can be used in its place. I did not go aft to it, because I thought my services would be more useful forward. After calling to get out the engine, I went to the life boat, and found some persons taking the tarpaulin off it. I caught hold of the lashing of the boat, and requested them not to let her go until we got a line fastened to her. I called to those at the forecastle to pass a line to make fast to her, which they did, and we fastened it to her bow. The fire was then burning through the promenade deck. I cut the lashing, and told them to launch the boat. I jumped from the promenade deck down on the forward deck, took hold of the hawser, and found it was not fastened to the steamboat. I told them to hold on to the rope, but they all let go one after another; the engine was still going, and I was obliged to let it go myself also. We then found two buckets, and commenced throwing water with them and the specie boxes; we got the water from over the side of the boat, which was then nearly stopped; while doing this, some others took the flag-staffs and parts of the bulwarks, and made a raft, to which we made a line fast and hove it over the side of the boat; we then threw the baggage overboard from four baggage cars, and made them fast with a line; the engine by this time was entirely stopped; it worked from ten to fifteen minutes going gradually slower until it ceased. We threw out every thing by which we thought any person could save themselves; and continued throwing on water in hopes that some relief might reach us.

"The main deck now fell in as far as the capstan, and the people had by this time got overboard, some of them drowned, and others hurried on to the baggage cars, the raft and other things. What was left of the main deck was now on fire, and got us cornered up in so small a space that we could do nothing more by throwing water. There were then only eight or ten persons astern on the steamboat, and about thirty on the forecastle. They were asking me what they should do, and I told them I saw no chance for any of us; that if we stayed there, we should be burned to death, and if we went overboard we should probably perish. Among those who were there, was Mr. Hoyt and Van Cott, another person named Harnden, who had charge of the express line. I did not know any one else.

"I then took a piece of spun yarn and made it fast to my coat, and also to the rail, and so eased myself down upon the raft. There were two or three others on it already, and my weight sank it. I held on to the rope until it came up again— and when it did, I sprang up and caught a piece of railing which was in the water, and from thence got on a bale of cotton where there was a man sitting; found the bale was made fast to the railing; I took out my knife and cut it off. At the time I cut this rope, I saw some person standing on the piece of railing, who asked me if there was room for another; I made no answer, and he jumped, and knocked off the man that was with me; and I hauled him on again. I caught a piece of board which was floating past, and shoved the bale clean off from the raft; and used the board to endeavor to get in shore at Crane Neck Point, in which I could not succeed; but I used the board as long as I could, for exercise. When I left the wreck, I looked at my watch, and it was just 12 o'clock. I think the man who was on the bale with me said his name was McKenna, and lived at New York; he spoke of his wife and children; how he had kissed them the morning he left home, and said he feared he should perish with the cold.—He died about 3 o'clock. After I had hauled him on the bale, I had encouraged him, and told him to thrash his hands, which he did for a spell, but soon pretty much gave up. When he died he fell back on the bale, and the first sea that came washed him off. My hands were then so frozen that I could hardly use them at all; was about three miles from the wreck when she sunk; and the last thing I recollect, was seeing the sloop, and raising my handkerchief between my fingers, hoping they would see me. I was then sitting on the cotton, with my feet in the water. The bale did not seem to roll at all, although there were some heavy seas.

"I was taken off the cotton by Captain Meeker, and brought to Southport, where I received every possible attention."

Charles B. Smith was a fireman on the Lexington. "The first time I heard the alarm of fire was about half past 7 o'clock in the evening. I was in my room asleep, on the guard; a man came in and told me that the boat was on fire; I got out of my berth; the door of the room was open, directly opposite the steam chimney, and I saw the promenade deck, and part of the casing around the chimney on fire; went immediately into the crank room and put on the hose, opened the cocks, and tried to get to the end of the hose to play on the fire, but the fire and smoke prevented me. The hose was lying alongside of the bulkhead, alongside of the air pump. I went aft of the shaft to get breath, and then tried to get the buckets down that hung over the shaft, which the fire prevented me from doing; I then went aft with the intention of getting into the boat; I there saw Capt. Child standing on the rail, by the crane of the boat, on the starboard side, and heard him sing out for the engineer; the engineer answered; and the captain asked him if he could stop the engine; he replied that it was impossible, as the fire prevented; I had now got to where Capt. Child stood, and saw the bow tackle of the boat cut away, with the boat full of passengers—the bows of the boat filled with water, and she swung round on her stern tackle. Capt. Child sung out to hold on to the boat, and slipped down to the fender, outside of the bulwark. I slipped over after him; he stepped into the stern sheets of the boat, and I put my foot on the stern of the boat, and hauled it back, and just as I got my foot back, the stern tackle was let go, but whether it was cut or not, I do not know. That was the last I saw of the boat or the captain. Capt. Child was in the boat at the time. I got over the stern then with the intention of getting on to the rudder; I hung by the netting, kicked in three cabin windows, and lowering myself down got on the rudder.

"I had been there but a minute or two, when I was followed by several others. There was a boy got over the stern, whom I told to drop overboard and get on a bale of cotton: he said he could not swim. I then told him to tell some of those on deck to throw over a bale of cotton. There was one thrown over, which I jumped after, and gave the boy my place. I swam to it, and got on it. I remained on it until about half past 1 o'clock. About that time I drifted back to the steamboat and got on board. There were then ten or twelve persons hanging to different parts of the boat. Mr. Hempstead was one of them, and one of the firemen by the name of Baum,—Job Sands, a waiter,—Harry Reed, and a small English boy,—another coal heaver, whose name was William,—and a deck hand by the name of Charles. These were all the names I knew; the rest were, as I suppose, passengers and some waiters,—there were no ladies. I staid there until 3 o'clock, when the boat sunk. I staid about midships, near where the fire originated.

"We stood on the top of the hips which are put on the boat to keep her from rolling, and are made of solid timber, running fore and aft of the boat nearly her whole length, under the guards; but the guards at this time were burnt off. I stood there until she sunk. After she began to fill, the rest jumped off. I then swam to a piece of the guard, and, with four others got on it,—they all perished before daylight. One of them was Harry Reed, and another, George, the fireman—the other was the boy to whom I had given my place on the rudder—the other I did not know; I think they all perished with the cold. I shook them all round, and tried to exercise them and rub them. I remained on the piece of guard until 2 o'clock in the afternoon, when I was taken off by the sloop *Merchant*, Captain Meeker, and was taken into Southport, where I had the best care taken of me possible. My feet were badly frozen, and my fingers touched a little with the frost."

Captain Chester Hillard was a passenger on the Lexington. "It was about an hour after supper that I first heard the alarm of fire. I was then on the point of turning in, and had my coat and boots off. I slipped them on. I then discovered the casing of the smoke pipe, and I think, a part of the promenade deck, on fire. there was a great rush of the passengers, and much confusion, so that I could not notice particularly. The after part of the casing was burning, and the fire was making aft. I thought at the time, that the fire might be subdued; but, being aft at the time, could not, therefore, see distinctly.

"I saw nothing of the commander, and from what I could hear of the crew forward, I supposed they were at work trying to rig the fire engine; I saw no buckets used, and think they were not made use of; I think the fire engine was not got to work, as I saw nothing of it. I shortly after went on the promenade deck; my attention had previously been directed to the passengers, who were rushing into the quarter boats, and when I went on the quarter deck, the boats were both filled. They seemed to be stupidly determined to destroy themselves, as well as the boats, which were their only means of safety. I went to the starboard boat, which they were lowering away; they lowered it until she took the water, and then I saw someone cut away the forward tackle fall; it was at all events disengaged, and no one at the time could have unhooked the fall; the boat instantly filled with water, there being at the time about twenty persons in her; and the boat passed immediately astern, entirely clear. I then went to the other side; the other boat was cleared away and lowered in the same manner as the first, full of passengers. This boat fell astern entirely disengaged, as the other had done; but fell away before she had entirely filled with water.

"By this time the fire had got under such headway, that I pretty much made my mind up '*it was a gone case.*' I thought that the best thing that could be done was to run the boat ashore, and for this purpose went to the wheel-house to look for Capt. Child, expecting to find him there. I found him there, and advised him to run for the shore. He replied that she was already headed for the land. The fire by this time began to come up around the promenade deck, and the wheel-house was completely filled with smoke. There were two or three on the promenade deck near the wheel-house, and their attention was turned to the life boat; it was cleared away. I assisted in stripping off the canvas, but I had no notion of going in her, as I had made my mind up that they would serve her as they had done the other boats. The steamer was then under head way. Before I left the promenade deck I thought it was time for me to leave; however, as the fire was bursting up through the deck, I went aft and down on to the main deck. They were then at work with the hose, but whether by the aid of the engine, or not, I cannot say. The smoke was so dense that I could not see distinctly what they were about. I think that the communication with the fore part of the boat was by this time cut off; from the first hearing of the alarm, perhaps twenty minutes had elapsed. The engine had now been stopped about five minutes. I recommended to the few deck hands and passengers who remained, to throw the cotton overboard; and told them that they must do something for themselves, and the best thing they could do was to take to the cotton. There were perhaps ten or a dozen bales thrown overboard which was pretty much all there was on the larboard side which had not taken fire. I then cut off a piece of line, perhaps four or five fathoms, and with it spanned a bale of cotton, which, I believe, was the last one not on fire. It was a very snug square bale, about four feet long and three feet wide, and a foot and a half thick. Aided by one of the firemen, I put the bale up on the rail, round which we took a turn, slipped the bale down below the guard, when we both got on to it. The boat then lay broadside to the wind, and we were under the lee of the boat, on the larboard side. We placed ourselves one on each end of the bale, facing each other; with our weight it was about one third out of the water. The wind was pretty fresh, and we drifted at the rate of about a knot and a half. We did not lash ourselves to the bale, but coiled the rope up and laid it on the bale. My companion did not like the idea of leaving the boat immediately, but wished to hold on to the guards; but I determined to get out of the way, believing that to remain there much longer it would become pretty hot quarters. We accordingly shoved the bale round the stern, when we left the boat and drifted away about a knot and a half. This was just 8 o'clock by my watch, which I took out and looked at. As we left the wreck, I picked up a piece of board, which I used as a paddle or rudder, with which to keep the bale end to the sea.

"At the time we left the boat there were but few persons remaining on board. I saw one lady, and the reason why I particularly noticed her was, that her child had got overboard, and was then about two rods from her; we passed by the child so near that I could put my hand on it as it lay on its back; she saw us approaching the child and cried out for us to save it. The child, which from its dress

From *Steamboat Disasters and Railroad Accidents in the United States.*

appeared to be a female, was dead when we passed it; nor can I recollect what was said by the lady,—it was hard to notice particulars at the time, as it was pretty rough, and I had as much as I could do to manage the bale of cotton. We then drifted away from the boat, and in ten minutes more we could see no persons on board, excepting those on the forecastle.

"We sat astride of the bale with our feet in the water; but were wet up to the middle from the water frequently washing over. We were in sight of the boat all the time till she went down, when we were about a mile distant. When we left the wreck it was cloudy; but about 9 o'clock it cleared off, and we had a clear night of it until the moon went down; I looked at my watch as often as every half hour, through the night; the boat went down at 3 o'clock. It was so cold as to make it necessary for me to exert myself to keep warm, which I did by whipping my hands and arms around my body. About 4 o'clock the bale capsized with us; a heavy sea came and carried it over end-ways; we managed to get on the bale on its opposite side; at this time we lost our piece of board, which had been useful as a paddle, and afterwards the bale was ungovernable; my companion had complained much of the cold from our first setting out; he appeared to have given up all hope of our being saved. On our first starting from the boat, I gave him my vest as he had on only a flannel shirt, and pantaloons, boots and cap. Cox remained on the bale after it had upset about two hours, or more, until it was about day light. For the last half hour that he remained on the bale, he had been speechless, and seemed to have lost all use of his hands, as he did not try to hold on. I rubbed him and beat his flesh, and used every effort I could to keep his blood in circulation. It was still very rough, and I was obliged to exert myself to hold on. The bale coming broadside to the sea, it gave a lurch, and Cox slipped off, and I saw him no more. He went down without a struggle. I then got more into the middle of the bale, to make it ride as it should, and in that way continued for about an hour, when I got my feet on the bale, and so remained until the sloop picked me up. The sea had by this time become quite smooth. On seeing the sloop I waved my hand to attract the attention of those on board. The sloop was the *Merchant*, Capt. Meeker, of Southport."

David Crowley, second mate on the *Lexington*, had similar experiences. At first he joined Stephen Manchester in throwing pails of water on the flames, but was soon driven back by the flames. He then went aft and, when he saw the passengers abandoning ship in the lifeboat, he "called out to them to put the plug in the boat." He helped one passenger throw overboard a hawser tub, and another the chaffing board. When there was nothing else he could do aboard the steamboat, he tossed a plank in the water and jumped on it. Later he swam to a bale of cotton which floated past him. On this makeshift raft he survived for *two days and two nights!* His saga was later paraphrased by a contemporary reporter.

"The morning after the misfortune, he saw the sloop *Merchant* pick up one or two persons; he endeavored, by holding up his waistcoat, to attract their notice, but without success. When the night of that day came on, he thought himself near Faulkland Island, and expected to drift ashore there, but finding himself exhausted, he, miraculous to state, composed himself on his bale of cotton, went to sleep, and slept soundly until morning! Much revived by his sleep, he continued, through the following day, to make every exertion his situation permitted, to reach the land, which, however, he did not do until night. When landed, he scaled the high bank on the shore, when a light at a distance attracted his notice; he followed its direction until he reached the hospitable mansion of Mr. Huntingdon, at the moment his son had just arrived there and was relating the particulars of the loss of the *Lexington*. His unexpected appearance, pale and wretched, with his waistcoat round his head, naturally created sensations of pity and astonishment; he received all the care and attention his helpless and miserable situation required." During his odyssey, David Crowley had drifted some fifty miles.

The burning steamboat drifted up the Sound until, around midnight, the flames could be seen from the Connecticut towns of Southport and Bridgeton. Rescue efforts from shore were hampered by low tide and ice. The sloop *Improvement* was out on the Sound that night, but although her master, Captain William Terrell, spotted a light which he later concluded must have been the flaming steamboat just before she sank, he was ten or twelve miles downwind and was therefore unable to render assistance even had he known of the awful tragedy then occurring. "The burning of the boat was seen from the Connecticut and Long Island shores; but all efforts to render assistance proved unavailing. She drifted up the sound with the tide, and was burning eight hours before she sank."

One eyewitness stated, "The boat was seen on fire, drifting past Stony Brook, about midway of the sound, the blaze shooting up from her in columns, lighting up the waters for miles around; a small boat put off, but returned after going a mile or two, it being too rough to venture farther."

The only vessel that actually rendered assistance was the aforementioned sloop *Merchant*. "Capt. Meeker discovered the steamer on fire soon after it broke out, and attempted to get out of Southport; but the harbor being shallow, and the tide falling, his vessel went aground, and he did not get out until the morning tide."

Upon hearing of the catastrophe, the owners of the *Lexington* appointed Captain Joseph Comstock to search the Sound "for the purpose of recovering the bodies of the ill-fated passengers and crew, and to search for and to protect whatever baggage and property might drift ashore, or otherwise be discovered." He began his search three days later, and reported:

"I went on board the *Statesman*: at day-break we started, and landed again at Old Field Point. It was at this time intensely cold, the thermometer varying from three to four degrees below zero. At the Point I now left six men to look out for luggage, as I had heard that a number of trunks and packages had come ashore in the neighborhood. During the night, the body of a child about four years old had drifted ashore.

"At 8 o'clock, A.M., I left in the steamer for the eastward. Every part of the bank was carefully explored as we progressed, and traced the shore around the bay. I left persons ashore at different points, and inquired at all the houses for information relative to property saved from the wreck. After running seven miles east, I learned that three bodies had been found. I had them sent to Old Field Point; I here learned that eighteen miles farther east, a man had got ashore alive.

"I then proceeded to explore the beach the entire distance of the eighteen miles, until I came to the place. During this distance we found numerous portions of the wreck, among which was one piece, on which was the entire word 'Lexington,' in letters two feet long.

"We learned that David Crowley, the second mate, had come ashore at 5 o'clock on Wednesday night. He stated to the people here that he had been forty-eight hours upon the bale of cotton, and had crawled several rods upon the beach through the ice, and after getting ashore, had walked three quarters of a mile to the nearest house. They said that his feet and legs were badly frozen. He was bare-headed, and in his shirt sleeves; and supposed himself to be the only one saved from the wreck. I have instructions to leave nothing undone to render his situation as comfortable as possible, and to procure for him all medical or other aid that might be necessary. They said he was in the best of hands, and that he was in want of nothing for his comfort."

There was quite a furor over the "melancholy occurrence" in which so many people died, and after which so many families were bereaved by the loss of loved ones. Local churches rang with dirges and indictments. To give the reader an idea of the rhetoric raised by preachers giving their Sunday sermons, here is a single extract of the many grandiloquent appeals for the souls of the dead: "No tomb shall plead to their remembrance. No human power can redeem their forms. The white foam of the waves was their winding sheet, the winds of the ocean shall be their eternal dirge."

The calamity inspired one anonymous poet to compose an elegy called "Burning of the *Lexington*." Of the 170 lines I quote but a dozen of the most evocative.

> What means the loud tumult,—the heart-breaking cry,—
> The shrieks that uprise to the dark vaulted sky?
> Why tremble the weak, and why cower the strong?
> Why rush they thus phrenzied and madly along?
> *The boat is on fire!* and they see that their grave
> Is the red flashing fire, or the cold dashing wave!
> "To the boats!" to the boats distracted they crowd,—
> And find the dark wave is their funeral shroud.
> "Lower the boats! lower the boats!" 'tis done in a breath,
> Down they sink in the icy embraces of death!
> Some struggle a moment and buffet the wave,—
> One shriek,—and they sink into one common grave!

Recriminations about the conduct of the *Lexington's* captain and crew were inevitable. The coroner's jury returned a verdict of malfeasance, stating in part, "It is our opinion, that had buckets been manned at the commencement of the fire, it would have been immediately extinguished. Also, inasmuch as the engine could not be stopped, from the rapid progress of the fire, with presence of mind of the officers, and a strict discipline of the crew, the boats could have been launched and a large portion of the passengers and crew, if not the whole, might have been saved. . . . From the facts proved before this jury, that the captain and pilot, in the greatest hour of danger, left the steamboat to her own guidance, and sought their own safety, regardless of the fate of the passengers: instead of the captain or pilot retreating to the tiller aft, when driven from the wheel house forward, and the ropes there being burned off—there being at that time a communication to the same tiller—there appeared to be no other thought but self-preservation. And it further appears to this jury that the odious practice of carrying cotton in any quantities on board of passenger boats, in a manner in which it shall be liable to take fire from sparks or heat, from any smoke pipe or other means, deserves the public censure."

Other testimony at the hearing provided the basis for much public debate. Frederic Hempstead was an engineer who had served aboard the *Lexington* on the passage previous to her loss, in place of his brother who was the vessel's regular engineer and who was ill at the time (and who died when the *Lexington* sank). Hempstead received warnings along with operational instructions from his brother. "My brother told me that the boat had been on fire before, and to look sharp after the fire along side the boilers, and that I should have trouble with the blowers. . . . My brother said he considered the *Lexington* a very dangerous boat, and cautioned me very strongly before I went up in her.— The caution he gave me was to look out against fire. He did not caution me against any other, excepting fire. Increasing the speed of the boat would make the sparks fly more, and consequently render the boat more dangerous. . . . My brother told me the casing of the steam-chimney had been on fire. The joiners were at work repairing it when I went on board, down in the boiler hatch."

Hempstead appears to have had a personal dislike of forced draft systems. He claimed in what seems unbelievable exaggeration that "the wind of the blowers blew the brick-work down. . . . I consider the boat safer without the blower. . . . I think the cause of the burning of the *Lexington* was the excessive heat and wind of the blowers. . . . The smoke pipe was often red hot during my trip. . . . When the damper was down, the return draft would throw live coal on the floor; the wood stowed away along side the boiler was on fire two or three times. The coal would come out whether or no, if the damper was up or down. This coal set the wood on fire."

How much of Hempstead's testimony was driven by grief over the loss of his brother is impossible to estimate.

William Comstock contradicted Hempstead when he wrote, "The *Lexington*, in the month of November, was put in the very best possible order for the winter service; she was completely overhauled, from the keel to the deck—including the engine and boiler. The work was done without any regard to expense. She was furnished with three good boats, (one a life boat), with fire engine and hose complete—force pump and hose to work by hand—also, two or three dozen fire buckets. She was also furnished with two separate and distinct steering gear—1st, she had iron rods extending the whole length of the promenade deck, with hide rope around the barrel of the wheel. 2d, she had a tiller, shipped through her rudder head, on the promenade deck, with iron chains and composition sheaves."

Comstock's revelations brought out two bones of contention, one of which was prescient. In relation to each other, the circumstance which was of lesser importance in the overall picture of the safety of steam navigation at sea, was the loss of steering. At the coroner's jury, Captain Manchester, the pilot, said, "At the rate the boat was running she might have reached the shore, if rightly headed, in about twenty minutes; it took some three or four minutes to get her head about: we were steering about east by north: we had not got the boat headed round before the tiller-rope gave way: when the rope gave way she was heading about south-east, and the land we were desirous of reaching lay about south, when I lost command of her by the giving way of the tiller ropes: the engine was at this time working. I don't know where the engineer was: the boat as she progressed, headed more to the eastward." The engine "worked some fifteen minutes after the fire broke out. It did not stop suddenly, but kept working slower until finally it stopped entirely. . . . I believe that the ropes were not parted by the strain, but were burnt off."

From this testimony can be extrapolated a scenario in which many more people could have survived the calamity had the vessel been grounded on or close to shore. Chains or wire ropes around the steering head would have made the difference.

Of greater significance to future casualties was the dearth of lifeboats aboard the *Lexington*, a haunting premonition of future catastrophes such as the sinking of the *Titanic* in 1912. The *Lexington's* three boats could accommodate a total of seventy people: less than half the number of passengers and crew aboard at the time of her loss. Yet, although the furor over the burning of the *Lexington* and the consequent loss of life fomented awareness and endless debate about steamboat safety and the quality of life-saving appurtenances then available, as well as censure of the conduct of Steamboat Inspectors for issuing certificates without strict adherence to the rules of safety or common sense, pleas to Congress for more stringent regulations did not result in immediate action. There was endless debate, as is government's way, but many years passed before wisdom prevailed over avarice. It took more than a few such catastrophes to inaugurate an era of concern for human safety.

The legacy of the *Lexington* lives on in the guise of merchant shipping laws, annual vessel inspections, and Coast Guard safety regulations.

On September 30, 1842, this brief paragraph appeared in a local newspaper called *The Long Islander*: "The Lexington.—The wreck of this ill fated vessel has been raised to the surface of the water, but, one of the chains breaking, she again sunk in 130 feet of water. The attempt is again in progress. The eight hundred dollars recovered from her were not in bills, as before stated, but in a lump of silver, weighing 30 pounds, melted by the fire, the box having been emptied on the deck to be used as a bucket for throwing water on the flames."

No other mention is made as to how the operation was performed. (Did hardhat divers descend to the wreck and sling chains under the hull? Did salvage vessels use the wire-drag method?) Nor have any follow-up reports yet surfaced that would shed light on the result of subsequent salvage attempts. Other reports made in later years may upon first sight appear to add information; yet a careful perusal of those reports divulges that the accounts actually refer to different vessels of the same name, one of which stranded in Lake Michigan in 1850, and another which was a schooner. Nevertheless, there exist allusions to the salvage of Vanderbilt's *Lexington* in 1850 even if not documented in official records or contemporary publications.

Whatever follow-up salvage operations may have been conducted went unchronicled, as salvage outfits are not in the business of making the results of their efforts known to newspaper reporters. However, much can be inferred by moving forward in time to 1983, when the National Underwater and Marine Agency, under the direction of Clive Cussler, undertook to locate the burned out hulk of the *Lexington*. After extensive research of extant documentation and extrapolation of the positions reported by the various witnesses to the event, NUMA narrowed the search corridor to a few square miles off Eaton's Neck. A side-scan sonar survey quickly resulted in the discovery of the wreck only half a mile from where the lighthouse keeper on shore saw the last flames disappear. That the site located constituted most of the main hull of the *Lexington* was verified by divers who reported the existence of charred timbers and the remains of the paddle wheels. Some of the burnt wood was recovered and analyzed by an expert in wood chemistry and wood anatomy identification; it proved to be yellow pine, of which the *Lexington* was constructed. A few other items were recovered (no specie) and were donated to the Vanderbilt Museum in Centerport, Long Island, for public display.

In a letter to the author, Cussler wrote, "I believe it *was* raised and then lost for two reasons. One, the wreck is broken in two and perhaps three pieces. The other is a bit of detective work I did after the divers reported the wreck wrapped in a weird green kind of wire. I tracked down the president of a cable company who collects all sorts of barbed wire and solved the mystery. It seems that in 1850 they could not extrude flexible wire, which sounds reasonable. So in order to make it bend, the iron strands were woven around a core of copper. Thus, when the iron cables used to lift the ship off the bottom eroded away over a 135 years, the now green patinaed copper core remained. An incredible feat to have raised such a large ship to the surface before losing it again in the middle eighteen hundreds. No one attempts a similar project even today."

Cussler passed along the following coordinates as sites of the wreck: 26647.4/43962.2, 26651.8/43962.8, 26647.1/43963.0, 26646.7/43963.0, 26626.0/43963.1, 26652.9/43963.4, 26647.0/43963.0, 26644.6/43963.4. He cautioned that "it is a rather dangerous dive considering the depth, strong current, low visibility and passing ships and boats." There is little or no ambient light on the wreck, so a powerful light is needed in order to see as far as a couple of feet. Disorientation comes easily, and relocating the anchor line is at best problematical without the use of a guideline. Divers should take Cussler's warning seriously.

Tim Coleman recorded two different sets of loran numbers which he obtained from Richard Taracka, who dived both sites. He found the bow in 140 feet of water at 26652.1/43962.8, and a paddle wheel in 78 feet of water at 26679.1/43979.9.

MAIDEN CREEK

Built: 1919   Sunk: December 31, 1942
Previous names: None   Depth: Unknown
Gross tonnage: 5,031   Dimensions: 390' x 54' x 27'
Type of vessel: Freighter   Power: Oil-fired steam turbine
Builder: American International Ship Building Corp., Hog Island, Pennsylvania
Owner: Waterman Steamship Company, Mobile, Alabama
Port of registry: Mobile, Alabama
Cause of sinking: Foundered
Location: 40° 10' North   72° 02' West

When war came to the United States the merchant fleet was put at great risk due to the depredations of German U-boats, which fired torpedoes without warning at unsuspecting civilian targets engaged in free commerce. Germany, in its second bid for military conquest of the world, respected no rights of non-combatants to pursue their livelihood in commercial transport. Thus the U.S. was forced to protect its ships by installing degaussing cables to thwart German magnetic mines and torpedoes, by emplacing guns and assigning armed guards, and by traveling in convoy under escort.

Installation of degaussing cables was completed on the *Maiden Creek* on July 12, 1942. One week later saw the emplacement of one 4-inch deck gun on her stern, four 20-millimeter machine guns (two forward and two aft), and two 30-caliber machine guns mounted on the bridge. The installation was accomplished by the owners, the Waterman Steamship Company, in Mobile, Alabama, which also oversaw the construction of splinter shields on the bridge and around the gun emplacements. The magazine constructed below deck aft was crammed with ammunition: 100 rounds for the 4-inch gun, 4,680 rounds for the 20-millimeter machine guns, and 3,000 rounds for the 30-caliber machine guns.

The armed guard unit assigned to the *Maiden Creek* consisted of nine men: one officer, one petty officer, and seven seamen. In addition the Navy assigned three enlisted men to work communications. Thus a dozen extra bunks were required and there were twelve extra mouths to feed.

The Navy also provided a weighted canvas bag in which to deep-six sensitive documents should there be any chance of such falling into enemy hands, flashlights, blinker signals, binoculars, vacuum bottles, semaphore flags, gas masks, lookout goggles, helmets, 45-caliber pistols, lanterns, medical kits, megaphones, a 16-power spyglass, foul weather gear, and an 8-inch searchlight. Extra safety equipment stowed aboard included four emergency life rafts, each with the capacity for eighteen people, and additional life jackets and rubber suits, the latter for cold water immersion. No expense was spared for the safety and comfort of the men as they steamed into dangerous seas.

Thereafter the *Maiden Creek* tramped the Caribbean, stopping at such ports of call as Key West, Guantanamo, San Juan, Ensanada Honda, and St. Thomas; this was at a time when U-boat activity was intense. Yet she managed to deliver her cargoes without making enemy contact. At the end of September the *Maiden Creek* began operating in the North Atlantic, principally between New York, Boston, and St. Johns, Newfoundland. December 22 found the *Maiden Creek* in Halifax. There was no premonition of disaster despite a flooded forepeak and submerged chain locker, and water in No. 1 hold. "This hold contained mineral concentrate, making use of the pumps impossible. Water in this hold was caused by the steam guards being broken from their mooring and being washed back and forth across their hatches, cutting the tarpaulin."

On December 27, the *Maiden Creek* sailed south in a convoy consisting of 12 merchant vessels, with three Canadian corvettes for escorts: HMCS *Matapedia*, HMCS *Rimouski*, and HMCS *Milltown*. The following day the convoy was joined by another convoy, also headed for New York. Although the *Maiden Creek* was capable of sustaining a speed of thirteen knots, a convoy travels only as fast as its slowest ship. In this case the rate of speed was seven and a half knots. Storm warnings were received on December 30. If the *Maiden Creek* had been traveling independently she would already have been anchored in New York harbor. Instead, she was laboring under heavy weather off the coast of New England.

Now events telescoped and recent frailties caught up with the aging freighter. Water in the forward part of the vessel pressed her down by the head as she bucked a rising sea. Steering became difficult due to the loss of headway and to the upward tilt of the stern, which brought the rudder partly out of the water. As put by Lieutenant (JG) Ralph Holland, officer of the armed guard, "She was taking water in No. 1 and 2 holds, as additional steam guards had broken and were cutting the tarpaulins. Ship was getting in worse condition by the hour, and the radio operator sent out S.O.S. at about 1630." The SOS was duly received by several U.S. Coast Guard stations: "Foundering require immediate assistance. Speed 10 kts. approximately. Holds forward filling, down by head, stand by." This transmission makes it appear that engine revolutions were increased in order to improve steering control, and that possibly the *Maiden Creek* had separated from the convoy and was headed for the closest point of land.

Holland: "The captain called the officers and myself to his cabin, and said that it looked like the ship would not last, and that we would have to abandon." Abandoning ship in stormy seas is no easy task, nor is pounding through the waves in a lifeboat a prospect to contemplate lightly. Yet there seemed no choice in the matter, for if the men did not abandon ship soon, the ship was likely to abandon them. What followed was an unfortunate set of circumstances which in military lingo is known as a "snafu" and which had dire results for nearly half the crew of the *Maiden Creek*.

According to Holland's armed guard report, "About this time a ship was sighted on the horizon, but our blinker failed to get across, so I fired 100 rounds of 20 m.m. tracer ammunition and finally attracted attention of this ship. The ship stood by and said that she would be glad to take the crew and would lay an oil slick to make it easy to lower the boat, if we abandoned ship before dark. About this time it seems that the Captain ordered the radio operator to cancel the S.O.S. The Captain, thinking possibly that there was a chance of saving the ship, asked this ship standing by if she could lay an oil slick to Block Island for him. The answer was 'No'."

When the Coast Guard received the transmission to "Annul SOS" it did so and forgot about the *Maiden Creek*. According to the Eastern Sea Frontier War Diary, "At 1830, the same day, the Convoy Escort Commander, HMCS *Matapedia*, received a message from Commander, Eastern Sea Frontier stating that an SOS had been intercepted from the *Maiden Creek* and that she was foundering. The *Matapedia* signalled the commodore vessel who stated that he had intercepted the SOS but had received the impression that a ship was standing by and therefore did not relay the message to the senior escort."

Holland: "About this time No. 3 lifeboat was lowered with twenty-three men, including five of the Navy personnel. It was safely launched. About this same time, we noticed that the other ship had hauled away, and that is the last that we ever saw of the ship that was to take us off. The first boat was launched at approximately 1700, and about 30 minutes later the remainder were lowered in another lifeboat. Two A.B.'s from the merchant crew lowered the last boat, and were to crawl down the boatfalls and join us, but, as the sea was very heavy, we were washed away from the ship, and one man dropped into the sea, and the other climbed back on deck. We tried very hard to fish this man out, but were unable to get him aboard. This was the last seen of these two seamen."

Although the *Maiden Creek's* radio message stated that her speed was two and a half knots faster than that at which the convoy was traveling, the Convoy Commodore considered her a straggler, meaning that she had fallen behind the rest of the convoy, but did not consider her to be in any danger of sinking. The Convoy Escort Commander aboard the *Matapedia* took a different tack concerning the vessels in his charge. He ordered the *Rimouski* to "retrace the course of the convoy and to institute a radar search for the *Maiden Creek*. The SS *Spero* was contacted 10 miles astern of the convoy, but had not sighted the *Maiden Creek*."

That night and all the next day the *Rimouski* continued her search for the missing steamer. The Navy dispatched two PBY's to the scene. At 9:35 in the morning of January 1, a Coast Guard plane from Floyd Bennett Field reported an unidentified merchant ship some one hundred miles west of the *Maiden Creek's* last known position, but somehow this information was either not communicated properly or was not followed up. At the end of the day, the *Rimouski* broke off her search and "rejoined the convoy without sending any dispatch to the effect that she had failed in her search."

By January 2 the search for the *Maiden Creek* and her survivors was forgotten. The ship and fifty-six men were in limbo.

Then, on January 3, 1943, an Army B-25 piloted by Lieutenant Norman Purdy, on routine anti-submarine patrol, spotted a lifeboat bobbing in tumultuous seas. When he flew close for a better look he saw that the lifeboat was filled with men, all waving frantically. Trotter called in his position and reported the situation. The Navy responded immediately by dispatching a PBY to the site. The seas were too mountainous for the Catalina flying boat to effect a safe landing. The best that the pilot, Lieutenant Commander Delos Walt, could do for the survivors was to drop emergency lifesaving equipment to them. "Flying low, back and forth over the boat, he dropped all the bundles he had brought and hovered around to see that they were all picked up." These bundles were filled with food, water, clothing, blankets, flares, and a portable radio.

The area was strewn with wreckage, including an empty lifeboat, a life raft, and a dead whale. The Coast Guard dispatched eight more aircraft to the scene. One of these, piloted by Lieutenant Edwin Ing, located a freighter some fifteen miles from the lifeboat. This was the SS *Staghound*. Ing communicated by blinker with the *Staghound* and directed her to follow him, which she did. So it was the *Staghound* which picked up the thirty-one men who had been fighting for their lives in icy, wind-swept seas for seventy-three hours, not knowing if they would ever be found or if death awaited them beyond the next comber.

Captain G.R. Cook, master of the *Maiden Creek*, Ralph Holland, and twenty-nine others were safe. Those who required medical attention were treated aboard the freighter. Now word was passed that another lifeboat had gotten away from the *Maiden Creek*. Worsening weather conditions precluded further aerial reconnaissance, but six surface craft spread out across the sea to search for the lifeboat containing the remaining members of the crew. These vessels were the *Sagamore*, *Modoc*, *Chaffinch*, *Niblack*, *Gleaves*, and *SC-672*.

Concentrated search efforts produced negative results until January 5, when the Coast Guard cutter *Modoc* came upon "a small gray lifeboat with red and white sails and the name *Maiden Creek* stenciled on the thwarts, awash in 39-04 N; 70-54 W with a body lashed inside. The body was lost while attempts were being made to recover it. Subsequently, the lifeboat was sunk by ramming and gunfire." Could this have been the body of the able bodied seaman who had climbed back up the falls after the second lifeboat was launched? Perhaps he managed to launch a small lifeboat by himself before the freighter took her final plunge.

The Navy issued orders to all vessels whose course took them past the

Maiden Creek's approximate location to post a sharp lookout. As late as January 8 this message was dispatched: "(For S.S. *African Star* and S.S. *Mount Aetna*) Life boat containing survivors from foundered S.S. *Maiden Creek* somewhere vicinity your route. Keep looking." However, "Nothing further was learned of the fate of the 23 survivors who had been reported in the second lifeboat. Under the circumstances of high winds and heavy seas, it is probable that the lifeboat capsized and that the already freezing occupants were tossed into the wintry sea." The final death toll was twenty-five fine men.

Holland reported how they had rowed all night that first night, then just drifted and awaited rescue. They spotted a plane the first day, "but plane did not see us." The second day at sea "one plane flew almost over us, but failed to see us." One can imagine the elation of believing rescue to be so close at hand, and the anguish at watching all chances of survival fly away. The *Staghound* was eastward bound, so the survivors were not landed until she reached her first port of call—Belfast, Ireland—which she made on January 13. The men were then cared for in a U.S. Army field hospital.

The wreck of the *Maiden Creek* has not been identified. Fixes obtained by Coast Guard stations placed the freighter at the time of the transmission at 39° 56' North, 70° 59' West. The ESF War Diary states, "SS *Maiden Creek* straggled in heavy weather, and was lost in the haze in approximate position 71-50 West, 39-55 North." The Navy Air Controller reported "the last known position of the *Maiden Creek* as 40-10 N; 70-35 W, about 66 miles SE of Block Island on the evening of December 30th." The Coast Guard plane from Floyd Bennett Field gave the position of the unidentified merchant ship it spotted from the air as 39-54 N, 72-58 W. It is possible that this was the *Maiden Creek*, abandoned but still afloat. A Naval message from January 4 stated: "Information from steamship *Staghound* indicates steamship *Maiden Creek* foundered in 40-10 North 72-02 West." More than likely none of these positions is correct.

This *Maiden Creek* should not be confused with another vessel of the same name and which was torpedoed off Bougie, Algeria on March 17, 1944.

MAINE

Built: 1892   Sunk: February 4, 1920
Previous names: None   Depth: 15 feet
Gross tonnage: 2,395   Dimensions: 302' x 44' x 17'
Type of vessel: Excursion steamer   Power: Coal-fired steam
Builder: Harlan & Hollingsworth, Wilmington, Delaware
Owner: New England Steam Ship Company, New Haven, Connecticut
Port of registry: New London, Connecticut
Cause of sinking: Stranded
Location: Off Execution Rock, Long Island Sound

The *Maine* led a long career as an fast excursion steamer, shuttling passengers and freight between New York City and ports in New England by way of the Long Island Sound. She was fitted with a four-cylinder engine at a time when most ocean-going vessels were propelled by engines having but three cylinders. Possessing two low-pressure cylinders instead of one gave the *Maine* an advantage in speed over her competitors, and made her the envy of commuters. Electric lights illuminated the private cabins and public rooms. A wireless set kept her in touch with port authorities and installations ashore, enabling her to radio ahead her estimated time of arrival so that docking preparations could get underway as she made her final approach. The *Maine* was not sumptuous as excursion steamers went, but she was reliable. She operated under a strict timetable and she kept to it faithfully for twenty-eight years.

On February 4, 1920, the *Maine* set out once again, as she had done so often in the past, to maintain her reputation for timely departures and arrivals. But at that time a fierce winter storm was raging along the coast. A strong wind was blowing, snow and hail were falling, and the Sound was clogged with ice. Into this frigid tempest the excursion steamer plunged.

The *Maine* was owned by the New England Steam Ship Company, and was operated by the U.S. Railroad Administration. When she left New York for Bridgeport, Connecticut she carried 142 tons of cargo consisting of general merchandise and nineteen horses. The number of passengers on board was recorded as both three and five. The crew totaled fifty-five, which seems like a lot considering the dearth of ticketed fares. The master of the ship was Captain Joseph Hancort.

Captain Hancort's report of the *Maine's* final hours is as lacking in detail as it is in punctuation. "Engines working full speed ahead but could not overcome resistance of heavy ice floes. Signalled to SS *C.W. Chapin* who was in vicinity to wireless owners of plight. Responded in shape of transfer tugs 3 and 19 *Alert* & wrecker Chapman Bros. but could not get within reach immediately account of heavy ice, surveying situation concluded no immediate danger, so stood by waiting moderation of weather conditions."

Beset in the ice. (Courtesy of Sharon Reese.)

Sailors often refer to a vessel's propulsion machinery in the plural despite the singularity of the engine, so that part I can understand. Aside from that, it is my interpretation of Captain Hancort's tantalizingly brief account that the *Maine's* radio was out of commission, perhaps due to the weight of ice which built up on the antenna and broke it, or possibly because the brittle wire snapped in the cold.

The *Maine* was not alone in her plight, for five other steamers were beset in the Sound as well. Three were mentioned in the papers by name: *Chester W. Chapin*, *City of Lowell*, and *New Hampshire*. And there they sat for three days. Eventually, the temperature moderated and the ice melted enough for the ships to get underway—except for the *Maine*.

According to one cryptic remark in the Coast Guard report, "Steamer *Maine* had already passed the point where she stranded and was two miles to the north'ard of same when she was caught by heavy ice floes and carried back onto the rocks." Expanded, this means that the ice pack slowly drove her back against her will until she ground onto Execution Rock, whose jagged underwater projections punctured her steel skin as if it were paper, after which her hull filled with water. The crew, passengers, and horses were in no danger of drowning because of the necessarily shallow depth. After the ship settled to the rocky bottom her upper deck stayed high and dry. But the people were stranded for three days without heat and water: the machinery spaces were flooded, and without power there was no way to melt the ice into which the drinking water had frozen.

Everyone was rescued without injury or loss of life. According to Coast Guard records, the estimated value of the vessel was $390,000. This represented a considerable loss to the company as the *Maine* was insured for only $211,000. Those same records allege that the cargo was worth $85,000, was insured for

Notice that the portholes have been removed. (Courtesy of Bill Quinn.)

$481,250, and represented a loss of only $6,000. There must be a mistake in there somewhere.

Most of the cargo was later salvaged, and so was much of the ship—in pieces. One document contained a scrawled annotation that "T.A. Scott Company's lighter *Transfer 19*" was brought alongside the *Maine* and that the salvage crew stripped the superstructure of its fittings and other valuables. Wreckers had plenty of time to work because the ship could not move—or be moved—off the pinnacle on which it was impaled. Once they licked off the icing, they went after the cake. A crane barge was lashed to the side of the *Maine* so her heavy machinery could be lifted from the hull. Out came the boilers, the four-cylinder engine, the propeller and shaft, even the bedplates and shaft supports.

When all was said and done, nothing of the ship remained but a bare metal hull and the gutted wooden superstructure. The superstructure was then set afire and burned right down to the metal beams which supported the upper deck. The hull was demolished until virtually nothing was left standing more than a few feet off the bottom.

After the wreckers were done with their work, nature took its course. Subsequent ice floes sheered off those portions of the hull which rose too close to the surface; constant wave action beat down the support beams still standing, and spread them about the bottom; oxygen and the acidic nature of the sea ate away at the metal plates, leaving them rusted and pockmarked. As you can imagine, there is not much left of the workaday excursion steamer which once appeared so stately—hardly enough, if you will pardon the pun, by which to remember the *Maine*.

Courtesy of Bill Quinn.

MALDEN

Built: 1907
Previous names: None
Gross tonnage: 5,054
Type of vessel: Freighter

Sunk: September 19, 1921
Depth: 40 feet
Dimensions: 373' x 52' x 29'
Power: Coal-fired steam

Builder: Fore River Ship Building Company, Quincy, Massachusetts
Owner: New England Fuel & Transportation Company
Port of registry: Boston, Massachusetts
Cause of sinking: Collision with SS *Jonancy*
Location: One mile offshore and one mile north of Montauk Light

The *Malden* had long been engaged in the coasting trade when she first came to grief in February 1920, when she ran aground off Fire Island during a passage in ballast from Boston to Norfolk. Damage to the hull was minimal. Because she was traveling light, the Coast Guard cutter *Seneca* managed to pull the freighter off the bar at high tide two days after she stranded. The *Malden* floated easily, but it was determined expedient to head to New York for inspection and repairs. Thus she remained in service for another year and a half.

The *Malden* did not escape her next accident so easily, nor on this occasion did the Coast Guard respond with the celerity which might have saved the freighter from disaster. September 17, 1921 found the *Malden* on a passage from Norfolk to Boston, deeply laden with coal. In command was Captain John Gertsen. Due to exceptionally heavy fog, he rounded Montauk Point by giving the headland a wide berth, precluding any possibility of running aground again on New York's sandy south shore.

Steering south at the same place and time was the small coastal steamer *Jonancy*. Her master was Captain Elisha Rogers; he was off duty at the time, and the bridge was under the command of Clarence Colbeth, the third mate. The *Jonancy* was owned by the Pocahontas Fuel Company. She was engaged in transporting coal from Virginia to ports in New England such as Boston and Portland. Thus her southbound passages, like those of the *Malden*, were return trips made with empty cargo holds.

Both vessels proceeded too fast for conditions through a thick, clinging fog. By the time the two colliers were within sight of each other, a collision was inevitable. The *Malden* and the *Jonancy* came together with the grating, grinding impact of steel on steel. Luckily, no one was injured in the crash. The *Jonancy's* bow was crumpled but she was in no immediate danger of sinking. The *Malden* suffered a devastating wound on the port side amidships. A quick inspection revealed that water was cascading into the hull at an alarming rate. The *Jonancy* hove to by the stricken *Malden*.

The gravity of the situation was transmitted to the world just one minute short of midnight, in a wireless message which stated succinctly and without punctuation: "In collision with SS *Jonancy* ten miles off Montauk ship leaking badly little hope of keeping afloat signed Gertsen." Less than a half hour later, at 12:28 a.m., came the mariner's ultimate request for help, complete with call letters: "SOS SOS DE KZV SS *Malden* sinking condition seven miles south Montauk Point Come Quick."

The *Malden's* wireless messages were intercepted by a Navy radio station, which relayed them to the Coast Guard cutters *Acushnet* (at Woods Hole, Massachusetts) and *Gresham* (at New York). The *Gresham* soon got underway, but the crew of the *Acushnet*, which was stationed much closer to the scene of the disaster, slept blissfully throughout the long, still night, unaware of ongoing events because the radio operator was off duty. Not until 6:30 in the morning did the telephone bell arouse the men and alert them to the *Malden's* plight.

This delay in communication created quite a row between the Navy and the Coast Guard; the Navy demanded an explanation for the *Acushnet's* lack of response. In its defense, the Coast Guard referred to written "Instructions to Radio Force" which spelled out the responsibilities of wireless operators aboard Coast Guard cutters. These instructions required that a continuous radio watch be maintained whenever a cutter was at sea; but that when a cutter was docked at her station, emergency messages were to be delivered by telephone. The Navy had been apprised of this protocol as far back as 1919, but had not yet properly disseminated the information.

Wrote the commanding officer of the *Acushnet*, P.W. Lauriat: "I have repeatedly emphasized the desirability and necessity for the prompt transmission of information. The *Acushnet*, while at her station, has a telephone on board and much time can be saved by forwarding urgent messages in this manner while we are at Woods Hole."

Interdepartmental miscommunication notwithstanding, the *Acushnet* belatedly got underway and arrived at the scene at 2:30 that afternoon, September 18. By that time the *Malden* had already been taken under tow by the Scott Wrecking Company's tug *Guardsman*; and both vessels were proceeding slowly toward shore. The *Malden* lay low in the water and yawed badly in the *Guardsman's* wake. The *Acushnet* placed a towing hawser aboard the *Guardsman* and towed ahead of the wrecking tug. This system worked until 7:25, at which time the hawser between the *Guardsman* and the *Malden* parted. As it turned out, the rope broke because the bow of the *Malden* had grounded in shoal water, with the port rail forward awash.

The *Gresham* was now also at the scene, and was asked to stand by. All three rescue vessels anchored in the vicinity of the *Malden* until 11:40 that night, when the rising tide lifted the freighter and sent her adrift. The tugs soon caught up with her and replaced the towing hawsers for another attempt at a tandem tow. From the *Acushnet's* log: "Steamer aground holding *Acushnet* and *Guardsman* against wind and tide." The tugs strained against the hawsers till 1:05 a.m., September 19, at which time towing operations were secured for the night.

Under tow. (Courtesy of Bill Quinn.)

The *Malden* came free at 8:20 the next morning. The *Guardsman* and *Acushnet* worked their engines as hard as they could in an attempt to reach the protected waters inside Montauk Point. They nearly made it. At 11:25 the *Malden* ground to a halt in seven fathoms of water about one mile offshore and one mile north of Montauk Light, and there she remained.

The *Gresham* returned to New York. The *Guardsman* went on her way. The *Acushnet* took aboard twenty-two men from the *Malden's* forty-two-man crew, but within the hour they were recalled to the freighter. At 5:20 the *Acushnet* "headed for New London, Connecticut, to receive stores and medical attendance for two members of the crew."

The condition of the *Malden* was summed up in a wireless transmission. "Grounded forward and afloat aft. Ship listed to port seventeen degrees and port bulwarks and port side of main deck under water for full length. Holds number one two three full four partly full five dry engine and boiler room dry. Steam on one boiler. Last high water vessel shifted position and *Acushnet* and *Guardsman* tried tow her in shore but failed. No holding her in favorable position and we are filling all double bottom tanks. Collision damage does not as far as seen appear serious for temporary repairs. Ship lies in exposed position and it is necessary to discharge port cargo and close all openings. Will advise later our decision after low water this afternoon crew still on board."

The *Malden* lay easy overnight and appeared salvageable. The next day, the *Acushnet* "returned to wreck and transferred aboard twenty-one men from *Malden* at the request of owners for transportation to New Bedford, Mass." The *Guardsman* also returned, this time with lighters and divers, and proceeded with the work of removing cargo and patching the hull. Had good weather prevailed, the *Malden* would undoubtedly have been saved.

By September 21, after a good thrashing, the hull was full of water except for the engine and boiler room, which were located aft; the stern was still afloat. At that time divers stated that the collision damage was not serious. The underwriters engaged the Scott Wrecking Company on a "no cure, no pay" basis as settlement for all services rendered.

Unfavorable weather continued. On September 23 the engine room bulkhead carried away, and with it went all prospects of total hull salvage. Salvage operations ceased. The next day the *Malden* was abandoned by the underwriters as a total constructive loss in the amount of $470,000. By September 26 the vessel lay on an even keel, with six feet of water over the main deck and with only the poop and forecastle exposed. Wrecking continued on into November, but it was piecemeal salvage only.

The damage sustained by the *Jonancy* amounted to $4,200. The ship was quickly repaired and returned to service the week following the accident.

The Steamboat Inspection Service conducted an investigation of the collision. Crew members from both vessels were called in to testify, at different times and places since the *Jonancy* was again plying the trade routes. The steamboat inspectors found sufficient evidence to bind over for trial the captains of both vessels and the third mate of the *Jonancy*. "Charges of violation of Article 16, International Rules, were preferred against John Gertsen, master, *Malden*, and Clarence W. Colbeth, third mate, *Jonancy*, who was in charge of the navigation of that vessel at the time of the accident; and charges of negligence and inattention to duty were preferred against Elisha T. Rogers, master, steamer *Jonancy*."

Article 16 of the International Rules of the Road reads: "Every vessel shall, in a fog, mist, falling snow, or heavy rainstorms, go at a moderate speed, having careful regard to the existing circumstances and conditions. A steam vessel hearing, apparently forward of her beam, the fog signal of a vessel the position of which is not ascertained shall, so far as the circumstances of the case admit, stop her engines, and then navigate with caution until danger of collision is over."

After deliberation, "Charges of violation of Article 16 against Gertsen and Colbeth were sustained. The charge of inattention to duty against Captain Rogers was sustained, and the charge of negligence against him was dismissed. The licenses of Gertsen, Rogers and Colberth were suspended for a period of 30 days, respectively."

The unsalvaged remains of the *Malden* still lie on the bar off Montauk.

Courtesy of Bill Quinn.

Courtesy of Sharon Reese.

MILES M. MERRY

Built: 1901   Sunk: February 17, 1909
Previous names: None   Depth: Unknown
Gross tonnage: 1,589   Dimensions: 215' x 43' x 20'
Type of vessel: 4-masted, wooden hulled schooner   Power: Sail
Builder: Percy & Small, Bath, Maine
Owner: J.S. Winslow & Company, Portland, Maine
Port of registry: Portland, Maine
Cause of sinking: Ran aground
Location: 700 feet east-southeast of the Moriches Life-Saving Station

There might be an excuse for the loss of the *Miles M. Merry* if this chapter could start with the trite beginning, "It was a dark and stormy night . . . " However, on February 17, 1909, the night the schooner went aground, the air was clear and the wind was blowing fresh from the west northwest--that is, from a direction which would tend to push a sailing ship away from a south facing shore. The reason for the stranding was recorded in the wreck report of the Moriches Life-Saving Station as "lost Recking," which I think can be interpreted to mean "lost reckoning."

What makes the stranding of the *Miles M. Merry* even more inexcusable is that she ran aground only a quarter mile away less than a year and a half before! That time, on September 10, 1907, she was refloated. As the station keeper noted, the schooner "stranded 200 yards S. of station at 7.45 p.m. Keeper saw her red light close in shore and burned a coston to warn her off, but she could not tack in time to go clear. Life-savers went on board in surfboat; master wanted a tug and a message was sent to New York for one. In the morning the wrecking tug arrived and, after working all day, floated her at 9 p.m., life-savers rendering all necessary boat service, using surfboat."

In 1909, she went down for the count, and so close to the station that she might have been steering for it on purpose. It was 4:30 in the morning that surfman Earl Swydam noticed the schooner "between the beach and a sand bar lying off shore and was sailing along the shore, her officers apparently unaware of their danger, although the weather was clear."

The *Miles M. Merry* carried no cargo and no passengers. She was "running light," as they say, or "in ballast," from Boston to Newport News, heading almost directly into the wind. Swydam burned a Coston flare to warn the vessel of impending danger. Instead of shaping a course away from shoal water, the schooner appeared to head for the light, for she soon turned east until she was nearly abreast the station, where she struck the bar and was driven high on the beach barely three hundred feet from shore. The life-saving crew wasted no time in bringing out the Lyle gun and setting up the breeches buoy.

"The vessel pounded heavily but did not spring a leak. So near was the vessel to the dry land that a line was quickly shot through her rigging and Captain J.O. Farrow of Saco, Maine, and eleven men composing the crew were taken ashore in the breeches without even getting wet in the sea. As the vessel stranded at high tide there will be difficulty in floating her."

Life-savers from the adjacent Potunk and Forge River stations arrived to lend a hand, and by 8 a.m. it was all over but the clean up. The saved and the savers sat down for a hearty breakfast provided by the Life-Saving Service. In fact, the food was so good that the erstwhile crew of the *Miles M. Merry* decided to hang around for lunch; then for dinner. They wound up staying for eighteen days.

During that time the owners hired a wrecking outfit to pull the ship off the beach, but she was too high and dry to be moved. When the job was given up, the life-savers assisted the schooner's crew in recovering the sails, blocks, and rope: precious little salvage for a vessel claimed to be worth $50,000.

Then, on March 15, came the curious coup de grace. The keeper of the Moriches Life-Saving Station, Charles Gordon, wrote, "The Schooner caught afire from a spark from her Boiler and Burnt to the waters edge. Received $36,00 for 180 meals from the owner to day March 16-09." (Transcribed as written.) Please note that at this stage in the evolution of wind-powered vessels, boilers were installed to provide steam for the winches which were used to raise and lower the sails, not for propulsion.

Another report of the incident from the Life-Saving Service files (this one typewritten) shed a different light on the matter. "To-day the Moriches life saving station crew discovered her ablaze. No one was on board and it was supposed she had been purposely fired to clear the beach as far as possible of the wreckage."

Thus circumstances or human agency conspired to run the schooner aground in the worst possible condition and at the worst possible time: with no weight in her holds and at high tide. Such is the way of fate.

Or is it?

Courtesy of the Suffolk County Historical Society.

MISTLETOE

Built: 1872
Previous names: None
Gross tonnage: 362
Type of vessel: Sidewheel steamer
Builder: John Roach & Son, Chester, Pennsylvania
Owner: Mistletoe Fishing Association, Inc.
Port of registry: New York, NY
Cause of sinking: Burned
Location: 26933.3

Sunk: October 5, 1924
Depth: 40 feet
Dimensions: 152' x 26' x 9'
Power: coal-fired vertical beam engine

43747.6

For much of her long career the *Mistletoe* belonged to the United States Light House Service, for which she performed so adequately that her accomplishments are clouded in anonymity. The work of a lighthouse tender was rather mundane, much like that of today's interstate trucks. Tenders delivered food, supplies, and mail, and exchanged personnel. They had no need to be at sea in bad weather.

At the time of her loss her certificate of enrollment listed her as a coastal freighter, but she was actually serving as a fishing vessel. She did not fish commercially; she transported anglers to and from the plentiful fishing grounds beyond New York harbor; today she would be called a "head boat."

She was 52 years old on October 5, 1924, when she left her slip for the last time bound for Davy Jones's locker. On board were Captain James Gully, master, nine crew members, and seventy-four passengers. The *Mistletoe* dropped anchor off the Ambrose Channel lightship, some two to two-and-a-half miles northeast of the whistling buoy, and settled down to let the people fish. The sea was smooth and the wind was blowing light from the south-southwest. There was no presentiment of disaster.

Without warning, fire broke out at 1:10 in the afternoon and instantly raged out of control. The captain's report was succinct: "Immediately sounded alarm, called crew to stations, water turned on, 2 streams, blew for assistance, flag inverted, transferred all passengers by 1:20 pm to various boats, tug, 1 steamer." He later elaborated his account: "Several fishing vessels took off passengers, tug *Marie Olsen* rendered assistance by taking off crew and playing hose on fire."

The aged wooden hull quickly burned to the waterline, and sank. Thanks to quick action on the part of the captain and his crew, no lives were lost and no injuries were sustained. The *Mistletoe* was valued at between $10,000 and $15,000.

The Steamboat Inspection Service conducted a three day investigation, "but the Board is unable to determine the origin of the fire. There was no difficulty in getting water on the fire immediately it was discovered by smoke making its appearance through the companionway. It was, when noticed, however, too

Courtesy of the Steamship Historical Society of America.

dense to allow of reaching the seat of the fire, which could not be distinguished [sic]. It is evident that the fire had been smoldering in some corner or behind woodwork until attaining sufficient force to burst through. There was no failure in the equipment of any kind, and the board found no negligence or other misconduct on the part of the licensed officers or crew. Case dismissed."

The *Mistletoe's* position in shallow water so close to the shipping lanes created a hazard to navigation, so federal engineers were called in to clear the harbor. Announced Superintendent A.E. Clark, "The removal of sunken ships from the harbor is one of the important functions of the army engineers. There are two wrecks which will have to be removed--the *Mistletoe*, a small steamer, owners unknown, which lies 12,000 feet off Rockaway, and the *Fort Victoria*, a Furness Bermuda liner, which was sunk last December off Ambrose channel." (For the circumstances of the loss of the *Fort Victoria* see *Shipwrecks of New Jersey*, by this author.) The *Fort Victoria* was a huge passenger liner whose removal was expected to cost "from $100,000 to $150,000.)

By comparison, the *Mistletoe* was small fish to fry. How much of the wreck was actually removed went unrecorded, but very little remains today of the once stately sidewheel steamer: worm-eaten timbers, scattered wreckage, and low-lying debris. The recognizable portions consist of the paddle wheels and shafts, the boilers, and the walking beam engine (which was knocked over and now lies on its side). Once away from this small midship section the wreckage disappears into the sand. Much might be discovered by digging.

OHIO

Completed: 1837
Previous names: None
Gross tonnage: 2,757
Type of vessel: Ship-of-the-line
Builder: Henry Eckford, at the New York Navy Yard in Brooklyn
Owner: U.S. Navy
Cause of sinking: Burned
Location: Peconic Bay

Sunk: April 1884
Depth: 20 feet
Dimensions: 197' x 53' x 22'
Power: Sail
Armament: None at time of loss

Life moved slower in the nineteenth century than it does today, and ships took longer to build. Construction on the USS *Ohio* began in 1817 and was not completed until 1837, twenty years later: and this before the formation of unions.

The *Ohio* was the brainchild of Scottish-born ship builder Henry Eckford, who emigrated to Canada at the age of sixteen and who learned his trade as an

Courtesy of the Naval Historical Center.

apprentice for naval constructor John Black, who was Eckford's uncle. At twenty-one Eckford moved to New York City, and within a couple of years set up his own shop as a ship builder. For large contracts he sometimes worked in partnership with Edward Beebe. In 1807, Eckford began building gunboats for the U.S. Navy. During the War of 1812, Eckford received many government contracts, which enabled him to expand his operations. His most notable achievement during the war was the reconstruction of Commodore Perry's Lake Erie fleet.

In 1816, Eckford designed a 68-gun ship-of-the-line to be armed with thirty-four 32-pounders and thirty-four 42-pound carronades. The keel was laid at the New York Navy Yard the following year, after he was appointed Chief Constructor of the yard. Work on the *Ohio* must have had low priority in relation to other vessels abuilding simultaneously, including those in Eckford's private business, for the hull was not launched until three years later, on May 20, 1820. Politics also seems to have interfered with Eckford's schedule, further slowing construction and causing him so much grief that he eventually resigned his position with the government. Eckford went on to build frigates for South American governments, with much more speed, but concentrated largely on the construction of merchant vessels.

The uncompleted *Ohio* languored at dock for a decade until she was commissioned, in 1830, and placed in ordinary. (In Naval parlance, to be placed in "ordinary" was the equivalent to being "laid up"; that is, not in use as a warship.) Not till 1837 did the *Ohio* leave her slip; she was partially manned and taken to Boston in order to be armed and fitted for sea. Finally she was ready to begin her lackluster career.

According to U.S. Naval records, "On 16 October 1838, *Ohio*, under command of Captain Joseph Smith, departed Boston for the Mediterranean Sea. Until her return to the United States, 17 July 1841, she afforded countenance and protection to United States commerce in the Mediterranean Sea, as flagship of Commodore Isaac Hull, commanding the Mediterranean Squadron. On 2 August 1840, Captain Smith was succeeded in command of *Ohio*, by Commander A.A. Lavette." There was no mention of action or firing of guns in anger.

"From 1842 to 1846, Ohio was in the Boston Navy Yard for repairs." *Five years for repairs?* "She was again commissioned, 7 December 1846, and on 4 January 1847, she set sail for the coast of Mexico. She arrived 22 March, and took station off Sacrificios Island, near the harbor of Vera Cruz, where she was actively employed until 9 May 1847." Finally, at the age of thirty, came action. "During this time, *Ohio* participated in the bombardment of the Castle of San Juan de Ulloa and the surrender of Vera Cruz. She assisted in the landing of troops and transported guns and carriages. She also rendered help to merchant vessels and sent a party of fifteen officers and three hundred men to USS *Mississippi*, to take part in an expedition against Tuspan. On 9 May 1847, she departed her station off Vera Cruz, sailing for New York."

After a quick turnaround of less than a month the *Ohio* set sail for the Pacific Ocean. She rounded the Horn, steered a northerly course, and joined the Pacific Squadron at Valparaiso, Chile. The next three years saw her under the command of three different captains. "She served with the Pacific Squadron until the spring of 1850, then returning to Boston where she was placed out of commission."

At that time Navy records indicate that her armament consisted of either eighty or eighty-four guns: either eight or twelve 8-inch guns, and seventy-two 32-pounders.

For the next quarter of a century the *Ohio* idled at dock. She was used as a receiving ship: that is, she provided temporary quarters for Navy personnel who were waiting for assignment. Her guns, useless in her capacity as a floating barracks, were removed. During the Civil War she was temporarily rearmed with one 8-inch Parrott rifle, four 100-pounder Parrott rifles, and twelve 32-pounders in order "to defend the city of Boston against an expected attack by Confederates, which did not develop." In 1875 she was again placed in ordinary, and that is how she remained during the rest of her Naval career.

By 1883, the *Ohio* was little more than a hulk and was roofed over so that she had very little resemblance to the ship-of-the-line she had once been. Now she bristled with grass instead of guns. On June 21 of that year the Navy condemned her and put her up for public auction. Her appraised value was given as $15,700, but on the auction block she managed to bring $17,100 under sealed bid. The lucky highest bidder was one Israel Snow, who beat John Thompson by a mere $100. The lowest bid received was $1,500.

Israel Snow must have recognized a lemon when he bid on one. "In a month she was re-sold for over $20,000 and towed to Peconic Bay, Long Island, to be broken up. Sightseers thronged aboard before the huge vessel was dismantled, and her figurehead, a bust of Hercules, was placed on Montauk Highway."

The ex-ship-of-the-line did not survive long enough to be broken up and sold for scrap. She soon caught fire, and her rotted wood burned furiously until practically nothing remained of the hull but a few charred timbers and some globs of melted metal fittings. What remains today is even less. After a long and mostly idle career, it should be noted that the *Ohio* is in no way historic or otherwise significant; it is simply old.

Courtesy of the Naval Historical Center.

OLINDA

Built: 1887
Previous names: None
Gross tonnage: 1,479
Type of vessel: Freighter
Builder: J. Blumer & Company, Sunderland, England
Owner: J.H. Andresen
Port of registry: Oporto, Portugal
Cause of sinking: Ran aground
Location: 26059.0

Sunk: June 11, 1895
Depth: 20 feet
Dimensions: 250' x 36' x 16'
Power: Coal-fired steam

43966.7

The slow loss of the *Olinda* is perhaps one of the most drawn-out shipwreck sagas in New York's history, taking more than four months from the time of her accidental grounding till she reached her disastrous end. Better that she should have been demolished in the beginning, and saved her would-be salvors a great deal of wasted time and money.

The *Olinda* was a freighter bound from Fall River, Massachusetts to New York City when she lost her way in a fog and crashed onto the rocks on the south side of Fisher's Island, at a place called Goose Hummock. Blame for the grounding was placed on the pilot, a Fall River native who should have known better than to run so close to shore. The date was June 11, 1895.

Sharp rocks tore through the iron plating of her bottom about fifty feet abaft the stem. The ruptured hull immediately began to take on water. No one was injured, nor was there any cause for alarm for the safety of the crew. The weather was mild, the seas calm. The *Olinda* lay impaled on the rocky hummock like a great beached whale, unable to move and, due to the shallow depth, unable to sink. She simply settled lower and lower until her hull filled with water.

The next day, the Chapman Wrecking Company arrived at the scene with the wrecking steamer *Hustler* and began the onerous task for which the outfit was so noted: saving ships and freight. The salvors began operations by lightering the cargo of corkwood and empty barrels, some of which was transported to New London, Connecticut during the next several weeks, and some of which was taken to New York aboard the barges *Panore* and *Nassau*.

On June 15, powerful salvage tugs managed to pull the freighter some twenty feet off the rocks "so that the stern lay on a better bottom." That was as far as they wanted to haul her until her hull could be patched and pumped free of water, lest she sink in deeper and dire straits. In addition to the vast, stove-in hole, an inspection found a couple of bad cracks in the hull plating of her bottom. During the next week, the *Olinda's* owners entertained the possibility that the vessel was doomed, and that they should cut their losses before incurring further expense from salvage. Consequently, on June 26 she was sold by the firm of Burdett & Dennis to the Ross Iron Works for the sum of $2,620. At the time of her grounding she had been valued at $150,000.

Salvage of the cargo continued. On July 12, an attempt was made to refloat the freighter, but it was unsuccessful. By the end of the month it was reported that prospects of saving the ship "grow less each day, and the probability is she will soon have to be knocked to pieces. During the past week her masts have worked up out of her four feet. This shows that the bottom of the vessel is on the rocks, and her sides are settling and pushing the bottom up toward the surface."

In order to prepare for another attempt at refloating the *Olinda*, on August 16, "part of the bottom of the steamer, which had been pushed up through the hull, has been broken away from her by dynamite. The owners have been particularly fortunate in having good weather, the steamer having rested as easily in her exposed condition as if she was in harbor." Despite the salvors' best efforts, the *Olinda* remained steadfast on her rocky perch.

Two days later a storm struck the area, "the most severe one since the steamer went on the rocks, and she rolled out her foremast and loosened some of the casks put in her hold. The attempt to save her, however, has not been given up." Nevertheless, all attempts to refloat the grounded freighter failed. Finally, on September 11 it was reported that the *Olinda* "will be broken up and the machinery, etc, that can be saved will be taken out."

Her death knell was reported on October 2. The ship "has broken in two and her stern gone ashore. Her bow is 100 feet off shore." Undaunted by this eventuality, salvors continued to try to recoup their losses. The final word on the vain but valiant attempt to save the *Olinda* came out on October 30: "After spending several months time and $50,000, efforts to save even half of the steamer *Olinda* (Br), before reported wrecked off Fisher's Island, has been abandoned. A bulkhead had been built and the vessel cut in two with intention of having the after part reconstructed when in a recent storm the bulkhead was stove, anchors refused to hold and the after part was thrown upon the rocks."

Salvors had better luck a year later when the *Tillie* went aground in nearly the same spot, only one hundred yards away from the *Olinda*, on July 30, 1896. The *Tillie* was hauled off the following day with very little effort. The *Olinda* remained.

Courtesy of the National Maritime Museum.

OREGON

Built: 1883

Previous names: None

Gross tonnage: 7,375

Type of vessel: Passenger liner

Builder: John Elder & Company (Fairfield Yard), Glasgow, Scotland

Owner: Cunard Steamship Company

Port of registry: Liverpool, England

Cause of sinking: Collision (probably with schooner *Charles H. Morse*)

Location: 26453.1

Sunk: March 14, 1886

Depth: 130 feet

Dimensions: 501' x 54' x 38'

Power: Coal-fired steam

43676.6

The *Oregon* is without a doubt the most well known and most frequently dived shipwreck covered in this volume, and is worthy of the broadest possible coverage in the greatest amount of detail. The *Oregon* is remembered not only by her unique place in history, as a first-class luxury liner which once held the record for the fastest transatlantic crossing, but by the wealth of memorable collector's items which have been, and continue to be, recovered from her rusted remains.

The *Oregon* was built for the Guion Line with the specific objective to construct the fastest liner in existence, faster even than her predecessors, the *Arizona* and the *Alaska*, the prototypes, also owned by Guion, on which the *Oregon* was patterned. Her hull was more streamlined both forward and aft so she could cleave the water more efficiently and leave less of a wake. Her triple expansion reciprocating steam engine was slightly larger than those fitted into the *Arizona* and the *Alaska*. The high pressure cylinder occupied the center position; it had a diameter of 70 inches, and was flanked by two low pressure cylinders each with a diameter of 104 inches. "The connecting rods are geared into cranks which balance each other and produce a smooth and equal motion. The piston stroke is six feet." The engine was capable of generating 13,000 horsepower, which is "equal to 191,517 tons lifted a foot high every minute."

Steam was fed to the engine from nine Fox patent double-ended boilers, each 16-3/4 feet long and 16-1/2 feet in diameter. Each boiler was heated by six furnaces, three at either end. The boilers were placed in three rows of three; in each row the boilers nearly touched each other, with the outer two boilers coming in close proximity to the sides of the hull. The uptakes for the center row of boilers were split so that the uptakes for the forward end of the boilers fed into the forward stack, and the uptakes for the after end fed into the after stack.

"300 tons of coal a day must be brought to the fires, and the ashes removed; 2,500 tons of fuel must be stored and handled. The confined area of the vessel seems to forbid the employment of anything except manual labor in the work." Of coal-passers and stokers there were many, but it was said that the engine could be operated by only two engineers.

The screw propeller was twenty-four feet in diameter; it pushed "the ship ahead with a power equal to that of twenty of the most powerful locomotives," and at maximum revolutions could maintain a speed better than eighteen knots. The shaft connecting the propeller to the engine was not a single cast, but consisted of fifteen separate parts made of "crucible steel."

Two enormous in-line smokestacks dominated the *Oregon's* profile, looking all out of proportion to the size of the ship, but raked so that they imparted a sense of speed. As was typical of the day when passengers did not yet have complete faith in the reliability of steam engines, the *Oregon* also carried masts, sails, and rigging. The two masts forward of the stacks were square rigged; the two masts abaft the stacks were fore-and-aft rigged. The masts were raked at the same angle as the stacks. It is unlikely that canvas was ever actually unfurled to aid the ship's propulsion, although staysails may have helped to maintain a heading in adverse wind conditions.

Although Lloyd's Register of Shipping lists the *Oregon's* length as 501 feet, by a different system of measurement the *Oregon* is sometimes listed as having a length of 520 feet, but this latter figure must be taken from the point of the stem to the counter. On the original builder's plans the "length between perpendiculars" and the "length on the load waterline" are both given as 500 feet, and the "length overall" is given as 518 feet.

The *Oregon* was "built of iron, with nine transverse watertight bulkheads, five iron decks, and a strong turtle-back deck forward and aft as a protection from the heavy seas. She was fitted to accommodate 340 saloon, 92 second-class, and 1,000 steerage passengers." However, in order to achieve accommodations for that number in steerage, the lower deck had to be stripped of partitions and appurtenances.

She did not enjoy the safety advantages of double-hull construction, which was known at the time but which was in general disfavor due to the added construction costs and to the reduction in speed caused by the increased weight of the hull. Scientific American noted that "probably no finer specimen of marine architecture than the *Oregon* has yet been produced. She was unsurpassed in strength and speed, and supplied with many requisites for safety, but lacking in flotation power and in devices suited for the temporary stoppage of leaks. She had no special means for preventing access of water to the furnaces."

Passengers traveling "saloon" or "cabin" were equivalent to what is called "first class" today. "Second class" passengers were sometimes referred to as "intermediates." There were no more steerage passengers (those who traveled in a giant bunkroom in the ship's after portion, where the noise and vibration from the propulsion machinery was the greatest, and who on some vessels had to supply their own food); they had been upgraded to "third class," and given berthing space below decks in small rooms which were cramped and without adornment; they received food and services commensurate with the ticket price. You get what you pay for.

The *Oregon* was elegantly ornamented. "The grand saloon, capable of dining the whole of the 340 cabin passengers, was placed in the fore part of the vessel, and was laid with a parquetry floor. The ceiling decorations were almost exclusively confined to white and gold. The panels were of polished satinwood, the pilasters of walnut, with gilt capitals. The saloon measured 65 by 54 feet, and was 9 feet in height in the lowest part. A central cupola of handsome design, 25 feet long and 15 feet wide, rose to a height of 20 feet, and gave abundant light and ventilation."

The saloon was forward of the engine. "The staterooms are large and well lighted and ventilated. Every facility for comfort is provided in the cabin. The ladies' drawing room is furnished in a costly manner, and is on the promenade deck. The latter extends nearly the entire length of the vessel. The wood work of the ladies' drawing room, the Captain's cabin, and the principal entrance to the saloons came from the State of Oregon. On the upper deck near the entrance of the grand saloon is the smoking room, which is paneled in Spanish mahogany and has a mosaic floor. Incandescent electric lamps, supplied by the Edison Company, are used in lighting the vessel." At the time, the light bulb was a recent and much touted invention which was in the beginning stages of replacing candles and gas lanterns.

The *Oregon* was built and fitted out at the Fairfield Yard of John Elder & Company, outside Glasgow, Scotland. The amount charged to Guion for construction was $1,250,000.

When the *Oregon* was launched with great fanfare, on June 21, 1883, she was advertised as the largest merchant steamer afloat. This statement was true only by default, or possibly by semantics, and was carefully worded so that it represented a technicality of language rather than the reality of marine construction. Without a doubt, at that time the largest steamer *ever* afloat was the *Great Eastern*, whose maiden voyage occurred nearly a quarter of a century earlier, in 1860. The *Great Eastern* stretched 693 feet from stem to stern and grossed 22,500 tons. Initially she plied the transatlantic lanes carrying passengers and freight, but then she was chartered for the task of laying submerged telegraph cables around the world, at which point she was no long occupied in the *merchant* trade. After a long and tumultuous career, by the time the *Oregon* was done building, the *Great Eastern* was laid up and no longer in active service.

The *Oregon* departed Liverpool on October 7, 1883, bound for New York. She was full of promise for her passengers and burdened with expectations from

THE GUION STEAM-SHIP "OREGON"—THE GREYHOUND OF THE SEAS.

From *Harper's Weekly*, with the original caption.

her owners and investors. She delivered on both responsibilities, but not with immediacy of action. Unlike other--sometimes more tragic--maiden voyages, the *Oregon* was not pushed to the limits in order to achieve fame straight off the building blocks. Captain James Price, master of the *Oregon* and commodore of the Guion fleet, coddled his charge like a newborn child. He ran the ship, and let the engineers run the engine. As a consequence, the engineers reduced speed several times because the bearings overheated. Nevertheless, the *Oregon* completed the westward passage in the respectable time of seven days, eight hours, and thirty-three minutes. The best day's run occurred on Captain Price's sixty-first birthday, when the ship made 456 miles in twenty-four hours.

Her shiny black hull, embellished with a broad streak of red paint at the waterline, like a modern-day racing stripe, cleaved the water effortlessly. "Her deck-houses and joiner-work were white as snow and the brass-work which covered rails and portholes shone like burnished gold in the rays of the sun." If a ship, being an inanimate object, cannot be proud, certainly her captain, officers, and crew could display such emotion as pride. Many notables among the passengers, today forgotten, commented to reporters on the ship's grace and elegance.

The *Oregon's* arrival in New York was not greeted with any kind of fanfare. She docked at Quarantine, a small island in the harbor, and waited there for several hours while health inspectors conducted their examination. The inspection was routine, and when the ship was cleared the *Oregon* moved on to the Guion pier at the foot of King Street. One reporter was so impressed by her size and magnificence that he described her as "a Broadway block moving through the water."

Not until her third voyage was the *Oregon* put to the test. By this time her engineers had full confidence in the performance of the machinery. She left Queenstown at noon on April 13, 1884. She ran into fog on the Newfoundland Banks, then encountered "considerable ice," which she avoided by taking a more southerly route than usual. She passed Sandy Hook on the afternoon of April 19, completing the passage ignominiously by running aground on a shoal in the Gedney Channel. However, she floated off with the rising tide without damage. The corrected time for the passage was six days, ten hours, and ten minutes, the quickest passage on record, and beating by more than eight hours the fastest crossing of the *Alaska* in either direction. So fast was the passage that she arrived in New York a day before the shipping line agents expected her.

Thus the *Oregon* achieved fame as a winner of the Blue Riband: a trophy awarded to the liner with the fastest transatlantic crossing, and held by that liner until usurped by another. This was the finest moment for both the *Oregon* and the Guion Line. But the moment was short-lived.

Despite the *Oregon's* success, the Guion Line was experiencing financial difficulties. Her vessels were not generating enough revenue to enable the company to maintain the payment schedule to the builder, to whom the ship was heavily mortgaged. Guion was forced to default on the loan, so the *Oregon* was taken back by John Elder & Company, to whom the ship became more of a liability than an asset: a white elephant which generated no revenues. Fortuitously, the Cunard Steamship Company was at that very moment contracting with Elder to build a pair of fast liners to compete with Guion's fleet. As the two ships were still in the design phase of construction, delivery of the completed vessels was a couple of years down the line. Elder offered to sell the *Oregon* to Cunard as an interim liner, and Cunard wasted no time in accepting the offer. Title to the liner was taken by Cunard on May 21, 1884.

No sooner had this occurred than the National Line put into service the latest addition to its fleet, the *America*, built by J & G Thomson of Clydebank, Scotland. On her maiden voyage she took the Blue Riband away from the *Oregon*, not on the westward passage, which commenced on May 28, but on the eastward. Thus the trophy was passed to the National Line.

A crucial if peripheral incident occurred on the *Oregon* in June. Her electrical plant broke down while she was in New York, and her departure had to be delayed until the dynamo could be repaired. A call placed to the Edison Electric Light Company produced no immediate result. Finally, a very frustrated shipping manager called Edison direct and demanded that he send an electrical engineer forthwith, with emphasis on the forthwith. The ship was losing money every day she stayed in port. Edison agreed, and hung up the phone. But it was an exceptionally busy day and all his engineers were out handling emergencies.

Who should walk into Edison's office at that very moment but a young Serbian immigrant who had arrived in America only the day before, aboard the *Saturnia*. He handed Edison a letter of introduction from British engineer Charles Batchelor, and, with excellent command of the English language, asked for a job. The reference seemed authentic, so Edison asked him if he could fix a ship's lighting plant. The Serbian proclaimed boldly that he could, so Edison hired him on the spot and brashly dispatched the man with some instruments and told him to fix the *Oregon's* electrical system. With the aid of the ship's crew the Serbian worked straight through the night, tracing short circuits and mending broken wires in the dynamo, until at dawn there was light.

That young Serbian engineer was Nikola Tesla. He worked for Edison for several more months, but the company was not big enough for two men of such vastly different talents, especially as their convictions about the generation of electricity differed so radically. Thomas Alva Edison, the man who was known as the Wizard of Menlo Park, was a staunch believer in direct current because he thought it was crucial to the sale of incandescent light bulbs, which he invented and on which he had the patent. Nikola Tesla was a genius in his own right who saw the advantages of alternating current, and who could not abide Edison's repudiation of a system which had so many obvious advantages. The two parted ways, and for years fought as bitter rivals over which type of electricity should prevail. In this Edison failed, and Tesla went on to form his own company, which designed, built, and installed alternating current generating systems throughout the land. Today, direct current is limited to only a few applications in which a one-way flow of electrons is superior to a reversal of flow.

The *Oregon* transferred her affections from Guion to Cunard without reserve. Her engineers tweaked her engine for every bit of power, and her machinery ran more smoothly with each succeeding passage. Soon she bested her own time. In August she wrested the fastest passage back from the *America* and claimed the Blue Riband for her new owners: first for the westward passage, then for the eastward. There was no faster liner in the world than the *Oregon*. By the end of the year she had trimmed the westward passage to six days, nine hours, twenty-two minutes, and the eastward passage to six days, six hours, fifty-two minutes. Cunard was justifiably proud of her new acquisition.

In March 1885, due to the escalation of hostilities in Afghanistan between England and Russia (the Second Anglo-Afghan War) the British government chartered some of the fastest Atlantic greyhounds to support the fleet. The *Oregon* was fitted out as a cruiser, but served primarily as a dispatch vessel. The political tension soon diminished, with the result that all the liners drafted for military service were returned to their owners except the *Oregon*. In July, she took part in naval maneuvers in Bantry Bay in order to "give the Navy a clear idea of just how useful these ships could be in their naval role."

Bigger and faster and more luxurious liners were on the ways, and while the *Oregon* continued to provide good reliable service for peace and war, it was only a matter of time before her speed record was broken. In August, while she was off fighting the war, her place was eclipsed by a newer Cunard liner, the "super hotel" *Etruria*, which took the Blue Riband for both passages on a single voyage. (However, the *Etruria* is also credited with what is perhaps the longest running time on record. During one voyage her propeller sheared off in mid-ocean, taking the rudder with it. The ship wallowed for days before a passing steamer took her in tow. She was twenty-eight days making port.)

At summer's end, the Admiralty returned the *Oregon* to Cunard, which quickly refitted the ship for passenger service. By November 1885 she was back on her familiar run between Liverpool and New York.

And so we come to 1886, and to the end of the *Oregon's* brief but prestigious career. Now in command was Captain Philip Cottier, a veteran master of the transatlantic liner service though only forty-five years old. On Saturday morning, March 6, final preparations for departure were made in Liverpool. Passengers queued up on the wharf and waited their turn to climb up the angled gangplank. Of the nearly 650 passengers, 186 were traveling first class, 66 were going second class, and the third class compartment contained either 389 or 395 (accounts differ). The number of officers and crew totaled 205, and all were busy performing their assigned duties and functions.

To add to the hustle and bustle, hordes of longshoremen filled the cargo nets with 1,835 tons of freight, which had to be hoisted, swung aboard, and lowered through the hatches into the holds. The various commodities were consigned to some 850 firms and individuals in New York City, and were valued at $700,000. This cargo consisted of silk, cloth, dry goods, books, dyestuffs, hardware, machinery, earthenware, fruit, whiskey, steel, tin plate, rubber, and building materials.

In addition to bulk cargo packed in crates and stowed below were several expensive consignments of diamonds destined for such famous jewel importers as Smith & Knapp, Peterson & Royce, W.S. Hedges, and A.H. Smith & Company. These were kept in the purser's safe.

Also being loaded were 598 bags of mail. The *Oregon* was designated by the British government as a Royal Mail Ship. This means that she was charged with the responsibility of carrying official documents and ordinary mail. While this sounds like a royal privilege, it is not, as most liners operating under the British flag were designated as Royal Mail Ships. The practice was as common as today's commercial airliners carrying airmail letters, and about as important.

Among these bags of mail were two official dispatch bags, 113 closed bags containing letter mail for the U.S. and Canada, 2,400 registered letters, and 470 bags of newspaper mail. The letter mail originated from countries such as France, Italy, Sweden and Russia. Money order posts came from England, Cape Town, Germany, Switzerland, Denmark, Belgium, and Portugal. Also packed in mail bags were more than $1,000,000 in negotiable coupons and greenbacks, and some $2,000,000 worth of stocks, bonds, and other securities (including 10,000 shares of Reading Railroad stock worth $500,000). None of this was out of the ordinary; it was regular commerce.

The *Oregon* departed Liverpool the same as she had many times in the past. It was a typical Saturday morning, the air was clear but cool. The weather continued fair most of the way across the Atlantic, except for a high swell and brisk southeast winds encountered off the banks of Newfoundland, which soon passed. No untoward events occurred during the passage to disturb the routine of the crew or to affect the activities of the passengers. If anything, the crossing was subdued by boredom.

Long Island hove into view during the night of March 14. As usual, the *Oregon* passed along the south shore at a distance of about five miles. A fresh wind picked up from the west, but not hard enough to appreciably stir the surface of the sea, which remained flat and calm according to some witnesses, and had a slight chop according to others. Captain Cottier retired, knowing that the ship was in the good hands of his Chief Officer, William George Matthews. The *Oregon* steamed west at a speed of better than eighteen knots. With anticipated arrival only hours away, the passengers' baggage was removed from the hold and stowed on deck in preparation for unloading immediately upon docking.

By 4:30 in the morning the *Oregon* was halfway between Shinnecock and Fire Island. Stated Chief Officer Matthews: "The fourth officer was on the bridge with me. He stood on the port side, and I stood on the starboard side. There were three men on lookout duty, two on the turtle back, and one on the forepart of the promenade deck. The latter was able to keep a lookout and pass the word along from the other men. The night was tolerably clear, but the day was not broken when the collision occurred. The first sign of the proximity of another vessel to our own was the sudden appearance of a bright light off the port bow. It appeared to me to be a light just held up for a time, for it disappeared instantly. It was just like a flash of light. I thought that it must be on a pilot boat with her masthead light out. Pilot boats do not carry side lights. Knowing that the Captain was not going to take on a pilot until we reached the bar, I had the helm put hard aport to bring the light more broad on the bow."

Today's readers need to understand that in the *Oregon's* time the convention for steering directions was opposite to what it is now. The steering wheel was linked in reverse to the steering gear, so when the top spoke of the helm was turned to the left (counterclockwise) the rudder--and consequently, the direction of the vessel--turned to the right.

When asked how high the light was held, Matthews replied, "I assumed that it was in the hands of a man standing on the deck. I saw no other lights at all; there were no colored lights. My first impression was that a vessel was there without any lights, and that somebody on her deck, suddenly perceiving the approach of the steamer, had grabbed the first light that came to hand and hastily held it up. . . . but the steamship did not have time to change her course before the collision occurred. I saw no sails nor the outline of the schooner until she was on the point of striking us. When I gave the order to change the ship's course I had not the slightest idea there was going to be a collision. I could not tell from the light whether the unknown vessel was moving or standing still, or in what direction she was headed. There were no regulation lights in sight. . . . I could not see her name or anybody on her. I could not even discern how many masts she had. I had no time to think between my giving the order to put the helm hard aport and the collision. The schooner struck the *Oregon* a few feet forward of the bridge upon which I stood. The blow did not careen the steamship over. It was a sort of glancing blow.

"The instant I heard the crash I signaled the engineer to stop the engines, which was done at once. Then I turned to look for the schooner. The *Oregon* was obeying her helm and swinging around. I looked all around the horizon, but could see nothing of the schooner. I heard no noise, no shouts, or talking among the schooner's men. No words were exchanged at any time between the two boats."

Mrs. W.H. Hurst saw the collision from a different perspective. "I had passed a sleepless night and was looking out through the deadlight into the almost impenetrable darkness. I could see the twinkling of a few stars away out where sea and sky seemed to meet. My husband awoke just then, and I spoke to him without turning my head. Suddenly the stars were shut out from view by some passing object. Then a brilliant red light shot by my cabin window, and I was calling my husband's attention to it when there was a terrible crash at the vessel's side, close to our stateroom. It was so severe as to nearly throw me off my feet, and it made the vessel shiver and tremble in a frightfully suggestive manner. My husband and I hurriedly dressed, for we knew that the steamer had been struck, and we supposed by another steamer. . . . While we were dressing there was a second crash, and then a grinding noise and the crushing of timbers. This last and most frightful of sounds was followed by the crash of a mass of falling timber. . . . There was only one stateroom between ours and the dining saloon, and it was immediately under this that the great holes had been torn in the *Oregon's* side. I could hear the water rushing into the hull of the vessel, or imagined I could, and was terribly frightened, for death seemed to me to be very, very near. The dining room was comparatively empty when we reached it and passed through it and up on deck, for we were among the first to get out."

A Mr. L.C. Hopkins was also up and about at the time of the collision. "I had been sick all through the voyage and could not sleep. I was taking some toast and tea, when I heard a crash and felt a shock that shook the *Oregon* from end to end. A frightful crash and clatter, as of the falling of an immense mass of iron plates, came from the port side. A moment later there was a second crash and shock. A third, but lighter, shock followed. . . . I went to my stateroom and called my wife out. Within eight minutes after the first crash and shock an officer of the *Oregon* came from the deck and cried out: 'Call everybody and order them on deck.' The women and children had begun to leave their rooms and, half clad, to crowd the passageways. They were urged out of them, and as fast as the passageways were cleared the iron doors were closed so as to make several compartments water-tight. The passengers were hurried to the deck, where they had to stand close together for warmth. Most of them were ill-clad. Some of the children were barelegged and barefooted. The mercury was at 32 degrees, and ice formed on the deck, but no one grumbled or screamed. The crew began to get the boats ready, and, to the praise of the company, they worked in a way that showed excellent discipline."

The rattle of telegraph chains alerted Captain Cottier that something was amiss. He raced up to the wheel house, where Matthews told him the situation, then relieved the Chief Officer and assumed command. This was a matter of procedure, not an indictment of performance. The forward momentum and the hard-turned rudder gradually brought the *Oregon* around until she completed half a circle and was heading back the way she had come. The reversed engine gradually brought the liner to a halt, after which the vessel drifted slowly seaward with the tide. Captain Cottier ordered an inspection of the damage. The news was not good. Two terrible gashes were torn in the side of the hull in No. 3 compartment, near the coal bunkers.

Captain Cottier at first thought that the *Oregon* would survive the ordeal, as only one compartment appeared to have been breached. But it soon developed that the point of impact was right on the edge of a watertight bulkhead, with the result that two adjacent compartments were flooding, and much faster than the pumps could eject the overflow. The situation did not look good.

Two men were lowered down the outside of the hull in boatswain's chairs: Second Officer Peter Hood and the ship's carpenter, John Huston. Mattresses and pillows were handed down to them, and they stuffed these into the jagged openings. But the mattresses and pillows were sucked into the ship by the fast flow of water which they were attempting to stem.

Next, a huge sail cloth or collision mat was worked down over the crash site. "An attempt was made to fasten these over the holes below the water line by the use of chains and toggles. Huston, divesting himself of all superfluous clothing, dove into the water and tried to make fast the chains. Three times he went down under the icy water in a vain attempt to find a method of stopping the inflow of the water. The efforts were fruitless, and Huston, much against his wishes, was deterred by Officer Hood from making a fourth attempt."

The collision mat was eventually secured by working ropes over the bow and under the hull, then bringing them up taut on the opposite side of the ship. The job was accomplished and the flow of water was somewhat diminished. By this time the ship was quite a bit down by the head and listing perceptibly to port.

From all accounts there does not appear to have occurred an outbreak of total pandemonium, but there was at the very least a great deal of activity and concern among the passengers and crew, and, understandably, a certain amount of confusion. One unidentified passenger claimed that "although he slept on the side where the break was he did not awake until called by a steward." Another passenger, Captain T.R. Huddleston, was either exaggerating or pulling a reporter's leg when he said that "he awoke three hours after the accident, blacked his boots, dressed himself carefully, and came out to breakfast, and only then heard of the collision." Perhaps, not hearing the thrumming of the engine or the vibration which ran incessantly throughout the metal hull, he thought the ship was docked at Quarantine.

Guns and rockets were fired to attract the attention of vessels in the vicinity. Hopkins noted, "They had not been in use long when a big steamship appeared. She was bound out, but she passed on, paying no heed to our signals." Hopkins also noted that in the light of dawn "we had a chance to see what damage had been done to the Oregon. There were three holes on her port side. One was above the water and was 12 by 9 feet. The others were smaller, but one of them was below the water line, and the sea was pouring into the hold." Another passenger thought the hole was large enough "that a horse and wagon could easily have been driven through it."

Worse than that, the sea surged through open hatchways whose watertight doors could not be tightly closed because the hinges were rusted or because the seals were choked with coal dust or because the bulkhead had been twisted in the collision. This permitted flooding of the boiler room, and soon the fires were damped by the rising tide, leaving the *Oregon* without means of propulsion or electric power to operate the pumps. Drowning the burning coal also created "a tremendous cloud of steam, so dense and thick that the firemen in the fire room dropped their shovels and rushed to the deck, where all the passengers had been summoned, many clad in their sleeping garments."

About two hours after the collision, Captain Cottier was forced to admit the strong possibility that the *Oregon* might sink, so he ordered the lifeboats prepared for launching. It goes perhaps without saying that the *Oregon* did not carry enough lifeboats to save the entire ship's complement. No vessel at the time did. In fact, even though the *Oregon* had on board only half the number of passengers she could have carried, there was space on the lifeboats for only half of them. This situation has existed since merchant shipping began, and posed the same problems as it always has: some people must be left behind to go down with the ship. Who would they be?

Chief Officer Matthews stated for the record, "I did not see any breaches of discipline on the part of the crew. There was no insubordination that I know of."

Mrs. Hurst again observed events from a different perspective. "The scene on deck was something awful. The people from the steerage were on deck, crying, screaming, and praying. It was a most awful combination of noises, and no one who heard it could by any possibility ever forget it. But above it sounded for a few minutes after I got on deck the curses and horrible oaths of the begrimed and half-attired firemen and stokers. They seemed to have mutinied, and the officers had no control over them. They were scattered all over the deck, and myself and other ladies and some children were so roughly pushed about that several of us were thrown violently to the deck. Finally the officers were reinforced by a number of the gentlemen cabin passengers and order was in some measure restored among those rough men. It took force to do this, though, and the minor officers had to use staves and belaying pins and fairly club the men to keep them from capturing the lifeboats, our only hope of salvation. As it was, one boat, the first away, was filled with them."

A *New York Times* reporter interviewed Captain Cottier on the matter. "In explanation of the story that some of the *Oregon's* stokers and firemen fought for the possession of two or three of the small boats immediately after the collision, Capt. Cottier stated that the only firemen who went near the small boats while they were being lowered were the men who were ordered by him to guard those boats. It is conceded that some of the steerage passengers rushed for the boats as soon as they found that the vessel was sinking, but they were driven back by the mates and crew."

As counterpoint, another passenger begged to differ with Captain Cottier's sanitized account of the orderly abandonment of the ship. This anonymous Englishman was quoted as saying, "A more cowardly set of rascals than some of the crew of the *Oregon* were never got together outside of a jail. A party of them --firemen, I think--took possession of a lifeboat and were preparing to get away without taking anybody else in her when a brave sailor ran at them with a big stick and belabored them soundly. But he didn't drive them out of the boat. They lay in its bottom and yelled for mercy. Then some passengers got into the boat. If I hadn't lost my purse I'd like to give that seaman something handsome."

Mr. F. Frost was even more graphic and vitriolic: "Those rascally firemen deserved drowning. When I approached the boat they had taken they threatened me with belaying pins. As I did not want my head battered I gave them plenty of room."

A passenger, Mr. Sturges, recounted his role in commandeering the boat away from the firemen. "I had not used a profane word since the first night of the Chicago fire until this morning. I cursed frightfully when I saw a party of fire-men going away from the ship with a boat not half filled. I called to them to come back. They would not return. Drawing my revolver and picking out the fellow who seemed to be their leader, I said, 'If you don't come back I will kill you.' They returned and we put 16 passengers into the boat. I believe I would have been justified in killing some of the rascals."

By comparison, Cunard's official press release was as innocuous as it was ingenuous: "With but few exceptions all behaved admirably, and with scarcely any trouble order was quickly restored. The partly dressed passengers were ordered to put on their clothing, and coffee was served to all."

It was estimated that not more than 400 people had been able to abandon ship in the ten lifeboats and three emergency rafts, crowded though they were, that the *Oregon* carried. That left upwards of 450 people awaiting their doom on the foundering liner. Even if they all managed to stay afloat when the ship went down, by wearing life belts or clutching life rings, it is unlikely that many could have long survived immersion in the frigid water before dying from hypother-mia, or drowning.

What to wondrous eyes should then appear but two glorious sails billowing brightly in the west wind. It was the two-masted pilot boat number 11, better known as the *Phantom*, answering the *Oregon's* rocket's red glare. It was a small boat, but it had deck space available for scores, perhaps hundreds, of desperate people. The time was 8:30, four hours after the collision. The heavily laden lifeboats had all remained in the vicinity of the wreck. Now they rowed for the

Phantom with all abandon and quickly discharged their human cargo so they could return to the drifting steamship and take off another boatload of survivors.

About an hour later, while the transfer of people was being effected, another ship, this one a schooner, approached the scene of the disaster. The *Fannie A. Gorham* was bound from Jacksonville to Boston with a cargo of coal. Captain Cottier waved her down and asked her captain to take the women and children from the overcrowded lifeboats so the boats could return to the ship for another load.

Now occurred one of the most absurd statements ever uttered, so ludicrous that it cannot be believed, and which is in any case more apocryphal than true, and probably a figment of the imagination of a reporter short on copy. As if it were a valid excuse for refusing to take on survivors, Captain Mahoney, master of the *Fannie A. Gorham*, declared, "I don't have enough provisions."

To which Captain Cottier supposedly replied, "I'm not asking for provisions, I'm asking for transportation."

Fortunately the seas were calm. Hundreds of people clambered from the lifeboats to the two sailing vessels and accomplished the task without a single injury and only little more than a dampened stocking. "Huston again distinguished himself by saving the lives of three passengers. He seemed ubiquitous while passengers were being assisted from the vessel into the boats. Several of these in their hurry to get into the boats fell into the water. Among these were the little son and daughter of an emigrant named Andrew NcNab. A fat woman and a baby fell into the water at the same time, but these two were easily pulled into the boat. The NcNab boy and girl were carried some distance from the boat.

From *Frank Leslie's Illustrated Newspaper.*

Huston saw their danger, and, throwing off his coat, with which he was trying to drive off the oil from his previous experience in the water, sprang overboard. It was the work of only an instant, with his strong, sure stroke, to reach the children, and both were brought back to the boat in safety. Subsequently Huston drew into the boat an elderly man who had fallen from the ladder into the water while trying to get into the boat."

Meanwhile, the lifeboats rowed back and forth between the *Oregon* and the two rescue craft. One lifeboat made as many as five trips, each one full to the gunwales with male passengers and crew who had been left behind. It took hours, but at least now there was space for everyone aboard the rescue craft, small as they were. (The *Fannie A. Gorham* grossed 324 tons, the *Phantom* less. But, as they say, any port in a storm.)

In the time honored tradition of the sea, Captain Cottier was the last man to leave his ship. By that time "her deck was so low in the water that he was able to step from the rail directly into one of the small boats." Now every soul was accounted for, the boats were so crammed with people that it was nearly impossible to maneuver them. So Captain Cottier dispatched Third Officer Taylor in one of the lifeboats to head for land and telegraph for help. Obediently, Taylor and his crew rowed north.

Yet another vessel hove into view, at 10:30. This was the North German Lloyd passenger liner *Fulda*, also bound for New York. By now the sea around the *Oregon* was filled with lifeboats, rafts, and rescue vessels, on which were packed some 900 people: a sight which Captain Ringk, master of the *Fulda*, undoubtedly had never seen before. The *Fulda* stopped within half a mile of the *Oregon* and immediately offered assistance. Then began the laborious process of transferring all the people previously transferred to the *Phantom* and the *Fannie A. Gorham* to the more commodious German liner. This also took hours.

By 12:30 it was all over but the short hop to New York. After the last remaining passengers and crew from the *Oregon* had been transferred to the *Fulda*, the Cunard liner made her last bow. Mrs. Hurst: "The last I saw of the *Oregon* was from the deck of the *Fulda*, when she plunged bow first down to the bottom, her great propeller screw being the last thing we saw of her."

Another passenger's description was much more graphic. "While the disappearance of the beautiful steamer we had learned to love was in one respect an awful sight, it was at the same time one of the most picturesque things I ever saw. She had listed well over to port before the last boatload, with Capt. Cottier, surgeon McMaster, and the ship's carpenter, left her. She lay there seemingly in a struggle for life against the waters striving to engulf her. Five minutes before she sank the great vessel rocked backward and forward and rolled from side to side, a great helpless mass. Then, as her bow dipped, the great waves rolled over her, and the slender foremast gave way and swayed to one side. Then the prow rose for the last time. it stood well up in the air for an instant and then, with a sort of spring from her keel as if preparing for a dive, the bow cut its way down into the waves she could no longer ride. There was a swirl of waters. Her dive was continued and the heavy stern swung well up, so that we could almost see her keel.

From *Frank Leslie's Illustrated Newspaper.*

Down she went head first, and the blades of the great propeller were thrown high and clear of the water. They, too, went down in the great gulf and the water boiled and bubbled and gurgled and lashed itself into a great mass of foam. We had seen the last of the *Oregon*."

Captain Ringk's observation was reserved: "When I first came up with her she was down at the head. Gradually she sank lower and lower, and all at once her head plunged out of sight under the sea and her stern came up like a teeter-totter. The stern rose so high in the air that you could see her screw-wheel. She remained in that duck-like position for a while, and then by degrees again she settled at the stern and went down as gracefully as though gliding off the cradles at a launch. It was all over in a minute or two, although as we all looked at the lovely creature in her helpless condition it seemed like a much longer time."

The *Oregon* had remained afloat for eight hours after the collision, time enough to conduct one of the most monumental rescue operations in the history of steamship passenger service, and without a single fatality. This enabled Cunard to continue advertising the fact that the company had never lost a life at sea. One passenger later quipped, perhaps in the euphoria of being alive, that "three dogs--a terrier, a bull, and a skyo--were saved." To which another chimed in, "But a Chicago man lost two magpies." Or perhaps they just flew the coop.

The *Phantom* and the *Fannie A. Gorham* were discharged from their duties and proceeded on their way. The *Fulda* continued on toward New York, her decks swelled with the addition of some 900 men, women, and children. Also on board were 69 sacks of mail which had been taken off the *Oregon*, and the entire consignment of diamonds which the astute purser, Robert Thorpe, had thoughtfully removed from the safe and stuffed in his pockets.

By this time news of some sort of casualty had reached Cunard's offices. The alert keeper of the Fire Island Life-Saving Station had noticed through his spyglass the great liner adrift, and thought he recognized her as the *Oregon*. He sent a telegram to Cunard noting his observations. Vernon Brown, agent of the Cunard Line, took immediate affirmative action without knowing exactly what the difficulty was. He chartered two tugs and himself boarded Cunard's *Aurania*, whose departure had been delayed by fog in the harbor, and all three vessels set out for Fire Island. (Remember that this was before wireless telegraphy and ship-to-shore radio.) Brown was working under the assumption that, since the *Oregon* had not arrived at her pier as scheduled, she must have been disabled. He issued orders to the *Aurania's* captain to tow the *Oregon* to New York with the help of the tugs, then disembarked onto another tug and went back to his office where he could keep apprised of developments and be able to execute the duties of his position.

Later that afternoon Cunard received another telegram from the Life-Saving Service, this one from the Forge River Station. According to the Service's annual report, the life-savers launched a boat through the surf and "pulled out half a mile from the shore to a small boat containing a party of men who were making signals for help. It proved to be a yawl with a pilot, and the third officer and three sailors belonging to the British steamship *Oregon*. A heavy sea was breaking on the outer bar with a dangerous surf running inside, and the third officer was the only one who would take the risk of landing with the life-saving crew. After waiting some time for a smooth chance a dash was made for the beach which was reached in safety. The yawl put out to sea again and was picked up by a passing steamer."

Third Officer Taylor gave a brief account of the accident and the fate of the passengers and crew, and pleaded for rescue craft. He did not know about the arrival of the *Fulda*, and by that time the *Oregon* had drifted out of sight from shore. Brown must have gone mad with the paucity of details. He sent a telegram to the Forge River Station for more information, but by that time (more than an hour later) Taylor had gone. Remember that telegrams were not instantaneous like phone calls. A written telegram had to be hand carried to a telegraph station, where it was transmitted by wire to another station, which then typed out the reply and sent the telegram by messenger to the addressee. The reply was just as long in coming.

That evening, after Taylor's terse telegram, the *Fulda* reached the outer bar of New York harbor and was forced to wait till midnight for the tide to change. She dropped anchor near the *Sandy Hook* lightship. A life-saving crew from the Sandy Hook Station boarded the liner and learned about the *Oregon's* demise. They returned to the station and, at 9:40 that night, sent a telegram to Brown at Cunard which contained only slightly more news than he already had: that the *Oregon* had definitely sunk and that the *Fulda* was bringing in the survivors.

By this time word about the casualty had reached the media. Responding to a hot tip, three enterprising reporters from the *New York Times* chartered a tug to transport them to the *Fulda*. This was not technically permissible because the ship had not cleared Quarantine. They did it anyway, and thereby scooped all the other dailies and carried particulars of the event a full day before any of their competitors. Afterward, the *New York Times* deservedly tooted its own horn by printing an account of how the story was obtained.

The tug *Ocean King* bypassed Quarantine entirely and headed right out of the harbor. "The tug's whistle sounded in a most important and businesslike manner. There was a strong dash of Health Officer in the toots and an air of ease and authority about every one on board the little vessel as she approached the big ocean steamer." When Captain Sam, master of the tug, shouted, "Make fast that line aboard the *Fulda*," his voice was imperious enough to carry conviction. No sooner was a line made fast than a rope ladder was tossed from the tug to the high rail of the liner. The reporters scrambled up the ladder as it swayed sickeningly back and forth, and gained the deck where "the extremely courteous officers tipped their caps to the reporters, who were amused, though rather mortified, to discover they were mistaken for Health Officer Smith and his assistants. Being in a hurry, however, they decided to defer explanations, as they had been informed by Health Officer Smith that under no circumstances would they be allowed to board the *Fulda*, though he had no objections, he said, to their holding a conversation with her officers or passengers from a distance."

The reporters quickly got away from the *Fulda's* officers, who were deceived about the purpose of the aggressive boarders, and lost themselves among the throngs of passengers in order to conduct interviews. They found Captain Cottier in a cabin so crowded that "its occupants were packed like figs in a box." While they were getting their stories, Captain Ringk learned the truth of their identity; he had more steam up than his ship. He ordered the tug's line cast off, then got the *Fulda* under way.

The reporters wrote their stories, but when they returned to the place where they had come aboard they found the *Ocean King* some distance away. They shouted for Captain Sam to take them off. As the tug closed on the liner, Captain Ringk rushed up to the reporters and said imperiously, "Nobody can leave this vessel."

The moment was tense. "Capt. Ringk was supported by a number of his crew. While all hands were looking at the reporters one of them, who had one leg over the rail, suddenly swung the other leg over. The Captain made a grab at the reckless young man's coat collar. He considered the young man reckless, but the young man knew better. He had rapidly calculated the distance between the *Fulda* and the tug, and had determined to make the jump. Before Capt. Ringk or his men could secure a hold on him the reporter had let go his hold on the *Fulda* and was in the air. A second later he had grasped the foremost stay of the tug and was safe on board. His brother reporters were grasped by a dozen hands before they could duplicate the feat, but in spite of the desperate efforts of the *Fulda's* crew The Times's men pulled their stories from their pockets and threw them at their fellow reporter on the tug. He caught them, and felt a great calm." There is much to be said for initiative.

Inevitably, under such circumstances as the loss of a vessel at sea, there are grave after effects even when no fatalities are involved. In the case of the *Oregon* the two issues of primary concern were determining the cause of the accident and adjusting claims arising from the loss of the hull, cargo, and personal possessions.

Although there seemed no doubt that the *Oregon* collided with a vessel, it was suggested instead that she struck the masts of the *Hylton Castle* (q.v.), sunk two months earlier. Quick calculations and reference to the nautical charts indicated that the sunken hull lay at least ten miles away from the site of the collision. This begged the question then of which schooner was struck and what happened to her and her crew. This mystery has never been solved with complete satisfaction because the schooner or any parts of her have never been found and identified.

Beliefs at the time ranged far and wide. The New York Maritime Exchange began combing the records for ships gone missing, especially those whose proposed routes intersected the *Oregon's* path at the approximate time of the collision. This was a slow and tedious process of discovery since sailing ships often cruised for weeks between ports of call, and it was not uncommon for them to be delayed by the lack of wind or to stop along the way for repairs or provisions or to wait out bad weather. In fact, at that very time more than two hundred loaded schooners were lying to in Hampton Roads because "the heavy northwest winds have made northern voyages in sailing vessels slow and perilous of late."

The job would have been half as difficult had it been known for certain that the schooner (if it actually was a schooner and not a square-rigger) was traveling east with the wind, implying that she was coming from a port to the south and heading toward a port in the north, and was at the time of the collision sailing with the wind in order to round Long Island. However, the lack of observation of navigation lights made some theorists wonder if the *Oregon* had not struck a ship which intended to proceed west but which, due to the strong head wind and ebbing tide, had dropped anchor to await more favorable conditions, in which case the *Oregon* would have stove in her stern. If that were true, the white light observed by the first and fourth officers could have been a binnacle light unmasked for a moment coincident with the collision, with the crew of the schooner unaware that they were about to be run down. This could explain why Matthews described the light as a "flash."

In the same scenario, the white light could have been an anchor light in the fore shrouds previously hidden from view by the masts and after shrouds, then momentarily made visible as the *Oregon's* angle of observation shifted. It should be understood that the elevation of the *Oregon's* bridge wing above the water could conceivably place the officers at a height from which they might have to look *down* at the masthead light of a coasting schooner of a size such as the one which came to the liner's rescue, the *Fannie A. Gorham*. This could explain why the schooner was not seen from farther away. A thin haze would cloak a ship which was miles away on the horizon, where it would ordinarily be silhouetted against the sky. Then, once the ship got close enough to be in visual range, it could only be seen against the dark background of the water. As every mariner and small boat operator knows, the distance of lights seen at night is incredibly deceptive.

The case for a near head-on collision seemed more persuasive. The evidence indicated that "the schooner was on the port tack, that is, with the wind blowing over her port side, and with her sails bellying out to starboard. The two vessels were approaching each other on the lines of an oblique angle." Mrs. Hurst's observation of a red light could be explained as a sailing ship's port running light. Among the dissenters of this interpretation of events was the Chief Officer of the *Dorset*, who was quite emphatic: "I am morally certain from my own experience of 20 years that she couldn't have seen it through the dead light of her cabin, but that she saw what often deceived old mariners--the reflection of the light in her state room. I won't believe such a red light was afloat on the unsupported statement of any woman."

While it is true that lights are often reflected on glass, his comment appears to be more an indictment of the sex of the observer rather than what she claimed to have seen. I wonder if he was man enough to admit his prejudice when it developed at the official inquiry that the red light was also seen by at least two seamen who were dragging up mail sacks. Several seamen testified to seeing a white light, and one, William Howgate, saw a green light. Seaman John Rogers saw the jib-boom strike the hull, and quartermaster John Cunningham, who was stationed in the wheel house, distinctly saw a three-masted schooner under all sail except the head sails, which had been carried away. Thus it was established that the *Oregon* collided with a three-masted schooner which was displaying the required navigation lights.

Moreover, from the testimony of witnesses there seemed no doubt that the unseen schooner rebounded after first striking the *Oregon*, then struck the liner's hull a second and a third time. Seafarers rushed to their blackboards and calculated that at the speed the *Oregon* was traveling she would have advanced a distance equivalent to her own length in about three seconds, which "would have carried her beyond a point at which a schooner could have struck her again." It might have looked good in chalk, but the figures did not fit the facts. With the schooner's sails full of wind and her masts in the act of crashing forward, by the evidence she must have recoiled with sufficient speed to account for the other two crashes.

Elsewhere it was estimated that the vessel "that struck the *Oregon* could hardly have been smaller than a one-thousand-ton schooner" which, loaded with coal, "would have gone to the bottom at once." The search for this unidentified schooner continued.

More outlandish theorists surmised that the *Oregon* might have struck a mine (at that time called a torpedo) which had gone adrift from "somewhere" or which had been placed by wreckers hoping to cash in on salvage; or that "dynamite or some other explosive in her hold was exploded." The *Oregon* carried neither dynamite nor explosive of any kind. A coal bunker explosion was also ruled out.

As can be imagined, the sinking of the *Oregon* created quite a furor in the press, in shipping circles, and among the general populace. There was the usual hue and cry about the liner not carrying enough lifeboats to provide space for everyone aboard. Both Cunard and the Board of Trade insisted that she carried more than was required by law for a vessel her size. Nor was there official condemnation of the shortage of life belts; the *Oregon* had but 813 , when she normally carried twice that many people. (She also had 205 life rings.) Why is it, I ask, that it makes perfect sense to every human being in the civilized world to provide enough lifeboats for *all* passengers and crew, except to those who run shipping companies and who are empowered to enact laws for the greater safety of life at sea?

One self-professed expert, R.B. Forbes, made some rather short-sighted criticisms based solely upon newspaper accounts of the accident. Much of his advice was academic considering the outcome. For example, he thought that rescue craft should have tied off to the *Oregon* to prevent them from drifting away, and that pumps should be fitted with manual overrides so that the muscle of steerage passengers (but not passengers of first or second class) could be used to pump out the holds by hand. Forbes also believed that ships should not slow down in fog, but should increase to their fullest speed because "the sooner we get over the many dangers in our path, the better in the long run." Imagine racing through a dense fog on the highway at eighty miles per hour in order to get out of the fog area sooner, and thereby lessening your chances of collision!

To give him credit where it is due, Forbes in his long career also proposed many sensible recommendations: the establishment of shipping lanes, the addition of airtight seats which would float off the upper decks when a ship went down, seat cushions which could double as floats (like those in commercial aircraft today), and a method of blowing off a ship's boilers not only to reduce the weight of the water they contained but to convert them to buoyant tanks which could conceivably extend the amount of time for a vessel to take its final plunge, thus allowing more time to launch lifeboats or to wait for rescue craft. If the *Titanic* could have remained afloat for a few more hours, the greatest maritime disaster in history might have become instead a famous rescue operation.

One British sea captain suggested that the *Oregon's* iron plating may have been made of a type called "pot metal" plate, which "has as much ductibility or pliability as plate glass," and which is therefore likely to shatter upon being struck rather than to dent or bend. This is not as outlandish a suggestion as it might seem, as many British vessels were constructed of such plate because it was cheaper to manufacture than the kind of plate which does not fracture when struck. Others promoted the use of steel plate for ships' hulls instead of wrought iron because steel is stronger, stiffer, and more elastic; also, more expensive.

Then there rose the question of why the *Oregon* did not steer for shoal water to the north, perhaps to be beached. The boiler fires were not instantly inundated. For this there was no answer. Only because everyone survived did this issue not take on more importance.

Now every port community was concerned about overdue schooners. The first one nominated as a suspect was the *Abbott F. Lawrence*, bound for Taunton, Massachusetts across the *Oregon's* path and a week overdue. This was three days after the accident. The next day more possibilities were added to the list: *B.C. French, C.A. Briggs, Mabel Phillips, Job Jackson, Eva L. Ferris, Taulane, Charles H. Haskell, Spartan, Maud Sherwood,* and *Kloto.* On March 19 the schooner *Hudson,* Philadelphia to Boston, became a potential victim.

Some concrete evidence came to light on March 20, when the fishing smack *Henry Morgenthau* picked up a schooner's yawl about twenty-five miles southeast of the wreck site. "The boat is a good one, built of cedar, and 30 feet long. The gunwale is painted black, the body white, and the bottom dark green. When found the boat was bottom up. There are indications that she was hurriedly cut loose from the vessel to which she belonged. The painter and gripes and all other connecting tackle had been hacked through clumsily with a knife, and a plug which fits the hole in the bottom of the boat was found in the locker. The yawl bore no name."

That same day a large lot of wreckage floated past Asbury Park, New Jersey, and one piece washed ashore: the cutwater of a sailing ship which "bore no marks by which it could be identified."

On March 24, fully ten days after the accident, and after many of the missing schooners had arrived at their destinations, their crews totally unaware of the collision or of the concern they had caused their shipping companies and loved ones, another vessel was posted missing: the three-masted schooner *Charles H. Morse* (sometimes erroneously reported as the *Charles R. Morse,* which is a different vessel entirely). The *Charles H. Morse* left Baltimore on March 6 with a cargo of coal bound for Boston. At Hampton Roads she joined the company of the schooner *Florence J. Allen.* The two ships were in sight of each other until the night of the accident and in the vicinity of where the collision occurred. The *Florence J. Allen* arrived in Boston two days later, but nothing had since been heard of the *Charles H. Morse.*

The *Charles H. Morse* was 152.7 feet in length, had a beam of 36.2 feet, and a draft of 13.8 feet; her tonnage was registered at 508 gross tons. She was built in Bath, Maine in 1880, and constructed of oak and yellow pine. She was under the command of Captain Alonzo Wildes. On board as a passenger was her former master, Captain Alfred Manson. A mate and a crew of six completed the complement.

The *Kloto* was still unaccounted for. She left Baltimore on February 22, bound for New York with coal. To place her at the collision site on March 14, she would have to have been held up a long time by bad weather and to have taken a long eastward tack. The *Kloto* was never seen again, but shipping circles were inclined to believe that the *Charles H. Morse* was the schooner in collision, and that the *Kloto* foundered.

A wooden schooner grossing 508 tons sinking an iron-hulled mammoth grossing 7,375 tons is equivalent to a tricycle taking out an eighteen wheeler. Stranger things have happened.

Then came a discovery which fairly well clinched the collision-with-a-schooner scenario. Three masts were discovered sticking out of the water southwest of Shinnecock Light. The Hydrographic Office assigned Lieutenant Field to investigate and take bearings. He found that the distance from the protruding masts to the wreck of the *Oregon* was sixteen and one half miles, with the sailing ship lying southwest of the steamer. The depth of water at the site of the sunken sailing ship was 138 feet.

The *Charles H. Morse* being a small vessel, her masts "would hardly show above water if she lay on the bottom. An explanation of this is offered by the theory that she may have caught on a ledge or that the masts may be wrenched from their fastenings, and are now hanging by the shrouds."

Unfortunately for history, no positive identification was ever made of the sunken sailing ship. It could have been the *Kloto* or some other, larger vessel. If only a diver could have gone down and read her nameboard the proof could be positive instead of circumstantial. But at that time all available divers were busily engaged in salvaging what they could from the *Oregon*.

Cunard engaged the services of the Merritt Wrecking Company the day after the liner sank. The wrecking steamer *Rescue* located the wreck quickly because two of the masts protruded above the surface, the mainmast as high as fifteen feet. A third mast was standing just below the surface. The wreck lay at a depth of 130 feet.

The sea was adrift with flotsam. "Several pieces of baggage, six cases of dry goods, three life rafts, and a lot of life-preservers were found floating in the vicinity. Several mail bags, which were being tossed about by the rolling sea about four miles southwest of the wreck, were also picked up." Everything was taken to Cunard's offices for safekeeping except the mail bags, which were turned over to the post office for drying and delivery. The post office had its work cut out. A few of the densely packed letters were found to be dry, but most were soaked nearly beyond recognition, especially those letters written on thin, nearly transparent paper. Some 100,000 letters had to be spread out on the floor and dried, then the bleeding inked addresses had to be deciphered. One letter from Cork was filled with shamrocks; three people showed up to claim it, but as the address could not be read none could have it, so it was sent to the Dead Letter Office. One package filled with cigars was confiscated because it was illegal to send cigars through the mail. One letter contained a will written on sheepskin; fortunately, the writing was still legible. Most of the newspapers were ruined.

Pilot boats and other wrecking vessels found "a large quantity of wreckage, consisting of cases, barrels, mail bags, trunks, &c. The crews of pilot boat *T.S. Negus*, No. 1, and of the brig *Fidelia* were engaged in fishing out the drift." The *Francis Perkins*, pilot boat No. 13, scooped up thirty-five bags of mail. The SS *Tonawanda* picked up one bag, the schooner *Henry Morgenthau* another. About twenty-five miles off Barnegat, New Jersey, the brigantine *Samuel Welch* came across "life preservers, beds, oranges, and other small articles." The schooner *Nellie J. Dinsmore* picked up two bags of mail and carried them to her destination, Portland, Maine, from which point they had to be shipped back to New York. The pilot boat *Loubat* brought in four packing cases marked B. & L. Two weeks after the collision the Coast Wreck Company's schooner *Edwin Post* fished up nine bags of mail. Eventually, more than half the mail was recovered, some by divers.

Pilot William Lewis was sailing in the vicinity of the wreck when he came across a mail bag which contained "$250,000 of Erie second consolidated bonds, addressed to L. Von Hoffman & Co. Mr. Lewis thought that he was entitled to salvage, and Von Hoffman & Co. offered him $500, which he declined to accept, deeming it an insufficient reward. His claim for salvage is still unsatisfied."

From *Harper's Weekly.*

Because the masts presented a hazard to navigation, the Lighthouse Board marked the wreck with a lighted buoy. This was soon superseded by mooring a lightship next to the wreck. The lightship remained on station until November 1, 1886, by which time the Merritt Wrecking Company had knocked down the *Oregon's* masts and funnels, and there was at least 60 feet of water over the obstruction.

Divers sent down to examine the wreck immediately ascertained that total hull salvage was out of the question, for the hull was broken in two "abaft the fore rigging." There followed a period of unusually bad weather which prevented divers from conducting a more thorough examination of the hull until mid-April. Then they "found that the vessel had broken in two between hatches Nos. 2 and 3. The after part of the hull had been twisted out of line from the forward part, showing that the vessel had probably sheered over as she went down and had then broken. About 25 feet aft of the break and in line with the fore part of the bridge was found the hole which had caused the vessel to sink. It was covered with canvas, which had been secured by two cords running under the keel, and five cords which had been attached to the rail. The canvas was cut away, and a break 6 feet long and 3 1/2 feet wide was found.

"The break commenced at two dead lights about 12 feet below the main deck. The iron plates of the side bulged in at the hole and had smashed in some of the cargo, which was evidently steel or iron in boxes. No debris was found near the wreck, but along the middle line of the side fore and aft there were long scratches in the paint, which appeared as if they had been made by the fluke of an anchor."

Cunard had full coverage on the *Oregon* so the only loss the company incurred was unearned future revenues, until a replacement vessel could be purchased or built. It was the responsibility of individual shippers and consignees to

A Merritt Wrecking Company diver at work on the *Oregon*, with the salvage vessels *Edwin Post* and *Rescue* in the background. (From *Frank Leslie's Illustrated Newspaper*.)

insure freight which belonged to them. But the passengers were left without recourse for the recovery of lost belongings beyond what Cunard was voluntarily willing to give them. Regarding such reimbursement, Cunard expressed the opinion that it would make fair compensation for losses if moderate claims were presented. The two key words here are "fair" and "moderate," for the implication was that if the claimants were too many or asked for too much, Cunard would pay nothing.

Consider the plight of the poor immigrants who were traveling steerage with all they owned, arriving in the United States to begin life anew with nothing but the clothes they wore on their backs. They lost everything. But Cunard did not have to deal with them because they did not have the financial resources to put forth their claims. Cunard replaced their lost train tickets, then sent them on their way west; most were settlers bound for Minnesota, Nebraska, and Dakota. Those who hung around the offices pleading for money for lost clothes and personal belongings received no satisfaction, nor could they afford the services of a lawyer.

The first class passengers were the ones who hired attorneys to seek restitution for personal effects which went down with the liner. And while I can certainly understand why one would not accept anything less than full replacement value for that fancy tweed suit or diamond brooch, I cannot help but point out the irony of the situation in which those who were so well off in life complained the bitterest about their losses.

Asked for an unofficial opinion on the matter, Chief Justice David McAdam replied, "The carrier across the seas of passengers or merchandise is not an insurer, and is not therefore liable for any loss of the goods intrusted to his charge without affirmative proof that the loss was occasioned by his fault or neglect. If the collision which caused the *Oregon* to sink was without any fault or neglect on the part of those in charge of the steamer, there is no responsibility on the owners either for the loss of goods shipped as freight or for passengers' baggage. If the ship had gone down by the 'act of God,' such as a tempest at sea or a stroke of lightning, it is clear that no liability would attach, but as such was not the case with the *Oregon*, the question of responsibility hinges upon the determination of the question as to whose fault caused the loss, and this is a question of fact rather than of law.

"As a general rule a steamer meeting a sailing vessel must take measures to avoid the latter, which has a right to keep its course. If, therefore, those in charge of the *Oregon* saw in time the vessel which collided, or if they might have seen it by the exercise of proper care and due diligence, then the collision was caused by the fault of those in charge of the steamer; but if, after exercising every care, those on board the *Oregon*, either by darkness or the fact that by reason of the sailing vessel not carrying proper lights, its presence could not be discovered in time, then, of course, those in charge of the steamer were not guilty of fault or neglect. In case of a suit against the owners, it would be sufficient, in order to establish a prima facie cause of action, to show that the baggage or merchandise was delivered to the steamer on the other side, and that the steamer failed to deliver it here. This would cast upon the steamship company the onus of excusing the non-delivery. The company could only do this by affirmatively proving the fact of the collision and that it occurred without its fault. If it proved this, it would be a valid defense. If it failed to do so, its owners would be held liable for all losses."

Cunard was also slammed with a suit from North German Lloyd, which sought to capitalize on the *Fulda's* rescue efforts. Although the company charged Cunard no money for its services, it filed a salvage claim against the diamonds which the *Oregon's* purser had saved. The diamonds were taken to the Customs House where Deputy Collector Berry assumed charge of them. This meant that their owners, some of New York's finest and most well respected jewelers, could not claim their goods until North German Lloyd's case against Cunard was settled.

These legal wranglings endured for years. Cunard's best defense against all claimants was a case then pending in the Supreme Court involving a collision between the *Scotland* and the *Kate Dyer*, which occurred in 1866. That's right, the courts had been trying to render a final decision for twenty years. The litigation was, as always, befuddling and labyrinthine, but the crux of the action was a statute which limited a ship owner's liability to the value of the owner's vessel after the accident (and not against any of the owner's other vessels or holdings). If the defendant vessel sank, as in the case of the *Scotland* and the *Kate Dyer*, the value of the vessel after the collision was essentially nothing.

To make a modern analogy, if you owned a beat-up jalopy worth $500 and you smashed up two Cadillacs and a Rolls Royce then careened through a store front and killed two people and started a fire which burned down the block, the most you would have to pay for damages would be the value of your vehicle *after the accident.* If the vehicle was totaled, you would walk away scot-free.

How supposedly sane minds managed to foist such an absurd statute on the civilized world is beyond me. Moreover, the statute was upheld, is still on the books today, and is often invoked in order to limit liability in maritime cases involving property loss.

Unfortunately, I was unable to find any court documents leading to a resolution of the *Oregon's* suit. However, since the British Board of Inquiry absolved the *Oregon's* officers from blame, the case was likely settled out of court to the dissatisfaction of all concerned. The passengers justifiably felt that, since the British court refused to hear testimony from the passengers, and heard testimony only from the officers and crew, the inquiry was a farce intended to whitewash the truth. Certainly, no reasoned and proper verdict can be reached in any case in which only selected facts are admitted into evidence.

Nor was that the only injustice dispensed. There was bureaucratic meddling as well. The Merritt Wrecking Company stored all salvaged goods and items in a warehouse owned by Bartlett, then, as was customary, filed a salvage claim against them. The lot was sold at auction and the proceeds deposited in the name of the court to await disposition and disbursement. The Custom House collector, named Heddon, "put in a claim for duties, and when a second lot of goods were landed and libeled by Capt. Merritt, the Collector decided that the manner of waiting for the Government to get its money was too long. He decided to step in, sell the goods, deduct the duties, and turn what was left over to Capt. Merritt. When the sale took place Marshal Tate was present and informed the purchasers that they could not have the goods, as they had been seized under an attachment. The buyers didn't scare a bit, but bid off the goods and paid their money. When they sent to the storehouse for the packages, however, Marshal Tate would not give them up and the purchasers came back to Collector Hedden to complain. 'Pooh,' said the Collector. 'Go get your goods. You have paid for them, and all you want is a "nervy" man to go and seize them.' A few days later the 'nervy' man went over to Bartlett's Stores, but there he met Marshal Tate and concluded not to take the goods. So the matter still hangs fire. The Marshal has the goods, the Collector has the money, and the purchasers have only receipts." Some things never change, and the petty contrivances of minor bureaucrats seems to be one of them.

Today the wreck of the *Oregon* is a broken down hulk, and it has been for quite a number of years.

Thirty years ago--in the mid 1960's--Michael de Camp wrote a popular article about what it was like to dive on the *Oregon.* That was eighty years after the sinking. Because the decks had long since caved in and the hull had completely collapsed, he described the wreck pretty much as it exists today. The major difference between then and now is not so much in structural deterioration as in the

Porthole, deadeyes, china galore. (Photo by Mike deCamp.)

sheer abundance of artifacts which lay scattered about at the time. Loose portholes lay among great piles of china plates, bowls, and cups; and glass bottles were as numerous as weeds in a poorly kept lawn. Relics were there for the taking, and divers did not recover individual items but collected them by the bagful. This is difficult to imagine for today's divers, who see barren rusty hull plates with circular holes which were once occupied by brass portholes, and who thrill over the discovery of a broken bottle or china shard. Yet it was so.

Despite the ease with which divers used to stock their shelves with *Oregon* mementoes, and the relative paucity in the volume of finds at the present time, the *Oregon* remains one of Long Island's most interesting and most visited dive sites--in addition to which divers now find artifacts far more unique and intrinsically valuable than any which have been found before. For those patient enough to pick a spot to "work" by fanning the sand or digging in the mud come the rare rewards of items which were previously buried or hidden by hull plates and therefore not accessible to the cursory explorers of yesteryear. Passengers' luggage, trunks, and suitcases have rotted away and left behind concentrations of personal articles such as gold rings, exquisite jewelry, brass buttons, silver coins, porcelain souvenirs, and innumerable belongings of unending variety. The major cache is in the starboard bow area, in what used to be the forward holds.

The wreck is so massive that it takes many dives to become familiar with the layout, especially when visibility is limited and when particulate matter prevents much light from reaching the bottom. The best way to learn the wreck is to start on the huge triple expansion reciprocating steam engine, which dominates the site from a height of thirty feet above the sea bed. As in all screw steamers, the boilers are placed forward of the engine. Compare this area with photographs of the liner in her heyday and understand that the smokestacks vent the heat and exhaust fumes from the boilers. The nine boilers lie on their bedplates justs as they were constructed, in three rows of three. All the superstructure above the engine and boilers has collapsed down and to the sides of this portion of the wreck.

Abaft the engine (behind it) many hull plates have fallen inboard, creating a tall mound which is equivalent to a collapsed house of cards with an added dimension of elevation. It is possible to crawl under some of these hull plates into what appear to be tunnels, but you must be careful of entrapments that you cannot back out of, and of becoming snagged or entangled--or lost, if the tunnels go on for quite a way. There is a particularly long tunnel along the port side of the engine. The propeller shaft is concealed by the collapse, but by trending due aft you will come to the massive propeller which is dug into the sand. Above is a huge metal structure which looks like a pie wedge: it is the steering quadrant, which was once several decks below the weather deck.

Most of the starboard hull amidships has collapsed inboard, while most of the port hull amidships has collapsed outboard. Once you learn to recognize these features you will be able to orient yourself while exploring along the edge of the wreck, even when the engine and boilers are out of sight. If you want to dig for china the most productive area is immediately forward of the boilers, in the long, broad flat area where you can see small tunnels and cavities under the decking or plating. Work your way to the bow, then turn around and work your way back; you might see items in one direction that you missed in the other direction because your eyes are facing forward and not back under plates as you swam over them.

A section of the bow is intact and tilted to starboard. You can swim inside and dig around, but remember that as you stir up the ever-present silt you might obscure the route you took going in.

This brief overview will get you started on your exploration of the *Oregon*. Take the time to learn the general layout of the wreck before you settle down to work particular spots. Especially, if the visibility is good, take a grand tour by

swiming just inside the perimeter from a height above the bottom that allows you to see the wreckage below you clearly, and turn your head slowly from side to side so you can create a mental image of the extent of the debris field off the edge and compare it to distinguishing features within the body of the wreck. Once you have a good picture of the wreck in your mind, the dive will not be so intimidating and you will gain confidence that you can relocate previously noted sites, and can get back to the anchor line when the dive is completed. And remember that the first objective of any dive is to have fun; any finds are an added bonus.

PETER RICKMERS

Built: 1889
Previous names: None
Gross tonnage: 2,989
Type of vessel: 4-masted full-rigged ship
Builder: Russell & Company, Port Glasgow, Scotland
Owner: Rickmers Reismuhlen Rhederei & Schiffbau Act. Ges.
Port of registry: Bremerhaven, Germany
Cause of sinking: Ran aground
Location: 26786.5

Sunk: April 30, 1908
Depth: Unknown
Dimensions: 332' x 44' x 25'
Power: Sail

43754.1

The *Peter Rickmers* was a steel-hulled full-rigged sailing ship which at the time of her loss was under charter to the Standard Oil Company. She left Sandy Hook on April 30, 1908 with 120,000 cases of crude petroleum bound for Rangoon, Burma. Within hours of embarkation on her eastward passage she ran into a storm and heavy seas which set in motion a course of events that eventually resulted in the loss of the vessel and came close to causing the death of every man on board and several dozen would-be salvors.

Said Captain George Bachman, master: "At two bells in the second dog watch--7 o'clock--the weather was thick and dark. I could not see any land or any lights so I gave orders to the chief officer to call all hands to 'bout the ship. She was then heading east by north, and paid off till she was heading north by west. Suddenly, without any noise or scarcely perceptible motion, the ship stuck on the sandy bar off this coast, about a mile to the eastward of where she now lies. The seas began to pound her soon after she grounded."

The *Peter Rickmers* ran aground on a shoal off Zach's Inlet, about one and a half miles southeast of the Short Beach Life-Saving Station. Life-savers from that station discovered the wreck within ten minutes of the grounding and began a series of rescue operations which they were more than a week completing. According to Life-Saving Service records, the "keeper called for help from Zachs Inlet and Point Lookout crews, who assisted in subsequent operations; launched surfboat on the inside, went down abreast the wreck and hauled boat across the beach, but were unable to board the vessel on account of the heavy wind and sea. Life-savers kept watch all night and stood by to board the wreck as soon as wind and sea abated a little."

Thus passed the first night of the drawn-out affair. While the life-savers maintained their all-night vigil, those aboard the stranded tall ship contemplated their fate. Despite the force of the wind and the state of the sea, the vessel lay easy; the steel hull absorbed the pounding of the waves and the grating of the sand without appreciable danger of sustaining damage.

Life-Saving report: "At 1 p.m. of May 1, made another effort to launch surfboat, but could not get her off in the face of wind and sea." Shortly thereafter salvage vessels from the Merritt & Chapman Wrecking Company arrived on the scene and took charge. For the moment the situation appeared to be well in hand, as the crew of the *Peter Rickmers* were in no immediate danger, and the salvors were confident that they could pull the ship off the bar at the next high tide. Thus the operation was one of salvage rather than rescue, and the release of the ship from the shoal was confidently assured.

However, the heavily-laden windjammer could not be moved despite the power of straining engines especially geared for power. Life-Saving report:

First aground. (Courtesy of Bill Quinn.)

"At daylight, May 2, succeeded in boarding vessel, but master and crew refused to leave." Every man was needed to assist the salvors in securing towing hawsers and lightering the ship's cargo. For the next five days cases of oil were offloaded from the *Peter Rickmers* and placed on barges. Each case removed was not only a case of oil saved, but less weight pinning the hull to the sea bed. "Much had been thrown overboard, and the residents along the south shore reaped a harvest by gathering up the cans and selling the oil for what they could get."

One reporter expanded, "The wreck, which has brought hardship and misfortune for her crew, has proved a modern Eldorado for the thrifty Long Islanders who are devoting all their time to salvaging the oil. Fishing boats, motor boats, duck boats, and, in fact, anything that can float has been commandeered for the purpose of going out to Short Beach for oil. Many Freeporters are making $50 a day easily. One fisherman has already made more than $500. The large boats pick up as many as 300 to 400 cases of oil in a morning and sell them to a contractor for 50 cents a tin.

"When the wreckers were jettisoning the cargo the hardy fishermen waited alongside and pulled the cases out of the water as soon almost as they were thrown in. There was oil, oil, everywhere in Freeport. Express wagons, buggies, and even automobiles are to be seen every minute of the day going through the streets, laden with tins of oil. The windfall, in addition to the prices that are being asked for rigs or boats, should make every thrifty inhabitant independent of the Summer boarder this year."

After a week aground, extrication of the ship seemed imminent. Then storm clouds gathered on the horizon, darkening the sky and whipping the sea to a froth as another front approached. Time was now a liability. The wreckers hauled on their hawsers in a last ditch attempt to pull the *Peter Rickmers* off the bar before the coming storm arrived. When the full fury of the gale struck, there were seventy-three men aboard the stranded ship: thirty-three crew men and forty wreckers, most of the latter being employed in lightering. They must have cheered when the ship pulled free.

But no sooner was the *Peter Rickmers* pulled off the bar than the salvage tug became unmanageable in the mountainous, quartering sea. Now both vessel were at risk of foundering. The towing hawsers were cut. With nothing to hold the *Peter Rickmers* off the beach, she was slowly but inexorably blown along the shore and closer to the dune covered strand. She drifted helplessly for a mile, then bumped over the inner bar and came to rest firmly gripped by the sand about half a mile from the beach. The wrecking vessel was forced to retreat farther offshore lest she too be wrecked.

Captain Bachman ordered distress signals fired in order to alert those on land of the *Peter Rickmers's* plight. The valiant life-savers responded immediately by setting up the beach apparatus and preparing the breeches buoy. But five shots from the Lyle gun proved that the *Peter Rickmers* lay too far offshore for the messenger lines to reach. "As a strong gale was blowing and sea running very high, there was no chance of reaching her by boat." Although the life-savers were powerless to render aid, at least thirty of them stood by throughout the night in case the ship broke apart or men took to the water in a daring attempt to abandon ship before it abandoned them. The men from the Jones Beach Life-Saving Station were called in as reserves.

A call went out to the Revenue Cutter Service, which at once scrambled a crew and dispatched the *Mohawk* to the scene. She was escorted by the salvage vessel *Rescue*. Their arrival was predicted for the dark hours of the morning, but head seas slowed their progress so much that by sun up they were still many miles from the scene of pending catastrophe.

The night of May 7 was one of danger and desperation for the men trapped aboard the *Peter Rickmers*, and one which none of them would ever forget. As one reporter described it, "Huge waves are washing over the big vessel's decks and causing her to pound viciously on the sands." Seams were ripped open between the steel plates, so that little by little, then at a greatly accelerated pace, the sea seeped into the hull. The ship was battered so hard by mountainous waves that the ship shivered with the concussion and the spars and masts were snapped one after the other like cordwood.

The men onboard "kept their eyes up aloft to see if possible where the next spar was going to fall. Sometimes the fall was so sudden that they had to take their chances of being swept overboard in jumping for their lives. The crew of the *Rickmers* wore their cork life jackets. . . . The forty men from the Chapman & Merritt Company wore their oilskins and sea boots. The sea on all sides of the wreck was covered with floating cases of the oil that had been jettisoned in the daytime."

Life-Saving report: "At daylight, May 8, as the ship had swung broadside to the beach, making a little lee, a picked crew from the four stations named above

Broken masts. (Courtesy of Bill Quinn.)

manned surfboat and in 3 trips landed the *Rickmer's* crew of 33 safely. The wreckers--40 men--who were on the ship launched their surfboats, which had previously been hoisted to the *Rickmer's* davits, and landed without mishap while life-savers were landing crew."

As usual, the official report lacked the graphic detail which appeared in the newspapers the following day. "After facing death in darkness and cold for ten hours, amid the crash of falling spars, the shrieking of a northeast gale, and the dull pounding of the green seas as they swept the vessel fore and aft, seventy-three men left the wreck of the four-masted German sailing ship *Peter Rickmers* at daybreak yesterday and landed on Short Beach, L.I. Thirty-three were members of the crew. The rest were men in the employ of the Merritt & Chapman Wrecking Company, who had been working on the stranded ship since Sunday night trying to salvage her cargo.

"The wrecking crew left the ship in their own boats. The crew were taken ashore in three trips by the surfboat of the Short Beach Station, steered by Capt. Steven Austin of the Point Lookout Station. Capt. George Bachman, skipper of the ill-fated ship, was the last to leave her. He made a pathetic figure as he turned to look once more at the handsome square rigger before the lifeboat sailors helped him from the surfboat to shore.

"The *Peter Rickmers*, with her lofty masts, except her lower masts and jigger topmast, gone by the board, with her yards hanging in confusion from the caps of the masthead, and her sails hanging loosely, and the German ensign flying at half-mast, is still fast on the beach. She seems likely to stay there till she goes to pieces.

"The wreck lies portside broad on the beach, the vessel's stern hard and fast in the sand, and her graceful clipper bow rising clear out of the water, about 500 feet from shore. Yesterday morning she showed plainly the havoc that had been made by the heavy seas of the preceding forty-eight hours. Her bulwarks on the starboard side had been swept clean away fore and aft, and there was not a deck-house in any part of the ship that had not been damaged by the falling spars. These had pierced the deck as if the latter had been made of paper as they fell from aloft in the night. It was only by great good luck and the exercise of the utmost vigilance that the men on board were not killed by the yards when they were carried away in the gale.

"The foretop gallant mast fell at 9:30 o'clock on Thursday night, crashing clean through the pilothouse, the galley beneath, and through the main deck, where it stuck fast. The maintopmast followed, piercing the deck over the sail-room, where the wrecking crew were sheltered. The bridges, fore and aft and athwartships, were all carried away, and the doors of the deckhouses smashed in.

"Yesterday morning the green seas still poured over the ship continuously with a heavy, sullen sound. Occasionally the life savers on the beach to-day could hear the frantic squealing of the three pigs which had been left on board in their pen on the after part of the galley, the only living things on the deserted ship that had sailed proudly out of the harbor of New York with all her canvas spread to the breeze just a week ago. 'Tibs,' the ship's black-and-white kitten, was carried ashore by one of the sailors. 'Nero,' the skipper's black retriever, sprang into the sea and swam ashore after he had seen his master safely into the surf boat.

"The sailors left their ship 'all standing,' in nautical parlance; that is, they had their oilskins, sea boots, and sou'westers on, but that was all they saved of their effects. The fo'c'sle, which was after under the poopdeck of the *Rickmers*, was full of water, and it was impossible to get at anything in or under the bunks. The messroom and cabins of the Captain and officers amidships were in the same condition. There was not a house or a locker on deck that was not full of water, and there were twenty feet of water in the hold. According to the Captain and the wrecking crew, the ship has been driven half a mile further in toward shore by the fury of the gale. Had she not been a stanch, well-constructed iron ship she would have gone to pieces long ago under the heavy, incessant pounding she received."

Captain Bachman believed that most of the water in the windjammer's hold had poured in through the open hatches, and not through broken seams. He maintained his belief that the hull was largely sound and that the *Peter Rickmers* could still be salvaged. However, she was now so high up on the beach that she was out of reach of wrecking vessels and lighters.

On May 19 it was reported in marine circles that "the big vessel was found to be on fire. Large quantities of oil were still believed to be in the vessel's hold and this no doubt would be destroyed. The origin of the fire was unknown." A local reporter elaborated, writing that the *Peter Rickmers*, "with 125,000 cases of oil as a cargo, took fire this afternoon and is likely to burn for many days. There were still 100,000 cases of oil on board. It is not known how the fire originated, but there is a theory that the oystermen set fire to the ship as the leaking oil was a menace to the oysters and clams along shore."

The Life-Saving Service report stated simply, "The *Rickmers* later went to pieces and became a total loss."

If anything remains today of the majestic tall-masted ship, it undoubtedly lies buried in the ever-shifting sands. The steel hull would be an easy target to locate with a magnetometer, or perhaps even with a hand-held metal detector. There is history under the surf.

PRINCESS ANNE

Built: 1897
Previous names: None
Gross tonnage: 3,629
Type of vessel: Excursion steamer
Builder: Delaware River Iron Works, Chester, Pennsylvania
Owner: Old Dominion Steam Ship Company
Port of registry: New York, NY
Cause of sinking: Ran aground
Location: 26968.3

Sunk: February 6, 1920
Depth: 20 feet
Dimensions: 350' x 42' x 27'
Power: Coal-fired steam

43758.1

The *Princess Anne* was a three-decked excursion steamer which transported passengers and freight between New York City and Norfolk, Virginia. When she left Norfolk on what proved to be her final voyage, she had on board one hundred four people: seventy-two crew and thirty-two passengers. This was February 4, 1920.

Captain Frank Seay, master of the *Princess Anne*, later related the circumstances leading up the stranding of his ship at the entrance to New York harbor. "We left Norfolk at 5 o'clock Tuesday afternoon on a trip which ordinarily takes nineteen hours. On the first day out we ran into the storm, which was so intense that observations were impossible and we had to go on dead reckoning. During the buffeting about of the vessel on Wednesday I was thrown from the ladder as I started up to the bridge and injured my knee. The first mate was on the bridge when the *Princess Anne* went aground. The sleet and snow came down so heavy that we missed the sea buoy which would have guided us into Ambrose Channel,

In regal days. (Courtesy of The Mariners Museum, Newport News, Virginia.)

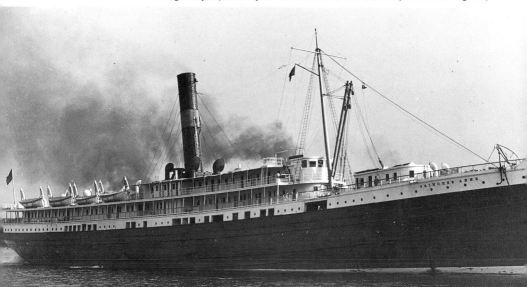

and before we knew it we were hard aground off Rockaway Point." The time was 2:30 Thursday morning: thirty-five and a half hours after departure.

A ship which runs aground in a fog may not be in serious trouble, as the weather is generally mild; but one which runs aground during a storm is in imminent danger of being pounded to pieces before salvage vessels can effect her release. The storm in which the *Princess Anne* found herself was not moderating, but worsening. Nevertheless, there was no alarm aboard the stranded steamer as the seas were not overly severe. Furthermore, the direction of the wind changed from northeast to northwest, which afforded some protection from the land.

Of more immediate concern was the extreme cold. "Several inbound steamships became jammed in the ice and many craft moored in the lower bay and outskirts of the harbor were driven ashore." The storm then raging was called the worst in twenty years. Long Island Sound looked like the Arctic Sea. Half a dozen steamships were frozen fast in the ice, including the *Maine*, which is covered elsewhere in this volume.

The situation on land was no better. The storm "did great damage to the Long Island shore in the vicinity of Rockaway and Long Beach. The Knickerbocker Hotel, Chase Avenue, Rockaway Beach, battered down by the waves on Thursday, was swept in to the sea yesterday morning. The beach bungalows on the Boulevard, off Hammel Avenue, which contained forty apartments, also were pounded to pieces and washed away. Thirty-six boats tied up on the bay side of Rockaway Point were carried away by the high tide." It was also reported that "the tide carried away portions of the boardwalk at Coney Island and wrecked some pavilions. Hundreds of rowboats at Sheepshead Bay were carried away or sunk at their moorings. Some of the waves were twenty to twenty-five feet high."

The New Jersey coast was particularly hard hit, with high tides sweeping over bulkheads, flooding roads and basements, and washing away sea walls, boardwalks, and cottages. The *George R. Skolfield* was driven ashore near Sea

In war paint. (Courtesy of The Mariners Museum, Newport News, Virginia.)

Isle City (for particulars of that rescue operation, see *Shipwrecks of New Jersey*, by this author).

While there was no immediate peril to life on the *Princess Anne*, neither could anyone be taken off the ship because the same thick snow which was responsible for her stranding prevented Coast Guard craft from rendering aid. "It was impossible for the Coast Guard to get to Rockaway Point by land or sea." Coast Guard Captain Joseph Meade "took one of the lifeboats from Arverne on a truck drawn by mules, and tried to get near enough to the water to make a launching. The snow and ice were four to six feet deep, and in some places the lead mules sunk in the snow to their ears and had difficulty in getting out again. Finally they refused to proceed, and the crew and newspaper men hauled the boat four and a half miles. They reached a spot two miles from the *Princess Anne* and got the boat afloat, but the crew could not get near the vessel because of the ice. The Coast Guard tried to get to Rockaway Point from the shore over the hills, but its members were blocked by gullies where the snow was eight to ten feet deep.

"Captain William Tucker of Coast Guard Station No. 92, also tried to get to the *Princess Anne* with a crew of eighteen men in his lifeboat but was unsuccessful. The snow fell heavily all day and at times the stranded craft was blotted from the sight of those on shore and officers of the *Manhattan*. The Police boat *Patrol* also made a trip out in the afternoon with the object of getting some pictures of the steamship on the sandbank and the seas pounding over her."

Aboard the *Princess Anne* some of the passengers were seasick. Their misery increased dramatically a few hours after grounding when the hull, which worked unceasingly on the shoal, split some seams and let the sea into the machinery spaces, with dire results. The last of some thirty messages received from Captain Seay succinctly outlined the gravity of situation: "Steamship's dynamo will not last much longer; after part of aerial down, mast broken, wires heavily coated with ice; half of bank of batteries gone and out of commission; will not be able to communicate much longer."

Shortly thereafter the dynamo room flooded completely and all power was lost. Without electricity there were no more wireless transmissions, no lights, no heat, and no way to prepare or heat food. Everyone donned extra clothing, and the people were reduced to eating hardtack and cold meals. That night it was cold, dark, and uncomfortable aboard the stranded steamer, but, human spirit being what it is under conditions of adversity, most people made do with what they had. "With a few oil lanterns shedding a faint light in the cabins they danced and sang, and when not doing that watched a continuous crap game in which the colored waiters and some of the passengers participated."

By the next day the seas had diminished to the point where boarding the stranded steamer appeared practical with a fair degree of safety. At least a dozen craft of all kinds surrounded the *Princess Anne*. Several tugs stood by with towing hawsers coiled and ready for deployment, and a Coast Guard cutter and two police launches maintained stations nearby. Captain Seay signaled that he preferred to wait until later in the day before commencing the disembarkation of the passengers (under the circumstances it can hardly be called a rescue) but Coast

Guard officers thought otherwise.

With Captain Meade in overall charge, the police launch *Patrol* nudged her padded side against the hull of the large steamer and took off the first boat load of passengers, all of whom wore life preservers in case they slipped on the ice-covered ladder and fell into the sea. "Three other trips were made by the launch and a coast guard cutter to the vessel without incident. On the fourth and last trip the launch towed in a lifeboat of the *Princess Anne*, which held nine members of the crew."

All told, sixty people were taken off the steamer: the thirty-two passengers and twenty-eight of the crew. "The members of the crew who had been permitted to leave were waiters and extra help and were not needed on board." Also removed was Captain Seay, who needed medical attention for his injured knee, and who was by that time threatened with pneumonia; he soon became delirious "and three physicians were called in consultation." One of the passengers, Mr. A.J. Pasternac, suffered from exposure and developed influenza.

For "admirable and efficient service," Mayor Hylan sent a congratulatory letter to Police Commissioner Enright, praising the harbor police who took part in the removal of the passengers and crew, with special commendations for Acting Captain Hallock of the *Patrol* and Lieutenant Dobert of Police Launch No. 6.

Wrecking vessels remained in the vicinity of the *Princess Anne* but were prevented by heavy seas from approaching close enough to initiate salvage operations. By this time No. 2 hold was filled with water to a depth of thirteen feet, spoiling the cargo of lettuce. By February 9 the ship was "flooded from stem to stern below the main deck, which is still above the sea." High hopes were held that the cargo could be removed, the hull pumped out, and the ship refloated.

Those hopes were abandoned that night. As waves continued to pummel the hull and wash away the supporting sand, the *Princess Anne* slowly broke apart. The crew "were thrown into a panic by the snapping of the steel plates of the hull, which they said sounded like machine-gun fire." First Officer C.W. Barker, who was in command in the absence of Captain Seay, "was compelled to draw his pistol to quiet them. The men were in the cabin trying to keep warm, as the fires were out, when suddenly the steamer shook from stem to stern, the vibration being accompanied by a series of loud noises. The crew ran to the deck, many of them going to the lifeboats, which they attempted to launch. Barker and William Heath, second officer, did their best to calm the panic-stricken sailors, and when they found their orders were being disobeyed drew their pistols. This action checked the men and they gathered into the cabin, where the two officers told them they were in no immediate danger. Barker said the snapping of the plates continued until midnight, when there was a two-foot break across the vessel just forward of the engine room.

"As soon as morning came Barker displayed the ship's flag upside down as a signal that immediate assistance was needed. The Coast Guard crew of Station 91, at Rockaway Point, saw the signal and immediately went out to the *Princess Anne* in a lifeboat. The crew, whose fears had been allayed with the coming of the day, were inclined to be stubborn and did not want to leave the ship unless their baggage was carried with them. The coast guards could not take the baggage and returned to the beach."

Conditions worsened aboard the stranded steamer, and soon the crew realized the folly of their inaction. Then came the power sloop *Stella C*, a fishing vessel whose captain, George Carman, recognized the upside down flag as a signal of distress. "He steered as close as the rough sea would permit and offered to take the crew ashore." This time there was no refusal. "It took him nearly an hour to manoeuver his boat alongside the stern of the vessel. Although licensed to carry only fifteen passengers, Capt. Carman found he had twenty-five men on board his sloop almost immediately. Most of the crew did not wait to climb down the rope ladder which had been let over the side of the *Princess Anne*, but jumped instead. Moreover, the men bent on taking their baggage with them were dropping trunks and hand baggage into the sloop. Capt. Carman had to issue sharp orders to prevent another wreck.

"The crew were taken to Lundy's Pier, in Sheepshead Bay, and their rescuer returned to the steamer for the remaining twenty. Barker and Heath decided to remain on board to protect the cargo, valued at $500,000."

The *Patrol* arrived at noon. On board were "J.J. Brown, general passenger agent of the Old Dominion Line, Captain Peter Nielson, former commander of the *Princess Anne*, and Dr. Edward L. Gainsburgh, medical examiner of the Railroad Administration," whose presence was anticlimactic in light of the recent abandonment by the crew, along with agents of the Merritt & Chapman Wrecking Company who surveyed the situation. After a thorough inspection they thought that some of the floating cargo might be salvaged, but hopes of saving the ship were virtually abandoned. Old Dominion Line officials "sent a wireless message to E.R. Richardson, Federal Manager of coastwise ships, requesting that a guard vessel be sent to prevent pillaging of the ship's cargo. The coast guards have arranged to take Barker and Heath off the ship if it becomes necessary."

The *Princess Anne* slowly listed to starboard as the sand was washed out from under her. She sank lower each succeeding day until her starboard gunwale dipped beneath the level of the sea. Eventually, after her upper works were battered to pieces by the waves, she was broken up where she lay. Today the wreck is little more and a lot less than a battered, scattered debris field, with potential interest only for those who are willing to fan away the sand in order to see what lies beneath.

Courtesy of Sharon Reese.

RODA

Built: 1897
Previous names: None
Gross tonnage: 2,516
Type of vessel: Freighter
Builder: A. McMillan & Son, Ltd., Dumbarton, Scotland
Owner: English & American Shipping Company, Ltd.
Port of registry: London, England
Cause of sinking: Ran aground
Location: 26740.4

Sunk: February 13, 1908
Depth: 25 feet
Dimensions: 315' x 44' x 20'
Power: Coal-fired steam

43757.2

The *Roda* was on a routine voyage from Huelva, Spain to New York City when she lost her way in a thick fog and ran aground three-quarters of a mile southeast of the Jones Beach Life-Saving Station, on February 13, 1908. She was soon discovered by the beach patrol, and with their usual aplomb and efficiency the life-savers quickly launched a boat through the surf and boarded the stranded steamer, and offered to take the crew ashore.

As the weather was mild and the seas smooth, Captain W.J. Beavan, master of the *Roda*, elected to keep his crew aboard in hopes that the ship could be pulled off the bar at the next high tide. He gave instructions for the life-savers to wire New York for wrecking vessels, which they did.

The Life-Saving report described subsequent events with that service's customary understatement which is so frustrating to historians who relish in

A contemporary postcard.

divulging details. "At 7 a.m. on the 14th, assisted by Zachs Inlet crew, again boarded her and her crew again refused to leave; sent dispatches to her owners. 1:30 a.m. of the 15th, heavy weather coming on, steamer sounded distress signals, life-savers boarded her and landed 12 men the first trip, 8 the second, and 3 the third. Master and 2 officers refused to leave the vessel at this time. Those who were landed were sheltered and fed at the station and given dry clothing from the W.N.R.A. supply where needed." (W.N.R.A. stands for Women's National Relief Association.)

Because the *Roda* was deeply laden with ore (one report states copper, another iron) she was firmly pinned to the sandy bottom. A long span of good weather was needed in order to offload the cargo onto lighters, or at least to throw it overboard. Only then could salvage vessels hope to pull the freighter off the bar. Captain Beavan knew this better than anyone; thus his reluctance to yield command. But the *Roda* was not destined to be saved.

Life-Saving report: "Storm increasing, at 11 a.m. master signaled for help and, assisted by Zachs Inlet crew, surfboat was launched and the 3 officers landed, made comfortable at station and supplied with dry clothing. The vessel became a total loss. Life-saving crews received valuable assistance in their operations from 15 wreckers who were sheltered at the station. Jones Beach station supplied shipwrecked crew and wreckers shelter and a total of 348 meals."

Efforts to salvage the *Roda* were by no means abandoned. On the 18th it was reported that "a barge was alongside and the tug *Wm E Chapman* was anchored offshore to render assistance." By then enough water had leaked or splashed into the hull to fill it to a depth of twelve feet. "Wreckers had been at work on the steamer for several days, but their efforts had been hampered by high seas and bad weather. A report from Jones Beach on Feb 21 said that the "str *Roda* had settled three feet in the sand and an examination that morning found her broken in two amidships."

The estimated value of the *Roda* was $80,000, of her cargo $22,680. She was sold on March 4 "for $735 and her cargo of copper ore for $200." Further salvage operations went unrecorded.

Captain Beavan and his crew were moved to write a letter of acknowledgment. "Gentlemen: We, the undersigned, members of the crew of the British steamship *Roda*, now stranded on Jones Beach, Long Island, beg to express our appreciation of the gallant conduct of the boat's crew employed in rescuing us from the above-named vessel on the morning of the 15th of February, 1908, in the very heavy weather and under exceptional circumstances. We must say that your conduct on this occasion is worthy of the greatest praise, and the manner in which the rescue was carried out worthy of American seamen.

"We also thank you for your kindness and hospitality extended to us while ashore in the life-saving station, and assure you we will never forget same.

"We trust you will accept this, our humble way of expressing our appreciation, in the spirit in which it is given."

For many years the wreck of the *Roda* was visible above the surface of the sea. Today her rusted remains lie barely submerged in 25 feet of water, looking more like an underwater junk yard than the ship she once was. Boaters beware of impaling your hull on sharp metal beams, and divers are cautioned to be extra careful when the surge is strong. There is enough vertical relief to funnel water through siphons which create ripping currents when the state of the sea is high. Calm ocean conditions must prevail before attempting to dive this man-made reef.

The structure provides a substrate for barnacles, mussels, anemones, and sponges, with all of which the wreck is thickly overgrown. Bottom dwelling fish such as sea bass, tautog, fluke, and flounder abound. Lobsters often find shelter under collapsed hull plates. And the smaller holes are a haven for crabs. The green rocks which litter the bottom are part of the cargo of copper ore; they make nice paperweights.

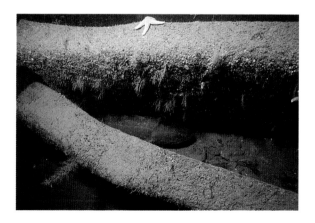

SOMMERSTAD

Built: 1906
Previous names: None
Gross tonnage: 3,875
Type of vessel: Freighter
Builder: R. Stephenson & Company, Ltd., Newcastle, England
Owner: A.F. Klaveness & Company
Port of registry: Christiania, Norway
Cause of sinking: Torpedoed by *U-117*
Location: 26425.2

Sunk: August 12, 1918
Depth: 170 feet
Dimensions: 340' x 47' x 27'
Power: Coal-fired steam

43456.5

By the summer of 1918 the United States was deeply embroiled in the war "over there." Massive ship and troop movements to the European front left the American mainland relatively unprotected from Axis onslaught. When the Kaiser found himself defending his homeland against Uncle Sam's military incursion, he retaliated by dispatching a small flotilla of U-boats westward. Half a dozen enemy submarines arrived off the east coast one at a time, "passing the torch" as it were from one to the other with just enough overlap to keep Allied naval intelligence guessing about how many U-boats were operating concurrently in local waters. The U-boats encountered little resistance from the depleted home fleet.

The primary goal of the U-boat offensive against the States was to attack merchant shipping in order to cut the flow of arms, food, and supplies with which the Allied armies at the front were being reinforced. In this the campaign was partially successful. During a six month spree--from May to October--U-boats were responsible for the loss of several hundred ocean-going vessels in Yankee waters. To be sure, many of these were fishing boats of little consequence in the grand scheme of war and world domination. But some were large ships: tankers, freighters, even a liner and an armored cruiser. (See *USS San Diego: the Last Armored Cruiser*, by this author.)

The second goal was to demoralize the citizenry and intimidate the public into backing out of a war which might prove to be too expensive to continue to wage. In this Germany failed miserably, for it misconceived the strength and virtue of American psychology. In order to achieve the Kaiser's nefarious objectives, U-boats captured merchant seaman and kept them as prisoners of war, torpedoed ships without warning and with substantial loss of life, laid mines in the shipping lanes, and in one instance lobbed shells on American soil--for the first time in over a century, when the U.S. and the U.K. fought the War of 1812. These depredations proved counterproductive, and served instead to instill civic pride, foment patriotism to a fever pitch, and incense the demand for just retribution: the foreign aggressors must be vanquished at all costs.

In light of the forgoing, it is ironic that when the *Sommerstad* (sometimes

misspelled *Sommerstadt*) was chosen as a target for a German torpedo, the freighter was registered to a nation which was not a participant in the war and was therefore protected by the laws of neutrality. This was not Germany's first aggressive act against non-belligerents, nor was it the last.

At the time of her loss, the Norwegian freighter *Sommerstad* was making a routine passage from Bergen, Norway to New York City. She crossed the North Atlantic along the great circle route, stopped briefly at Halifax, Nova Scotia, then continued south and west toward her intended destination, where she expected to fill her holds with corn, a commodity much needed by the people of Norway. August 12 found her some twenty-five miles southeast of Fire Island: well outside the "danger zone" or "blockade zone" proclaimed by Germany, and therefore not fair game for unrestricted submarine warfare. The *Sommerstad* was traveling in water ballast, which means that she carried no cargo and that her deep tanks were filled with sea water in order to provide proper ballast.

Unknown to the thirty-one men aboard the *Sommerstad*, their ship was being stalked by Kapitanleutnant Otto Droscher in the *U-117*. The U-boat had already sunk several ships since its arrival in American waters, and had laid mine fields off the coasts of New Jersey and Maryland. The well-seasoned crew manned their action stations, awaiting orders, while Droscher took sightings through his periscope despite prevailing fog.

Droscher wrote in his log with characteristic military brevity (translated): "Fog has lifted slightly -- attacked submerged. Steamer has a gun on the stern. <u>Torpedo shot -- Hit</u>. Tube III, depth setting 2 m, firing range 400 m (G6AV & Torp.). Steamer sinks quickly. Size estimated at 3000 tons. Course 300°, 9 knots, bound for New York. Lifeboats disappear from sight in the thickening fog." (Droscher's observation notwithstanding, the *Sommerstad* carried no gun.)

If the *Sommerstad* had gone down with all hands, the above annotation is the only account that would be available to historians today. Fortunately, there were no fatalities on the Norwegian ship, and the entire crew was interrogated after being landed in the States.

Captain George Hansen, master of the *Sommerstad*, gave the most complete description of the morning's events (ellipses denote the interrogator's questions): "A little after eight o'clock I came out on the bridge, where my chief officer and second officer were at that time. I went over to the port side of the bridge and looked out, and I thought I saw something in the water. I went and took the glasses, but I could not make out what it was. I stood for a few minutes looking through the glasses, and then saw a torpedo coming along a little aft from abeam of the ship. . . . As soon as I saw the torpedo I stopped the vessel, and ordered the engines reversed and full speed astern. The torpedo went under the vessel, barely missing it, a little on the fore part of the bridge, and came up on the other side. . . . I walked across to the other side [of the bridge] and I then gave orders for full speed ahead. . . . When I saw the torpedo start to swerve around I gave orders for full speed astern; and when it passed the bow it made two turns, making a complete circle, and then struck our vessel aft on the port side exactly between the third and fourth hold right at the bulkhead."

From Captain Hansen's testimony it appears that the torpedo was fired accurately but that it traveled too deep for the *Sommerstad's* draft--given as seven feet--then, perhaps having its gyroscope disturbed by the wash during the near miss, it made a complete circle counterclockwise around the bow of the ship and came back for another try at a shallower depth, this time being successful in its mission. The captain's account was corroborated by Chief Officer Johan Albert Haltlid, Second Officer Ludwig Nilson, Fireman Halden Helvorsen, Able Bodied Seaman Charles Nelsen, and Mess Boy Sverre Svang.

As soon as Able Bodied Seaman Eyvind Balstad Olsen saw the torpedo pass under the hull, and before it began its errant curve, he warned the men below decks and shouted for them to make for the lifeboats. "I thought the submarine might appear and shell us."

Down below in the engine room Chief Engineer Benedix Andersen ran around like a one-armed paperhanger trying to follow telegraph orders from the bridge. "The signal was turned to full speed astern, and I tried to get the engine to go full speed astern, but before I could do it, the signal was full speed ahead, and then it was changed to full speed astern again. I then got it to full speed astern, 4 or 5 revolutions, and then it was full speed ahead again. I got it working full speed ahead and immediately after that the explosion happened with the engine working full speed ahead. . . . The water came through the tunnel hatch, and when I saw the water come through I understood the ship had been torpedoed and was starting to sink. . . . The water came with great force through the tunnel hatch, and filled up the engine room. The water came up to my knees, and I was afraid to stop any longer. I tried to stop the engine and got it working dead slow ahead, but I didn't have time to stop it. I then went up the ladder and the water came from the deck down into the engine room. When I came on deck the boat was ready to go away and I jumped right into it."

Captain Hansen stated, "Several of the watch on deck were knocked down by the force of the explosion, and the cook was blown clean out of the galley." He quickly parroted the seaman's panicked proclamation and gave the official order to abandon ship. All hands who had not already done so went immediately for the boats. It was fortunate that they did, for the *Sommerstad* went down by the stern two or three minutes after the torpedo struck.

Nelsen described his experiences: "I then run to the boat deck, and cut the tackles that keeps the boats in. This permitted the boats to swing out; then I run to the forward boat fall, and lowered the boat half way out, and then I could not lower them any further because the ropes were fouled, and I made my end fast. . . . I then run down to the midship's deck; by this time the ship was sinking, and when it got close to the water, we cut both tackles; this permitted the small boats to leave the vessel, and I was left on board. . . . Then I run forward, and when I got down to the forward deck, the head of the ship was rising out of the water, and then I run up on top of the engine room skylight, and tried to get hold of the tackle to get down to the boats; then an explosion started while I was on top of the skylight of the engine room, and had to leave there and go to the midship's deck; then I jumped into the water, and swam to the boat."

As the men pulled at the oars they spotted a periscope cleaving the calm surface of the sea; it dipped beneath the ripples and did not reappear. The freighter's bow was still visible when last seen before being enveloped in fog. Then the men were alone in the broad, blue Atlantic, with nothing to comfort them but their thoughts.

Said Second Officer Nilson to his interrogator, "I have been torpedoed two times before." This was an extraordinary statement for a citizen of a neutral country to make. Nor was he the only crew member to have been torpedoed previously.

The *Sommerstad* was not equipped with wireless, and even if it had there had been no time to transmit an SOS. This meant that no one with any regard for the survival of the crew knew of their plight, and that their best prospect for rescue was to row toward land. For nine and a half hours they plied the oars. Captain Hansen: "Toward sundown we heard Fire Island's siren, and made directly for the shore. Soon afterward we were sighted by the naval patrol vessel which brought us to this city [New York]. The men were tired with rowing all day, and were taken care of for the night on the patrol boat."

The rescue vessel was the USS *Aramis* (SP-416). The men were later taken to the Norwegian Sailor's Home in Brooklyn, where they received food and lodging and the kind care of people from their own country.

The Norwegian Minister was outraged. The *Sommerstad* was the twelfth Norwegian vessel sunk by U-boats off the American coast. And this does not count the number of Norwegian vessels deliberately sunk by U-boats in other parts of the world. Germany's continued disregard for neutral rights was intolerable, especially as it came on the heels of a proclamation from Berlin which guaranteed safe conduct for Norwegian vessels "running outside the blockade zone with imports to Norway."

Quoted one official document, "The Norwegian Minister, who has applied to the German department of foreign affairs on account of the sinking of the steamer *Sommerstad* has been assured that the German government does not at all intend to prevent Norway's import of food supplies outside the stop-zone and that Norway will be righted as much as possible if the steamer, contrary to expectations, has been torpedoed without any warning." German assurances, of course, were not worth the paper they were printed on, unless the assurances were hostile.

After sinking a number of other vessels, the *U-117* returned safely to Germany. It stayed inactive for the short time remaining before the Armistice was signed, on November 11, 1918. Under the terms of surrender, Germany was divested of its entire fleet of warships and U-boats. Most of the U-boats were scuttled in water deep enough to preclude salvage, but some were kept afloat by Allied command so that submarine experts could disassemble them and examine their intricate mechanisms. Six U-boats crossed the Atlantic with U.S. Navy crews at the controls; the *U-117* was one of the six.

When the Navy completed its studies, the *U-117* went on another cruise off the eastern seaboard. This time, instead of spreading death and destruction, it toured American ports as part of the Victory Loan Campaign. Thousands of curious citizens were invited to walk its decks and explore its inner workings--and asked to buy bonds to help float the country out of its war debt.

In July 1921, the *U-117* was towed to a site off the Virginia coast and sunk as part of a bombing test conducted by Brigadier General Billy Mitchell. For more details see *Shipwrecks of Virginia*, by this author. (Since the publication of that book the wreck of the *U-117* was discovered and identified by a team of wreck divers, one of whom was this author.)

The wreck of the *Sommerstad* is more popularly known as the Virginia, a name given to it before its identity became generally known. The wreck appears to have been the object of a major salvage operation: it looks as if a great amount of explosives was used to blow apart the hull, leaving it flattened and spread out over a broad area. Furthermore, the triple expansion steam engine is missing: there is an obvious empty space where the engine should sit, between the boilers and the end of the propeller shaft.

The depth to the bottom is 170 feet. Occasional structural members stick up eight or ten feet, but for the most part the relief is five feet or less, especially around the perimeter of the wreck where beams and hull plates yield to a white sandy bottom. Visibility is usually superb: a bright 40 to 50 feet with high reflectivity off the sand.

Although the wreck is largely demolished, this condition has the advantage of exposing items of interest which are often unseen or inaccessible due to their location deep within the hull. Orientation may be difficult because the wreck is so broken up, so divers should be prepared to do a remote decompression if they cannot find the way back to the anchor line.

The greatest hazard on this site is monofilament. The wreck is fished heavily for cod and pollock; because these fish are large, high pound-test line is used to catch them. So many hooks have snagged in the debris throughout the years that fishing line lies across the wreck like a single immense, interconnected net; viewed from above, one gets the impression that a gigantic spider spun a web of thick strands horizontally across the wreck. Large lobsters proliferate.

One of many sisters. (Courtesy of the Naval Historical Center.)

SUB CHASER 209

Built: 1918	Sunk: August 27, 1918
Previous names: None	Depth: Unknown
Gross tonnage: 85	Dimensions: 110' x 14' x 5'
Type of vessel: Submarine Chaser	Power: Three gasoline engines
Builder: Mathis Yacht Building Company, Camden, New Jersey	
Owner: U.S. Navy	Official designation: SC-209
Cause of sinking: Accidentally shelled by SS *Felix Taussig*	
Location: 40° 08' North	73° 12' West

When it became obvious to America that her participation in the war in Europe was inevitable, one way of preparing for that eventuality was the passage of a Naval bill which allowed for increased warship construction. In addition to capital ships, the Navy needed small and maneuverable escort vessels--such as destroyers--as well as a craft specially suited to take the offensive against Germany's greatest waterborne threat, the U-boat. German submarines took an enormous toll of Allied shipping in the eastern Atlantic, and in 1915 sank five Allied merchantmen in international waters off the coast of Massachusetts. Thus the Navy maintained no illusions about what kind of craft was needed to send to the front and to protect the home waters.

The design for a suitable submarine chaser was refined to a vessel with a wooden hull whose overall length was 110 feet, and which could reach a speed of 18 knots; it was powered by three gasoline engines each turning its own pro-peller. These sub chasers were mass produced by numerous small yards which ordinarily built private yachts and fishing boats. By war's end 440 were com-pleted and placed in service in both the American and French navies. In addition to two machine guns, they were armed with either a 6-pounder or a 3-inch deck gun. Submerged listening tubes could detect the sound of a U-boat's motors and get a bearing on its direction. A sub chaser's normal complement consisted of two officers and twenty-four crew men.

So successful proved the sub chaser that the model was brought back during World War Two and another thousand or so were built, the only major difference being the addition of more sophisticated listening devices.

Sub chasers were not given names. Each had a number and that number was painted on the bows. In Naval shorthand "submarine chaser" was abbreviated

"S.C." and was often written without punctuation. Sometimes the designation was spelled out, such as "submarine chaser *No. 209*". All these variations were accepted and were used in official correspondence, apparently dependent solely upon the whim of the writer.

Sub Chaser 209 was received by the Navy on October 22, 1917. Her acceptance was only preliminary because her auxiliary generator had a cracked flywheel. During the winter this was repaired, and the vessel was armed and stocked with ammunition. She was commissioned in March 1918. In command was Lieutenant (JG) Henry Bowes; the executive officer was Ensign George Randolph.

In May the first of the dreaded U-boats arrived off the American coast, and for the next six months as it and its inhuman brethren wreaked havoc among the merchant fleet the Navy was hard pressed to protect coastal shipping. Lookouts scanned the horizon for that familiar low-lying silhouette topped by a slender conning tower, and Naval gunners kept their fingers on the triggers of their weapons, ready at a moment's notice to pound the enemy to pieces before it could launch a deadly torpedo.

This was the state of alertness aboard the freighter *Felix Taussig* on the night of August 26, after the long Atlantic crossing from Bordeaux. Furthermore, tension mounted as the freighter neared the American coast because she encoun-

Another sister. (Courtesy of the Naval Historical Center.)

tered an unidentified steamship whose blinker light flashed the letters "T.N.T." at ten minute intervals. Captain Wade, master of the *Felix Taussig*, believed the signals "may have been meant for enemy submarines which might have been in the vicinity." Captain Wade passed the word among his crew to be especially alert, especially as the light fog would aid the enemy in disguise.

A few hours later, at 2:30 a.m., with the blinking signals still visible astern, a lookout shouted that an object resembling a submarine lay off the port beam a mere two hundred feet away. Captain Wade sounded the general alarm. The gun crews were already at their stations and were ready for action. The unidentified vessel showed no lights in the dark. It was traveling in the same direction as the *Felix Taussig*, then passed with superior speed and crossed the freighter's bow. The order was given to commence firing.

The freighter's forward 3-inch gun fired at once, but the shell went wide of its mark. A moment later the after 4-inch gun fired, and also missed the target. Then the forward gun scored a hit, then another miss. Suddenly, the target vessel flashed a red signal light. Captain Wade gave the order to cease firing, but before the order reached the forward gun crew another shell was expended and scored a direct and devastating hit which resulted in a violent explosion and which set the vessel afire. Flames fanned for the sky for only three minutes before the vessel slipped smoking beneath the waves.

A submarine hunting group led by the U.S. destroyer *Patterson* (DD-36) was operating in the vicinity. Eleven sub chasers were part of the group. One of these, *SC-188*, drove in to the scene of the recent action and found the sea littered with bodies and floating debris--not from a German U-boat but from a sister sub chaser, the *SC-209*. The profile of a sub chaser charging fast through the water was unfortunately similar to that of a U-boat, with the wheel house too easily mistaken for a conning tower.

The carnage on the *SC-209* was awful. Both officers and fifteen men were killed outright, and one man later died from his injuries aboard the U.S. hospital ship *Comfort* (AH-3). Four other men were severely wounded by shrapnel. One crew man, Claude Kalmey, at the risk of his own life, pulled two injured men from the burning wreckage of the wheel house and dragged them to safety, one to the bow and the other to the stern; unfortunately, both later died. In the few short minutes that the sub chaser remained on the surface after the terrible shelling, the four who were uninjured managed to save the four wounded men by helping them overboard and by supporting them with life preservers and floating wreckage. George Wiegand and Claude Wilde kept Thomas Haran's head out of the water. Haran, who was severely wounded, shouted, "I can't make it. Let me go. Look out for yourselves." But neither man would relinquish his hold, and kept Haran afloat until help arrived. The survivors, such as they were, were picked up by the *SC-188* and transferred to the *Patterson*.

The *Felix Taussig* remained in the area for two hours, aiding in the forlorn search for survivors but finding none. It was later surmised that her final round had detonated a depth charge and set off secondary explosions which consumed the unsuspecting sub chaser. Nor was this the first incident of sub chasers falling under friendly fire; but it was the first occasion which resulted in casualties.

On October 5, 1918, Secretary of the Navy Josephus Daniels "commended Claude Wilde, machinist's mate second class, U.S. Naval Reserve Force, for the courage displayed and the heroic work done by him."

On December 30 and 31, minesweepers swept the area where the *SC-209* went down. The found no sign of the sub chaser. Subsequently, on June 26, 1919, "The sub-chaser #209 having been sunk and no trace of her having been found after a careful search the Bureau of Navigation will prepare the necessary orders striking this vessel from the Navy list."

In 1920, the parents of some of those who went down with the *SC-209* undertook a private search for the wreck. There is no record that their efforts were successfully rewarded. Nor do I know of anyone today who has knowledge of the wreck's location. Being constructed of thin wood which was much damaged by fire, the hull undoubtedly fell apart in short order. The gasoline engines were not large, like steam engines, and would not present much of a target for modern electronic search equipment. If the wreck of the *Sub Chaser 209* is ever found, its identity can best be established by the three shafts and propellers and by the gasoline engines.

The *SC-209* never fired a gun in anger, but she did rescue the airmen from seaplane number 990, which "was forced to land on the sea off Barnegat when its engine went dead on June 10."

The *Sub Chaser 209* was remembered in World War Two, when a new construction program launched the building of a new fleet of submarine chasers which were practically identical to those of the generation before. The prime mover in this case was H. Liggett Gray, who served aboard the *SC-209* as chief petty officer. He was detached from the vessel only a few days prior to her loss. Apparently, the violent end which came to so many of his companions made quite an impression on him, and he paid service to their passing twenty-four years later, as stated in a Navy memorandum dated June 9, 1942: "Mr. H. Liggett Gray is desirous of donating to the first vessel of the subchaser class which distinguishes itself in action a memorial trophy. This trophy is to be in remembrance of the officers and men who lost their lives in the loss of the S. C. 209 in the first World War."

Truly, the heroic dead never die, for they live on in the hearts of those who are thankful of the sacrifices they made in the cause of freedom.

As William Vanderbilt's private yacht. (Courtesy of the Vanderbilt Museum.)

TARANTULA

Built: 1912
Previous names: None
Gross tonnage: 159
Type of vessel: Patrol yacht
Builder: George Lawley & Sons, Neponset, Massachusetts
Owner: U.S. Navy
Cause of sinking: Collision with SS *Frisia*
Location: 26608.9

Sunk: October 28, 1918
Depth: 115 feet
Dimensions: 128' x 19' x 8'
Power: Two gasoline engines

Official designation: SP-124

43609.6

The *Tarantula* began her career as a private yacht built for William Kissam Vanderbilt, scion of the nineteenth century financier Cornelius Vanderbilt who built a vast commercial empire from his shipping and railroad interests.

At the time of her construction the *Tarantula* represented the latest word in mechanical and electrical advances. She was fitted with two gasoline engines, one 4-cylinder and one 6-cylinder, which together generated 600 horsepower and propelled the hull at the respectable speed of 14 knots. Wrote Vanderbilt, "Up to the time of her construction gasoline propelled ships never had storage capacity for over 1500 gallons of gasoline in their tanks. The *Tarantula* had over 7,000 gallons and was capable of cruising over a radius of 3,000 miles at well over 12 knots per hour." (Note: there is no such measurement as a "knot per hour." The correct measurement is either "knots" or "miles per hour."

To supply electricity the yacht was provided with three 110-volt generators. Vanderbilt must have purchased generators with the same strategy used in stock market investment--diversification--for each generator was supplied by a different manufacturer: the 10-kilowatt set came from Westinghouse, the 7.5-kilowatt set came from Winton, and the 5-kilowatt set came from the Gas Engine and

Power Company.

Vanderbilt undoubtedly enjoyed the *Tarantula*, but when war appeared on the horizon of American shores he made no complaint about doing his part for the Allied effort against Germany. He loaned the yacht to the Navy for the duration of hostilities, with the proviso that she be returned to him when the Navy had no further use for her. On April 25, 1917, the *Tarantula* was delivered to Third Naval District headquarters in New York. She was converted to a patrol vessel by the addition of two 6-pounder anti-aircraft guns, one forward and one aft, two 30-caliber machine guns, and a Naval reserve crew of two dozen men. She was designated as the SP-124 (SP stands for Section Patrol) and for the next year and a half she conducted routine patrols along the Long Island Sound and in the coastal waters off New York and New Jersey.

Vanderbilt himself commanded the newly commissioned gunboat until December 17 of that year. "Then Chief Boatswain Mate L.A. Jeffrey, Jr. became her Commanding Officer until October 14, 1918, when he was replaced by an Ensign." In hindsight, with the armistice only weeks away, it would have been better for all concerned had Jeffrey, who was already familiar with the operation of the vessel, remained in command.

The *Tarantula's* end came on the fog-shrouded night of October 28, 1918. At the time Ensign Edward Parsons Corning was in command, the Officer of the Deck was Boatswain's Mate John Duncan; Seaman Second Class K.O. Redfield was at the wheel; three lookouts scanned the darkened skies, three engineers watched over the engines, and a radio man was posted on station to monitor the air waves.

Due to the limited visibility, the engines were running at half speed when "the signal of a steamer was heard at intervals beginning at about 8:45 p.m. The *Tarantula* responded each time with her signal, and as the course of the steamer could not be determined the course of the *Tarantula* was altered to NNW on which she proceeded at slow speed, and a sharp lookout kept." At this time, the *Tarantula* was about eight miles southwest of the *Fire Island* lightship, heading toward New York harbor some forty miles distant.

After twenty-five minutes of careful watching and maneuvering, a lookout reported a ship's masthead light off the port beam. Ensign Corning ordered full speed astern just about the time the oncoming vessel's green side light came into

After conversion to a Navy gunboat. (Courtesy of the Vanderbilt Museum.)

view. The time was 9:13. The bow of a large steamship loomed out of the fog and drove into the *Tarantula's* port side at a right angle, piercing the hull a distance of two or three feet just forward of the bridgewing and abreast of the pilot house, which was some twenty feet abaft the bow.

If the steamer had been going full speed she no doubt would have sliced through the yacht's metal hull like a knife through warm butter. But the *Frisia*, a Dutch passenger ship of the Royal Holland Lloyd Line on route from New York to Halifax, was creeping through the fog at a mere knot and a half, feeling her way carefully through the murk. So slight was the collision that most of her passengers were unaware that a collision had occurred; and so strong was her stem that it suffered little more than the loss of a few layers of paint.

The force of the impact on the *Tarantula* was more severe. In extreme slow motion the yacht heeled sharply to starboard, then was shoved sideways through the water by the momentum of the steamer, which was still moving forward. The yacht's bow was slued around until the two vessels grated together side by side. In a scream of sparks and tortured steel the *Tarantula's* port lifeboat was torn from its davits and crushed.

All this did not occur instantaneously, but took three or four minutes. Ensign Corning climbed through the smashed front window of the wheelhouse and went down to examine the damage. The *Tarantula* had suffered a gash in her hull which was three feet across and which extended below the waterline. The sea rushed in with such speed that the men were chased out of the forward compartments by the rising flood. While the drawn-out engagement between vessels was taking place, some members of the crew managed to launch the yacht's dingy. But before anyone could climb aboard, the rope painter was severed by the friction of the two hulls, and the dingy went adrift.

Finally, the two vessels drifted apart. The *Tarantula* was down by the head and settling slowly, but Ensign Corning thought that the watertight bulkheads should keep the vessel afloat. Despite his impressions, however, he ordered the starboard lifeboat to be launched, and half the crew boarded it and struck out for the *Frisia*, which was hove to nearby. By the time the lifeboat returned for the remainder of the crew, the *Tarantula* appeared to be settling more rapidly. Ensign Corning regretfully abandoned ship with the rest of his men. No one observed the yacht's final demise.

All from the *Tarantula* were accounted for, and only one man suffered a slight injury. The men were well taken care of aboard the *Frisia* until later in the night, when they were transferred to the newly commissioned U.S. destroyer *Montgomery* (DD-121), which transported the *Tarantula's* survivors to New York. At the subsequent court of inquiry the investigating officers found that "the collision was due to the fog and the inexperience and poor seamanship of the Commanding Officer of the *Tarantula*."

The *Frisia* was so little damaged by the collision that she continued on her voyage to Halifax. Since the steamer was at sea it was impossible to properly assess the cost of repairs; an agent of the steamship line stated that the actual loss was "immaterial," although the Navy, in its wisdom, estimated the cost of repairs at $10--undoubtedly the price of a can of marine paint. The Royal Holland Lloyd Line did not sue for damages.

Since the *Tarantula* could not be returned to him, Vanderbilt was reimbursed for the loss of his yacht. In addition to the appraised value of $75,000, he was paid $3,034.86 for the amount of consumable stores on board at the time of delivery to the Navy. Thus Vanderbilt's yacht was written off and forgotten, to become little more than a footnote in the annals of the Great War.

The wreck was not located until the 1980's, by a private dive club known as the Aquarians. I first heard about it in 1985, when I received a query letter from club member Ronald Barnes, who informed me that fellow club member Billy deMarigny had recovered a bell from a wreck known as the Gunboat (so called because of the Naval armament) on which was stamped the vessel's name and the date 1902. I had no file on the *Tarantula*, but a glance through my reference library quickly turned up the information Barnes was seeking. It also turned up a mystery.

The *Tarantula* which the Aquarians found was built in 1912 (or 1913 according to one source), so why did it have a bell dated 1902? I eventually discovered that another yacht named *Tarantula* was built ten years earlier, in 1902, by Yarrow & Company in Scotscoun, in the United Kingdom, for Member of Parliament Colonel Harry MacCalmont, and subsequently acquired by William Vanderbilt. This *Tarantula* was a steam yacht propelled by Parsons turbines, "the second ship of its kind to be equipped with turbines, the *Turbinia* being the first." She was equipped with three turbines, one high pressure and two low pressure. The high pressure turbine rotated the central shaft, and the two low pressure turbines rotated the outer shafts. Perhaps unique was the experimental design in which three propellers were mounted on each shaft; thus the yacht was driven by nine propellers, and could attain a speed of 24 knots.

W.K. Vanderbilt wrote, "I had her towed from England to within fifty miles of the Virginia Capes by a tramp steamer. From there on under her own steam she completed the voyage, arriving at Newport News in August 1903. She was the first turbine propelled ship to operate in the western hemisphere. She was loaned to the Navy Department for a period of one week or so, to allow them to obtain certain data which they were desirous of obtaining. This data I have been told was used in the Naval Academy at Annapolis for a number of years thereafter, in making, I believe, a comparison between reciprocating engines and turbines. I found by various experiments that the three propellers attached to each shaft did not increase the speed of the ship as was originally figured, the two after propellers working in broken water. They were replaced by a single propeller to each shaft and a 26 1/2 knot speed obtained thereafter."

Vanderbilt loved to race his yachts. There was stiff competition among the members of the Seawanhaka Corinthian Yacht Club to which he belonged, and of which he was the Commodore in 1904. He was extraordinarily proud of the fact that in 1905 the *Tarantula* "defeated Howard Gould's *Niagara IV* in a race on Long Island Sound." Stories of his racing misadventures are legion. He drove the *Tarantula* so hard and fast along the East River that her huge wake often damaged shore property and boats tied to the piers. Claims for damages pelted him like rain. It finally reached the point where any wake damage was automatically assumed to have been caused by the *Tarantula*, a custom which kept his lawyers busy "proving that she hadn't been in the East River at the time of such-and-such a claim."

In 1912, Vanderbilt ordered a new yacht from the yard of George Lawley & Sons, in Neponset, Massachusetts. He named her *Tarantula* after his other yacht, which he sold to J.K.L. Ross in 1914. Ross renamed the steam yacht the *Tuna*. In 1916, the *Tuna* was sold to the Canadian Navy, which desperately needed fast patrol boats for the prosecution of the war. The *Tuna* was thereafter known as the HMCS *Tuna*, and at this point she passes out of this history of Vanderbilt and the *Tarantula*. The question that comes to my mind is this: did Vanderbilt keep the bell from the first *Tarantula* then mount it on the second? No documents at the Vanderbilt Museum in Centerport offer clarification on this point. Nor have I been able to decipher the meaning of the initials "S.Y.C." which are inscribed on the bell beneath the date. It has been suggested that the initials stand for Seawanhaka Yacht Club. While it is true that Vanderbilt was a long-time member of the Seawanhaka Corinthian Yacht Club, and was its commodore in 1904, this explanation does not account for the lack of the letter "C" in the initials.

Purists should also note the differences in the *Tarantula's* length and depth which are ascribed by different sources. *Merchant Vessels of the United States* gives the length as 116.6 feet and the depth as 10.7 feet, yet Navy records give the length as 128 feet and the depth as 8 or 9 feet (depending upon which Navy source is used). These differences are more likely a matter of the type of measurement used rather than a change after accession by the Navy. For example, the MVUS figure could be waterline length and the Navy figure overall length.

Little remains recognizable of the *Tarantula* today. The hull is contiguous but almost completely broken down. Machinery amidships offers the highest relief of about six feet. The bow sticks up barely three feet; one anchor is snugged in its hawsepipe, but the hawsepipe is not connected to any considerable section of hull plating. About fifty feet off the starboard bow lies what appears to be a fuel tank. Aquarian Tommy Soriano made an interesting observation: the top deck has been flipped over, probably by a trawler, so the bow faces aft and lies upside down. The stern peters out to a badly scattered debris field without definition or any recognizable features.

For souvenir collectors, abaft the diesel engine is the place to dig, for this is where much china, silverware, and ornate brass fittings have been found. Miscellaneous items have also been found in the sand off the port side amidships, but be prepared to fan the sand with great energy if you look here. The magazine lies about fifteen feet back from the starboard bow. The small arms locker contains 45-caliber shells, while in the main armament ammunition locker are found long, narrow shells for the deck gun. Paper labels are sometimes found inside the large shells, and on them lettering may be legible which spells out where the shells were last packed: St. Juliens Creek, Virginia. Marine life is abundant and lobsters are plentiful, so the wreck is worth a visit and an occasional return.

TURNER

Commissioned: 1943
Previous names: None
Displacement tonnage: 1,630
Type of vessel: Destroyer
Builder: Federal Ship Building & Dry Dock Company, Kearny, New Jersey
Owner: U.S. Navy
Cause of sinking: Magazine explosion
Location: 26936.4

Sunk: January 3, 1944
Depth: 60 feet
Dimensions: 348' x 36' x 17'
Power: Oil-fired steam turbine

Official designation: DD-648

43725.6

The destruction of the U.S. destroyer *Turner* is all too swiftly told in consideration of the large number of fatalities involved in her loss. She was commissioned on April 15, 1943, and was immediately assigned to convoy duty for which she was very much needed in order to protect the merchant fleet from marauding German U-boats. In the performance of this task she escorted Allied ships across the Atlantic Ocean and back again. At 3:00 a.m. on January 3, 1944, after nearly nine months of this exacting service, and after escorting a westbound convoy for sixteen consecutive days, the *Turner* dropped anchor on the east side of the Ambrose Channel. The night sky was overcast, the air was freezing, and a light snow was falling. Ten-mile-per-hour winds stirred a moderate sea.

Aboard at the time were 293 men: 17 officers and 276 enlisted men. In command of the destroyer was Commander Henry Wygant, Jr. Anchored nearby were four other destroyers (*Stevenson*, *Stockton*, *Swasey*, and *Thorn*) and two destroyer escorts (*Inch* and *Stanton*).

That morning the *Turner* was due to unload most of her ammunition, a job done periodically because explosive devices tend to become inoperable when impregnated with salt from sea spray or the ocean atmosphere after a long period of disuse. What actually occurred aboard the *Turner* shortly after dawn is a matter of speculation, since no one who had direct knowledge of what triggered the fatal blast survived the event. A Court of Inquiry found that the most probable cause of the initial explosion was improper disarming of the fuzes of the 7.2-inch rockets, which launched hedgehogs. This conjecture was based upon evidence that "Schlessinger, H.A. (TM1c), while enroute to breakfast, discussed Mark 22 Projector ammunition with a shipmate and that he (Schlessinger), after breakfast, informed Gray, M.G. (TM2c), in the forward mess hall, that he was going to defuze the ready Mark 22 Projector ammunition, in No. 2 Handling Room; whereupon Schlessinger left the mess hall. That, within a short period of time after Schlessinger's departure from the mess hall, the first explosion occurred." The Court of Inquiry also noted that "none of the torpedo personnel attached to the U.S.S. *Turner* on 3 January 1944, ever had disassembled Mark 22 Projector ammunition prior to that date." It was further speculated that the han-

Courtesy of the National Archives.

dling and stowage room explosions touched off the forward 5-inch magazine.

A Coast Guard document described the beginning of the *Turner's* demise: "To Coxswain Fred A. Williams, on anchor watch on a Coast Guard 83 foot subchaser at the pier of the Sandy Hook Coast Guard boat basin, who happened to be looking at her at the moment, she appeared to jump clear out of the water and a great ball of brilliant red fire hovered over the midsection of the ship. A second or so later the terrific sound of the explosion rolled across the bay."

It was reported that "sleepy householders awakened to hear pictures rattling, chandeliers clinking, doors opening or trying to open. Scores of persons along the Jersey shore and the Long Island coast told of a weird whistling gust sweeping through their homes or aparatments." In nearby buildings, hundreds of windows were blown out of their frames. "Thousands of persons seemed convinced that something had blown up either in their own homes or somewhere down the street. Hundreds of suburban dwellers were positive that their oil burners had exploded." Vibrations from the blast were felt as far away as thirty miles inland.

The flames following the explosion were seen "from the lookout tower at Sandy Hook and Rockaway Coast Guard Stations. Lt. Comdr. George F. Morin, the Coast Guard station skipper at Sandy Hook, took personal charge of the disaster mobilization plan that immediately went into effect at the station. All available floating equipment was ordered to prepare for immediate departure to the scene."

The first explosion occurred at 6:17 a.m. "in the vicinity of No. 2 Upper Handling Room and the Anti-Submarine Projector Ready Stowage Room." At that time the rooms contained fifty 5-inch shells and forty-nine fuzed rounds of Mark 22 projector ammunition. The accidental detonation blew out the sides of the hull from just above the waterline to just below the forecastle deck, ruptured the forecastle deck plating, demolished the rear portion of the forward gun's shrapnel shield, and distorted the entire bridge structure leaving it "a mass of burnt and twisted steel." The ship took a four degree list to starboard.

In the fraction of an instant the middle third of the *Turner* was converted to a raging inferno. No one knows how many men died in that initial titanic blast, but it was around one hundred, and included every officer except for two acting ensigns who were Naval reservists; scores of others were burned and severely injured by flying debris.

The survivors in the bow and the stern could not communicate with each other. The bow lost all electric power, plunging the below deck spaces into utter darkness; no water was available to fight the flames which threatened to overtake the forward compartments.

Despite the lack of officers to take command, the crew aft rallied themselves in a valiant effort to try to control the conflagration and save the ship. Only a limited supply of water was available for the after fire main; nor was there adequate pressure to force it through the hoses. In desperation, the men connected the bilge pumps and flushing pumps to the fire main. This enabled them to extinguish small, isolated fires, but their major efforts were hampered by factors which were out of their control: a wind from ahead fanned the flames aft; flying, burning debris landed helter-skelter on the deck; fuel oil seeping from fractured tanks floated to the surface and caught fire, surrounding the ship in a sea of flame and blistering the hull, causing the paint on the ship's sides to peel and burn like tissue paper.

Meanwhile, secondary explosions literally tore the ship apart. More casualties were incurred as men died screaming in the flames, or were suffocated in the dense, hot smoke, or were forced overboard where, in their weakened condition, they drowned. The intense heat sporadically cooked off 40-millimeter ready ammunition, which caused additional casualties and which hampered rescue operations.

The first rescue craft to reach the scene of the explosion was a 77-foot Coast Guard cutter attached to the Sandy Hook Pilot Command, the USCG *83306*. The cutter's commanding officer, Lieutenant (jg) John Dean, threaded a path through debris surrounding the destroyer and "laid his vessel alongside the port bow of the U.S.S. *Turner* with her stern abreast the blazing section and successfully removed thirty-nine men trapped in the forecastle."

Fireman Jack Paulsen was blown through the side of the destroyer into the freezing water. He lolled in a state of semi-consciousness and miraculously found himself floating on a mattress. Shipmate Gustave Delonnoy, Jr. leaped overboard and, amid windswept sleet, swam to Paulsen's aid and "pushed the mattress over to a Coast Guard boat which took them both aboard."

Soon, half a dozen more "Coast Guard craft had arrived and were circling the stricken ship and removing the dying, the dead, and the wounded from the water. Shells of the 20 and 40 millimeter variety were exploding throughout this period of the rescue work." One Coast Guard cutter tied up to the *Turner's* stern to take off survivors; some of the coastguardsmen leaped onto the hot deck of the destroyer to search for injured personnel who could not make their own way aft because of their injuries.

The USS *Swasey* pulled anchor and maneuvered to within sixty feet of the burning destroyer, then "dispatched fire and rescue parties that landed alongside a Coast Guard craft secured to the U.S.S. *Turner*." When the officer in charge of the boarding party could locate no person in authority aboard the destroyer, he took command and directed his team to do what they could to help extinguish the fire which still raged out of control. Discovering that no electricity or water was available, the party soon retreated.

Gradually, the crew in the after part of the vessel was driven back to the very stern. "Fire was breaking out in one of the after gun turrets and had begun scorching torpedoes more than thirty feet from the fire." Coast Guard Ensign Peter Chase, from the sub chaser whose coxswain had observed the explosion, "gave the order for all hands on the *Turner* to abandon ship. The remaining members of the crew, still on board, went over the side to be picked up by the flotilla of Coast Guard rescue craft. Forty-six men scrambled aboard the 83 footer, skippered by Chase, which was still tied to the blazing destroyer. . . . The lines were cast off and the sub-chaser backed clear and headed for Sandy Hook, with her cargo of burned and injured survivors." Forty-five minutes had elapsed since the first explosion had rent the *Turner* apart.

The *Turner* continued to burn for another forty-five minutes, the heat cooking off ammunition continuously. "Then with another terrific explosion that sent debris flying all around the rescue ships, the destroyer settled deeper into the water and with a sudden hissing sound, quickly sank beneath the surface of the sea." The destroyer rolled over and sank on her starboard side, but subsequently "an explosion in the after boiler room blew out the port side of the hull and righted the after section of the ship."

When the final count was taken, the number of fatalities totaled 139. Among those saved was the *Turner's* mascot, an unpedigreed rat terrier named Turn To. In order to care for the survivors, a complex emergency operation of heroic proportions was mobilized without delay. The American Red Cross and the New York Police Department assisted the Navy with all the resources at their command, providing doctors, nurses, ambulances, and medical supplies. The commodity most needed was blood plasma; 200 units were donated from Red Cross stocks, another 200 came from the Marine Hospital on Staten Island, and additional units were contributed by various Army hospitals in the area.

One of the most dramatic

A shoeless survivor clutches a blanket around his upper body for warmth. Notice the falling snow and ice-covered deck. (Courtesy of the National Archives.)

and significant events that occurred in response to the call for help was the flight of a Coast Guard helicopter. At that time, helicopters were in the experimental stage of development: untried and untested rotary-winged machines in which few people had much faith. Nevertheless, when blood plasma was desperately needed--and needed quickly--to save the lives of some of the *Turner's* injured crewmen, Commander Frank Erickson, head of the Coast Guard aviation unit at Floyd Bennett Field, "had no difficulty in taking off one of the experimental helicopters from that station and landing it at the Battery. Fourteen minutes later it settled gently on the beach at Sandy Hook with two cases of blood plasma for the survivors of the explosion." Not only did Erickson fly his machine in conditions which kept fixed-wing craft firmly grounded, he was able to make pinpoint landings in places where no airstrips existed. Delivery by boat or car would have taken an hour or more. Thus the whirligig announced its usefulness for special operations, and by this advent entered human consciousness as a machine impervious to the snow squalls and sleet through which it was forced to fly.

Upon arrival at Sandy Hook, the blood plasma "was administered to the badly injured." There the barracks and sick bay were "a beehive of activity, and under the direction of pharmacists' mates, seamen and carpenters, signalmen and yeomen, were preparing to receive the victims and survivors." In addition, sixty-five men were treated at the Army Post Hospital at Fort Hancock, New Jersey, the Naval Hospital at Brooklyn, and the Marine Hospital on Staten Island.

A Court of Inquiry was convened the day following the accident, and continued for several days. After listening to 930 pages of testimony from survivors and expert witnesses, the Court was forgiving in its opinion and found no fault in command or in action to which it could attach blame. There were recommendations, to be sure, such as better training for personnel involved in defuzing ammunition, replacement of the defective fuze type with a modified type which was less sensitive to handling, and segregation of ammunition to be defuzed from all other ammunition. Lieutenant John Dean, Coast Guard Reserve, was commended for his heroic action of placing the cutter in his command against the *Turner's* bow, which action resulted in the saving of so many lives.

The most important recommendation of all, however, was "that future design provide suitable and adequate quarters for officers and chief petty officers in at least two parts of the ship widely dispersed and that every practicable effort be made to effect such a dispersal in ships of current design."

On January 16, a memorial service was held in the auditorium of the Navy Receiving Station in New York, to honor the men who were killed on the *Turner*.

Navy divers examined the wreck shortly after the disaster. They found that the *Turner* had broken "into two major sections -- a forward section and an after section; the portion of the ship between frame 35 and frame 67 has not been found, but a mess of unidentified tangled wreckage lies generally between the two major sections which are about 100 feet apart."

Subsequently, the Navy conducted a major salvage operation on the *Turner* in order to remove the larger portions of submerged structure because the wreck posed a hazard to safe navigation. Brought in to do the job was *Crane Ship No.*

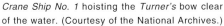

Crane Ship No. 1 hoisting the *Turner's* bow clear of the water. (Courtesy of the National Archives.)

1: the hull of the old battleship *Kearsarge* (BB-5) whose guns and turrets had been replaced with a huge rotating crane capable of lifting 250 deadweight tons. Extra ballast and side bulges (or blisters) provided the stability required to hoist heavy objects without the ship toppling over.

The crane ship was moored over the site for weeks. Massive sections of steel wreckage were raised out of the water and deposited onto barges for removal. What portions of the wreck were not salvaged in this manner were blown flat with explosives. Today, little remains of the *Turner* other than a broad, low-lying field of rubble.

The wreck site provides a substrate for encrusting marine organisms and a home for bottom dwelling fish and crustaceans. Although very little is recognizable as part of a ship--the wreck looks more like a metal scrap heap--it is not uncommon to find small brass items such as engine parts, locks, shell casings, and so on. Underwater orientation is practically impossible. Dive on an incoming tide when the water is cleaner; otherwise visibility is practically nil as the wreck is covered in the outflow of the Hudson River.

On October 21, 1945, in conjunction with Navy Day festivities celebrating victory over the Axis powers, a wreath-laying ceremony was held over the site of the *Turner*, in memory of those who lost their lives in that titanic explosion nearly two years previous. John McCue, former torpedoman on the *Turner*, tossed the wreath into the water where so many of his fellow men perished.

On September 24, 1994, another celebration was held over the site of the *Turner*. On this solemn occasion the Eastern Dive Boat Association hosted a wreath-laying ceremony in which former crew members participated. Also in attendance was the grandson of Commander Henry Wygant, Jr.

The wreck of the *Turner* continues to exemplify the futility of war and the folly of hostile aggression. Let us not forget the lessons which previous generations fought so hard to learn.

WILLIAM C. CARNEGIE

Built: 1900
Previous names: None
Gross tonnage: 2,664
Type of vessel: Wooden-hulled five-masted schooner
Builder: Percy & Small, Bath, Maine
Owner: J.S. Winslow & Company, Portland, Maine
Port of registry: Portland, Maine
Cause of sinking: Ran aground
Location: 1/2 mile south southwest of the Moriches Life-Saving Station

Sunk: May 1, 1909
Depth: Unknown
Dimensions: 289' x 46' x 22'
Power: Sail

For Captain Mitchell Reed, master of the *William C. Carnegie*, it was a routine voyage from Newport News, Virginia to Portland, Maine: one he had made many times in the past, and one he expected to make many times in the future. In fact, the coastal voyage was so routine that in cliché it might be called a milk run, except that the schooner did not carry milk. The cargo which filled the holds to capacity--4,400 tons of bituminous coal consigned to Randall & McAllister-- was worth $12,000 upon delivery.

All sails were set on all five masts as the windjammer bucked very high seas and tacked against a fresh northeast wind which reached near gale force. The rain-swept decks were slippery underfoot, so the twelve-man crew exercised caution when getting about. None wanted to climb the shrouds in the wintry weather then blowing.

The night of April 30, 1909 was not only dark, it was misty. Captain Reed was unable to take a fix on the stars with his sextant, so he followed a course

Courtesy of The Mariners Museum, Newport News, Virginia.

based upon deduced reckoning--which has been corrupted by generations of mariners to "dead reckoning" with more prescience than intended. The noise of the wind drowned out the sound of approaching breakers, so there was no warning that the schooner was headed for shoal water until the bow ground onto the bar and the vessel shuddered to a sudden stop. The *William C. Carnegie* was hard aground about half a mile from the Moriches Life-Saving Station. The time was 2:50 in the morning of May Day, and a mayday it was.

Forty minutes later surfman Charles Albin was completing his patrol of the beach when he spotted the stranded schooner in the distance. He ran to the life-saving station and alerted Keeper Charles Gordon of the windjammer's predicament. Gordon: "I immediately called all hands and went with beach cart to the scene of the wreck." At 3:45 a.m. the life-savers fired the first shot with the Lyle gun, but the shot fell short. The *William C. Carnegie* stood about 600 yards from shore. Another shot fell short, then another, and another, and another. In all, the life-savers fired seven or eight shots with varying thicknesses of line and increasingly larger charges of powder, all to no avail. The schooner could not be reached, so the breeches buoy was not set up.

Gordon called the adjacent stations as backup, and soon the crews from the Potunk and Forge River stations arrived to help in launching the surfboat. At 4:40 the boat was shoved through the breakers. "We launched all right--but took a big sea between bar and shore filled + capsized the boat, two men were caught under the boat but freed themselves in a short time, the boat drifted ashore bottom up and was then righted."

A newspaper reporter wrote an account which was more graphic and more grammatically correct: "The seas were breaking twenty feet high but the big self-bailing boat was headed out, with Captain Gordon at the steering oar, and Captain Gildersleeve, of the Potunk station, acting as supporter. Eight of the hardiest life savers took the oars and as many more lined up to give her a good start. She rode the first half dozen seas gallantly, making about one-third the distance, when a huge comber knocked her end over end and sent the ten men headlong into the sea."

This near tragedy made the life-savers pause for thought. It was their job to take necessary risks in an attempt to save the lives of helpless mariners; it was not their job to take unnecessary risks against all odds of success. They called the Revenue Cutter Service and explained the situation. The Revenue Cutter *Mohawk* was dispatched immediately to the scene of impending disaster.

Meanwhile, seeing the best efforts of the life-savers come to naught, Captain Reed rallied his crew around the *William C. Carnegie's* yawl, which also served as a lifeboat. With the ship continually being battered by huge waves of water which washed completely over the weather deck, and with the hull breaking up beneath them, the crew boldly opted for a plan of self-rescue. The men gathered on the upper deck and lowered the yawl over the side. With good luck and great seamanship all twelve men managed to get the boat away without capsizing. Because of the high surf running, the only safe course available to them lay out to sea. The men bent over their oars with a will, rowing hard until they reached calmer water about a mile and a half from shore. And there they remained for the entire day.

The *William C. Carnegie* was blown broadside to the beach where "she began to break up under the pounding. Fragments of her were driven ashore, cabin furniture, bits of her torn sails, planks from her decks and all kinds of flotsam. Before nightfall the beach was strewn with the wreckage, and finally the schooner sank, with decks awash."

The life-savers stayed by the wreck all day. As nighttime neared they lit a bonfire on the beach as a signal to guide the *Mohawk* to the vicinity; they also aimed a searchlight toward sea. Not until 6:00 p.m., however, did the revenue cutter heave into view through the misty, darkening sky. "When she poked her nose through the fog another cheer went up from the lifesavers, for the men in the long boat had been having a sorry time of it as the huge waves tossed it about like a cockleshell. Swinging broadside on to the windward of the *Carnegie* the *Mohawk* soon had the captain and crew aboard and promptly headed for New York."

Every man was alive and well.

The following day an agent for the owner visited the site of the wreck. "The *Carnegie* was a very valuable vessel and cost $125,000 when she was built nine years ago and was estimated to be worth about $70,000 before the accident. The *Carnegie* was managed by J.S. Winslow & Co., who also owned her with several other parties in Portland including Captain Reed, who owned a large part of the vessel. There is very little insurance on the vessel, only a few of the owners being protected. The cargo of coal was valued at $12,000 and was covered by insurance."

The *William C. Carnegie* was given up as a total loss. Coincidentally, J.S. Winslow & Company owned the *Miles M. Merry* (q.v.) which went aground twice off the Moriches Life-Saving Station. Winslow's agent was getting all to familiar with the life-savers there.

Courtesy of Sharon Reese.

YONKERS

Built: 1864
Previous names: *Ocean Signal, Tennyson, Deutschland*
Gross tonnage: 1,265
Type of vessel: Wooden barge
Builder: E. & A. Sewall, Bath, Maine
Owner: Lewis Luckenbach
Port of registry: New York, NY
Cause of sinking: Foundered
Location: 26128.9

Sunk: January 26, 1898
Depth: 150 feet
Dimensions: 187' x 38' x 23'
Power: None

43793.8

The *Yonkers* is not known by that name at all, but as the *Tennyson*. This is because when John Dudas recovered the bell from an unidentified wooden snag in 1967, the words cast in bronze read "Tennyson 1864". Said Jay Porter, captain of the fishing boat *Jess-Lu*, "I was returning from a job I was doing for the Army engineers when my underwater sonar detected the wreck. I catalogued the spot as a good place for fish to gather and determined that someday I would return with divers to take a closer look at the wreck." Four years later, Porter took Dudas to the site and, as they say, history was made.

The *Yonkers* was built at the yard of E. & A. Sewall, in Bath, Maine. The three-masted full-rigged ship on the ways was supposed to be called *Ocean Signal*, the name chosen by the Sewall company. Usually, Sewall built ships only for themselves, but in this instance they sold the vessel foreign while she was still on the stocks. The British buyer was A. Malcolmson, who registered the ship in Lloyd's as the *Tennyson*; her home port was Liverpool, England. When the ship was sold to William Orr in 1868 the port of registry was changed to Greenock, Scotland but the name was retained.

In 1875 the *Tennyson* was extensively rebuilt. She was sold German in 1877 for use in the oil trade, and renamed *Deutschland* by her new owner, Robert S. Carr; she was registered in the port of Hamburg, Germany.

In 1887 the *Deutschland* went aground off Red Hook, New Jersey. "Her timbers were so strained that she was unfitted for sailing, and was made into a coal barge." That is, her sails were removed and her masts were dismantled with the result that she no longer had motive power of her own, and had to be towed. She embarked on her new if somewhat ignominious career as the *Yonkers*.

In January 1898 the tug *Walter A. Luckenbach* left Newport News with two barges in tow: the *Yonkers* and the *Halycon*. "A hawser 150 fathoms in length was made fast to the bow bits of the *Yonkers* and from her stern bits a line of the same length extended to the *Halycon*."

A rather confusing report of the circumstances encountered on the night of January 13 explained, "Capt. Willen of the *Luckenbach* reported that he had encountered heavy seas throughout Saturday night, and that at 6 o'clock on Sunday morning he observed that the tug was making better headway. Upon going astern he felt the towline slack with nothing attached to it. [By which is meant that Captain Willen walked to the stern of the tug, not that the tug was put in reverse.] He at once put [the tug] about to ascertain the nature of the trouble, and his vessel narrowly escaped collision with the *Halcyon*, which had been the rear barge.

"On the *Halcyon* as little was known about what had become of the *Yonkers* as on the tug, she being far astern of her, and in the darkness she would scarcely be discernible. The men on the *Halcyon*, however, thought they saw something dark rise in the air a short distance in front of them a few minutes before the tug came up. It is supposed that the *Yonkers* foundered in the heavy sea raised by the strong gale blowing, or was struck by a passing steamer a short time before the discovery of the parting of the tow line. The *Luckenbach*, after the accident, put into New York and reported the loss to her owners, and then went on to Providence."

The four men aboard the *Yonkers* apparently went on to Providence, too, but not to the capital of Rhode Island. "That the *Yonkers* was wrecked and did not simply part her lines and drift away is looked upon as certain in view of the report made by Capt. Black of the steamer *Hogarth*, which arrived here last Sunday afternoon. He reported at that time that at 10 o'clock Sunday morning at a point about twenty miles south-southeast of Sandy Hook he sighted a vessel's deckhouse, on which was an object resembling a man.

"Although the sea was running high he lowered a boat in charge of his chief officer. The boat swamped before it had gone many feet, and was hauled aboard. A larger boat was substituted, which reached the wreckage, but the object resembling a man had disappeared. He also sighted a tug, believed to have been the *Luckenbach*, picking up another barge. Although no marks of identification could be found about the wreckage, it is believed that it was the remains of the *Yonkers*, and that her crew were lost."

It was not uncommon for deck houses to float off a wooden vessel when the hull plunged to the bottom. Sometimes the entire weather deck broke loose from the gunwale. Many a sailor owes his life to wooden ship construction and fastenings whose accumulated strength was less than equal to the amount of reserve buoyancy integral to the building materials of the upper deck or deck houses.

In the present case, however, the true fate of the *Yonkers* was not ascertained until 69 years after the event. One can but wonder what other maritime mysteries will be solved in the future by curious boat captains and exploratory wreck divers.

The *Yonkers*, or *Tennyson*, is a typical snag, similar to hundreds of other dismasted sailing ships which ride the sand off the coast of Long Island. It abounds with lobsters and bottom dwelling fish because it is seldom visited due to its depth. Thickly encrusted and badly worm-eaten timbers rise no higher than a few feet from the sea bed. But these same timbers provide the cavities in which game animals hide.

SUGGESTED READING

Berg, Daniel (1993) *Long Island Shore Diver*, Aqua Explorers, 2745 Cheshire Drive, Baldwin, New York 11510.

----- (1990) *Wreck Valley Vol II*, Aqua Explorers, 2745 Cheshire Drive, Baldwin, New York 11510.

Braynard, Frank O. (1963) *S.S. Savannah: the Elegant Steam Ship*, University of Georgia Press, Athens, Georgia.

Clark, William Bell (1929) *When the U-Boats Came to America*, Little, Brown, and Company.

Forbes, R.B. (undated, but circa 1886) *The Loss of the Oregon*, J.F. Cotter & Co, Printers, 165 Devonshire St., Boston, Massachusetts.

Gentile, Gary (1988) *Shipwrecks of New Jersey*, Sea Sports Publications, Norwalk, Connecticut.

----- (1989) *Track of the Gray Wolf*, Avon Books, New York, NY.

----- (1989) *USS San Diego: the Last Armored Cruiser*, GGP, P.O. Box 57137, Philadelphia, Pennsylvania 19111 ($20 postage paid).

Glick, Les (1990) *Divers Guide to Long Island Waters*, Amphibian Enterprises, P.O. Box 391, Manorville, New York 11949.

Heyl, Eric (1952-1969) *Early American Steamers* (six volumes), Erik Heyl, 136 West Oakwood Place, Buffalo, New York, 14214.

Howland, S.A. (1840) *Steamboat Disasters and Railroad Accidents in the United States*, Dorr, Howland & Company, Worcester.

Kaasmann, Herb (1993) *Oregon: Greyhound of the Atlantic*, Old Walrus Productions, P.O. Box 665, Navesink, New Jersey 07752.

Keatts, Henry C. (1992) *Guide to Shipwreck Diving: New York & New Jersey*, Gulf Publishing Company, Houston, Texas.

Keatts, Henry C. and Farr, George C. (1990) *Dive into History: Warships*, Gulf Publishing Company, Houston, Texas.

Northrop, H.D. (1904) *New York's Awful Steamboat Horror*, D.Z. Howell.

Quinn, William P. (1988) *Shipwrecks Along the Atlantic Coast*, Parnassus Imprints, P.O. Box 335, Orleans, Massachusetts 02653.

Quinn, William P. and Morris, Paul C (1989) *Shipwrecks in New York Waters*, Lower Cape Publishing, P.O. Box 901, Orleans, Massachusetts 02653.

Raguso, John N. (1992) *Atlantic Wrecks: Book One*, The Fisherman Library, 1620 Beaver Dam Road, Point Pleasant, New Jersey 08742.

Rattray, Jeannette Edwards (1955) *Ship Ashore!*, Yankee Peddler Book Co.

----- (1973) *Perils of the Port of New York*, Dodd, Mead & Co.

Schmitt, Frederick P. and Schmid, David E. (1961) *H.M.S. Culloden*, The Marine Historical Association, Inc. Mystic, Connecticut.

Sheard, Bradley (1991) *Beyond Sportdiving!*, Menasha Ridge Press, P.O. Box 43059, Birmingham, Alabama.

Voynick, Stephen M. (1984) *The Mid-Atlantic Treasure Coast*, The Middle Atlantic Press, Wilmington, Delaware 19899.

LORAN NUMBERS – ALPHABETICAL

120 Wreck	26873.4	43468.3	Barge	26788.5	43716.9
2 x 4 (barge)	26929.8	43755.2	Barge	26911.8	43494.5
3 Fares	26651.5	43605.2	Barge #1	26530.0	43865.0
3 Sisters	26791.6	43642.3	Barge #2	26838.1	43538.6
59 Pounder	26632.4	43601.1	Barge #3	26788.5	43716.9
AC Ridge	26942.0	43920.0	Barge #4	26870.4	43734.7
Acara	26800.9	43750.8	Barge #5	26869.5	43738.5
Ace	26940.0	43745.7	Barge #6	26737.0	43728.5
Acid Barge	26794.8	43484.4	Barge #7	26881.5	43728.5
Across Wreck	26832.8	43550.1	Barge (closed)	26587.5	43659.8
Addie Anderson	14424.0	43989.9	Barge (steel)	26870.5	43734.7
Adelle	26883.4	43478.2	Barnegat Inlet R "2"	26878.0	43278.0
Adonis	26950.2	43598.8	Barnegat Ridge North	26785.0	43240.0
Airplane	26605.9	43716.8	Barnett	26926.8	43771.2
Airplane Engine	26922.6	43768.8	Barraitai	14863.9	43965.9
Ajace	26956.6	43754.1	Bass	14560.4	43817.4
Alan Martin	26792.0	43482.4	Bass	25829.5	43817.4
Algol	26794.8	43484.4	Bayville Barge	26847.1	43938.2
Ambrose Light	26910.0	43700.0	Bayville Engine	15324.0	43941.0
Ambrose Ridge	26912.5	43703.0	Benson	26859.5	43566.9
Ambrose Tower	26910.0	43700.0	Bidevind	26357.6	43280.4
Ambrose Wreck	26912.5	43703.0	Big Wood	26828.8	43571.3
Anastasia	26853.5	43359.0	Black Diamond	25998.1	43895.1
Anchor Chain	26847.7	43320.0	Black Point (bow)	25796.1	43940.3
Andrea Doria	25147.7	43480.0	Black Point (stern)	14456.2	43938.6
Andrea Doria (stern)	26148.5	43481.0	Black Warrior	26951.8	43755.3
Angler Bank	26784.4	43655.3	Blackfish Schooner	26116.5	43978.6
Annapolis	14535.4	43945.9	Blue Box	26814.7	43508.2
Annex	26891.0	43558.0	Boat Mold	26912.0	43492.6
Apple Tree Wreck	14540.0	43836.5	Bomb	26831.2	43620.7
Aransas	13837.0	43909.1	Bonanza	26779.4	43363.5
Arundo	26796.9	43534.8	Bone Ship	26921.4	43289.8
Arundo	26796.3	43534.0	Bone Wreck	26886.7	43289.7
Arundo (engine)	26791.8	43514.7	Brick Barge	26875.9	43245.4
Asfalto	26831.2	43620.8	Bridge Rubble	26906.2	43509.9
Atlantic Beach Reef	26870.6	43735.0	Bridge Rubble	26910.6	43506.7
Atlantic Princess	26508.0	43294.0	Bridge Rubble	26910.5	43505.1
Austin W.	26705.9	43515.9	Bridge Rubble	26910.4	43495.1
Ayuruoca	26842.3	43547.7	Broadcast	26752.3	43600.2
B.A. Buoy	26876.5	43630.5	Bronx Queen	26968.8	43735.1
BA Wreck	26874.7	43619.6	Brunette	26916.4	43476.0
Baby Doll	26880.3	43954.8	Bumps	26865.5	43561.4
Bacardi	26308.1	43310.6	Cadet	26916.4	43475.8
Balaena	26799.8	43521.8	Cape Fear	14394.7	43993.5
Bald Eagle	26861.5	43640.4	Cape Fear	25779.0	43993.5
Bald Eagle	26831.2	43640.3	Car Float #52	26911.0	43500.7
Bald Eagle	26061.6	43640.2	Carlson II	26912.3	43497.6
Barge	26909.3	43756.6	Cassoon	26895.4	43350.1
Barge	26869.8	43739.2	Cedar Creek Wreck	26921.8	43339.2
Barge	26868.6	43738.0	Celtic	26798.7	43989.6
Barge	26865.8	43733.7	Chaparra	26847.6	43239.9
Barge	26737.0	43728.5	Charlemagne Tower, Jr.	26921.8	43339.2
Barge	26881.5	43728.5	Charles E. Dunlap	26929.8	43755.2
Barge	26772.4	43718.4	Charles Morse (?)	26507.5	43600.9

Name			Name		
Chester A. Poling (stern)	13840.9	44327.8	Fallon	26886.7	43266.5
Choapa	26863.6	43590.8	Farms	26887.0	43595.0
Cholera Bank	26772.1	43672.3	Fifty-nine Pounder	26632.4	43601.1
Cindy	26831.2	43620.8	Fire Island Lightship (not)	26599.0	43644.7
Cities Service No. 4	14806.9	43970.7	Fire Island Reef	26635.9	43735.4
City of Salisbury	13974.4	44283.3	Fire Island Wreck	26674.1	43754.3
Clam	26944.6	43754.8	First Chance	26949.9	43751.4
Coal Barge	26930.5	43945.7	. Fisherman's Buoy	26919.0	43679.9
Coal Barge #1	26932.3	43789.3	Fisherman's Buoy (barge)	26919.9	43677.2
Coal Barge #2	26939.7	43793.7	Florence	26680.6	43574.7
Coal Schooner	26860.0	43559.6	Fran S	26873.6	43733.7
Coal Wreck	26796.4	43671.6	G & D	26671.4	43574.3
Coal Wreck--West	26798.0	43713.2	G-1	14386.8	44010.7
Coimbra	26203.6	43576.8	Galley	26788.0	43484.4
Coimbra (near)	26242.9	43695.0	Gate City	26420.6	43790.3
Concrete Rubble	26945.0	43653.0	Giant Whistler	26943.5	43717.5
Concrete Rubble	26945.0	43651.0	Gina	26968.3	43758.1
Concrete Rubble	26944.2	43650.2	Glen Island	23893.6	43937.6
Concrete Rubble	26944.0	43649.0	Gloria & Doris	26671.4	43574.3
Concrete Rubble	26944.0	43649.0	Glory Grounds	26841.6	43712.5
Concrete Rubble	26945.0	43649.0	Gluckauf	26546.9	43765.3
Concrete Rubble	26943.0	43649.0	Gong Grounds	26975.0	43748.0
Concrete Rubble	26943.0	43647.0	Goulandris	26853.9	43576.8
Condor	26831.9	43984.7	Gov. Mansion	26926.4	43349.6
Coney Island	26792.0	43481.3	Gov. Mansion	26918.1	43317.0
Continent	26884.7	43637.4	Granite	26954.7	43759.1
Cornelia Soule	26954.7	43759.1	Great Lakes #78	26915.6	43683.3
Cornelius Hargraves	26854.8	43296.8	Grecian	25823.8	43830.8
Coyote	13920.8	44266.4	Grecian	25823.8	43838.8
Crane	26853.5	43361.0	Greek	26863.6	43590.8
Crane Barge	26424.3	43516.1	Guard	14623.8	43967.3
Cranford Ferry	26906.3	43503.3	Gulftrade (bow)	26886.8	43260.6
Deck Barge	26911.1	43502.7	Gulftrade (stern)	26821.3	43318.3
Delaware	26928.4	43467.5	Gunboat	26608.9	43609.6
Derrick Barge	26964.3	43759.8	Gwendoline Steers	26798.7	43951.3
Dodger	26617.9	43673.4	H C Tank	26912.0	43241.7
Dragger	26795.6	43725.9	Halfway	26894.5	43842.8
Dragger	26806.6	43250.6	Hammies Junk Pile	26911.0	43306.1
Drumelzier	26674.1	43754.3	Hang	26532.0	43568.0
Dry Dock Reef	26908.8	43506.8	Hankins	26884.5	43340.6
Drydock	26779.4	43718.8	Happy Days	26674.8	43602.0
Drydock #4	26631.1	43733.5	Henry Endicott	13967.7	44081.1
Dual Wrecks	26950.2	43598.8	Herbert	13961.2	44297.1
Duke	26781.5	43737.0	Hercules (tug)	25973.7	43953.6
Durley Chine	26308.1	43310.6	Heroine	14525.7	43946.0
Durley Chine (false)	26671.2	43572.7	Hilda Garston	14283.8	43953.3
Dwight	25514.5	43922.3	Holiday	26268.7	43434.0
Eagle	26891.0	43531.0	Horatio Hall	13856.2	43897.0
East Ridge	26788.3	43267.3	Howard	26773.7	43753.4
East Wreck	26933.3	43747.6	Humpty Dumpty	26795.0	43434.0
Edna	26705.9	43516.1	Hylton Castle	26569.4	43695.3
Edwin Duke	26781.5	43737.0	Iberia	26855.5	43736.2
Emerald Wreck	26873.5	43394.8	Ida K	26855.1	43422.5
Engine	26913.0	43727.1	Immaculata	26801.8	43584.0
Essex	25838.0	43872.4	Imperial	26873.6	43395.0
Essex	25838.1	43872.2	Inshore Schooner	27030.1	43774.5
Eureka	26752.3	43600.3	Ioannis P. Goulandris	26853.9	43576.8

LORAN NUMBERS -- DESCENDING 4 LINE

Chester A. Poling (stern)	13840.9	44327.8		Pendleton	13867.7	43914.0
Herbert	13961.2	44297.1		Aransas	13837.0	43909.1
Romance	13969.4	44290.6		OC Reef--towers	27015.0	43907.0
City of Salisbury	13974.4	44283.3		Two Brothers	25872.1	43902.3
Coyote	13920.8	44266.4		Montana	25871.2	43900.7
Kiowa	13991.6	44265.5		Horatio Hall	13856.2	43897.0
Pinthis	13924.4	44175.3		Black Diamond	25998.1	43895.1
June K	13935.4	44127.7		U-853	25776.0	43894.8
Mars	13956.8	44093.5		Seneca	14019.6	43891.9
Henry Endicott	13967.7	44081.1		Lightburne	14535.6	43872.6
G-1	14386.8	44010.7		Essex	25838.0	43872.4
Cape Fear	14394.7	43993.5		Essex	25838.1	43872.2
Cape Fear	25779.0	43993.5		Barge #1	26530.0	43865.0
Addie Anderson	14424.0	43989.9		Pinnacle Rock	14547.7	43865.0
Celtic	26798.7	43989.6		Scallop Barge	26560.0	43860.5
Condor	26831.9	43984.7		NE of Varanger	26721.5	43852.8
Lansford	13782.7	43981.6		Snug Harbor	25942.5	43843.0
Blackfish Schooner	26116.5	43978.6		Halfway	26894.5	43842.8
Lake Hemlock	14902.3	43978.1		Grecian	25823.8	43838.8
Yankee	14205.6	43975.9		Apple Tree Wreck	14540.0	43836.5
Cities Service No. 4	14806.9	43970.7		Grecian	25823.8	43830.8
Poling Bros. No. 2	26894.8	43970.6		Bass	14560.4	43817.4
Uncle John	14200.0	43970.1		Bass	25829.5	43817.4
Lobster Hole	26900.0	43970.0		Panther	26248.7	43802.0
Guard	14623.8	43967.3		Tennyson	26128.9	43793.8
Olinda	26059.0	43966.7		Yonkers	26128.9	43793.8
Onondaga	14627.7	43966.4		Coal Barge #2	26939.7	43793.7
Barraitai	14863.9	43965.9		Gate City	26420.6	43790.3
Stacks Reef	26979.5	43965.3		Coal Barge #1	26932.3	43789.3
St. Francis	14307.0	43964.6		Shinnecock Reef	26288.1	43787.5
L-8	14423.1	43959.1		Inshore Schooner	27030.1	43774.5
Baby Doll	26880.3	43954.8		Moriches Reef	26431.1	43771.6
Hercules (tug)	25973.7	43953.6		Barnett	26926.8	43771.2
Hilda Garston	14283.8	43953.3		John C. Fitzpatrick	26135.6	43770.4
Gwendoline Steers	26798.7	43951.3		Jug	26135.6	43770.4
Larchmont	14616.4	43949.0		Airplane Engine	26922.6	43768.8
Heroine	14525.7	43946.0		Gluckauf	26546.9	43765.3
Annapolis	14535.4	43945.9		Derrick Barge	26964.3	43759.8
Coal Barge	26930.5	43945.7		Robert A. Snow	26964.3	43759.8
Lake Crystal	14598.4	43944.9		Cornelia Soule	26954.7	43759.1
Bayville Engine	15324.0	43941.0		Granite	26954.7	43759.1
Unnamed	14455.3	43940.4		Gina	26968.3	43758.1
Black Point (bow)	25796.1	43940.3		Princess Anne	26968.3	43758.1
Black Point (stern)	14456.2	43938.6		Roda	26740.4	43757.2
Bayville Barge	26847.1	43938.2		Barge	26909.3	43756.6
Glen Island	23893.6	43937.6		Margaret	26901.2	43756.5
Maine	26938.5	43937.6		Black Warrior	26951.8	43755.3
Vineyard Lightship	14289.6	43931.3		2 x 4 (barge)	26929.8	43755.2
Port Hunter	14097.7	43930.7		Charles E. Dunlap	26929.8	43755.2
Dwight	25514.5	43922.3		Two By Four	26929.8	43755.2
John Dwight	14238.0	43922.3		Clam	26944.6	43754.8
Kershaw	14094.6	43922.1		Seawolf	26413.2	43754.4
Trojan	14291.4	43921.4		Drumelzier	26674.1	43754.3
AC Ridge	26942.0	43920.0		Fire Island Wreck	26674.1	43754.3

Quadrant	26674.1	43754.3	Wreck #12	26913.0	43717.1
Ajace	26956.6	43754.1	Barge	26788.5	43716.9
Italian	26956.6	43754.1	Barge #3	26788.5	43716.9
Peter Rickmers	26786.5	43754.1	Airplane	26605.9	43716.8
Howard	26773.7	43753.4	Coal Wreck--West	26798.0	43713.2
Scow	26773.7	43753.4	West of Coal	26798.0	43713.2
First Chance	26949.9	43751.4	Walcott	26518.1	43712.6
Acara	26800.9	43750.8	Glory Grounds	26841.6	43712.5
Tea Wreck	26800.9	43750.8	Martin's Misery	26932.3	43707.1
Rockaway Reef	26927.3	43748.6	Stilson	26932.3	43707.1
Gong Grounds	26975.0	43748.0	Steamer #3	26932.4	43707.0
Rockaway Reef	26926.0	43748.0	Steamship	26932.3	43707.0
East Wreck	26933.3	43747.6	Sandy Hook "R" 2	26959.0	43704.0
Mistletoe	26933.3	43747.6	Ambrose Ridge	26912.5	43703.0
Ace	26940.0	43745.7	Ambrose Wreck	26912.5	43703.0
Victory	26812.4	43743.5	Pilot Boat	26908.3	43700.5
Tin Can Grounds	26972.0	43740.0	Sandy Hook	26908.3	43700.5
Barge	26869.8	43739.2	Ambrose Light	26910.0	43700.0
Pipe Barge	26869.7	43738.6	Ambrose Tower	26910.0	43700.0
Barge #5	26869.5	43738.5	Steel Wreck	26794.5	43697.2
Scallop Ridge	26917.7	43738.5	Lizzie D	26828.9	43696.5
Barge	26868.6	43738.0	Rum Runner	26828.9	43696.4
Tug Boat #2	26881.5	43737.3	Lizzie D	26829.0	43696.3
Tugboat	26881.5	43737.3	Scotland Buoy	26948.2	43696.3
Duke	26781.5	43737.0	Lightship Relief	26903.5	43695.9
Edwin Duke	26781.5	43737.0	Relief Ship	26903.5	43695.9
Iberia	26855.5	43736.2	WAL-505	26903.5	43695.9
Zeeliner	26622.9	43735.8	Hylton Castle	26569.4	43695.3
Fire Island Reef	26635.9	43735.4	Coimbra (near)	26242.9	43695.0
Bronx Queen	26968.8	43735.1	San Diego (USS)	26543.4	43693.2
Atlantic Beach Reef	26870.6	43735.0	Seventeen Fathoms	26889.0	43684.0
Scallop Ridge	26930.0	43735.0	Great Lakes #78	26915.6	43683.3
Barge #4	26870.4	43734.7	Phillips Wreck	26915.6	43683.3
Barge (steel)	26870.5	43734.7	Two Story Wreck	26915.6	43683.3
Tennyson	26174.0	43734.3	Pentland Firth	26923.3	43682.4
Barge	26865.8	43733.7	N.B. Buoy	26837.3	43680.6
Fran S	26873.6	43733.7	Fisherman's Buoy	26919.0	43679.9
Drydock #4	26631.1	43733.5	Fisherman's Buoy (barge)	26919.9	43677.2
Ocean Prince	26631.1	43733.5	Oregon	26453.1	43676.6
Barge	26737.0	43728.5	Vivian	26405.4	43675.2
Barge	26881.5	43728.5	Dodger	26617.9	43673.4
Barge #6	26737.0	43728.5	Cholera Bank	26772.1	43672.3
Barge #7	26881.5	43728.5	Coal Wreck	26796.4	43671.6
Stone Barge	26782.1	43728.3	Mohawk (RC)	26867.6	43670.8
Engine	26913.0	43727.1	Mohawk (Revenue Cutter)	26867.6	43670.8
Karen K	26903.0	43727.1	RC Mohawk	26867.6	43670.8
Rickseckers	26913.1	43727.1	Revenue Cutter	26867.6	43670.7
Unidentified	26913.0	43727.1	Barge (closed)	26587.5	43659.8
Suffolk	14468.7	43726.2	Reggie	26594.3	43659.2
Suffolk	25644.7	43726.0	Reggie	26593.9	43658.9
Dragger	26795.6	43725.9	Angler Bank	26784.4	43655.3
Rainbow	26795.7	43725.9	Mud Dump Buoy	26903.8	43653.3
Valerie E	26863.6	43725.9	Concrete Rubble	26945.0	43653.0
Turner (DD-648)	26936.4	43725.6	Concrete Rubble	26945.0	43651.0
Drydock	26779.4	43718.8	Concrete Rubble	26944.2	43650.2
Barge	26772.4	43718.4	Concrete Rubble	26944.0	43649.0
Giant Whistler	26943.5	43717.5	Concrete Rubble	26944.0	43649.0

Concrete Rubble	26945.0	43649.0	Yankee	26671.4	43574.3
Concrete Rubble	26943.0	43649.0	Durley Chine (false)	26671.2	43572.7
Sub Chaser	26935.0	43649.0	Irma C.	26660.4	43571.6
Concrete Rubble	26943.0	43647.0	Big Wood	26828.8	43571.3
Macedonia	26941.7	43645.3	Hang	26532.0	43568.0
Fire Island Lightship (not)	26599.0	43644.7	Benson	26859.5	43566.9
Kenosha	26599.0	43644.7	Unknown	26859.5	43566.4
Lightship	26599.0	43644.7	Pinta	26880.7	43564.1
Tug	14927.1	43644.4	Bumps	26865.5	43561.4
3 Sisters	26791.6	43642.3	Coal Schooner	26860.0	43559.6
N.A. Buoy	26603.5	43642.2	Schooner	26672.7	43559.2
Three Sisters	26791.6	43642.2	Annex	26891.0	43558.0
Bald Eagle	26861.5	43640.4	Train Wheel Wreck	26671.2	43557.7
Bald Eagle	26831.2	43640.3	Unidentified	26671.1	43557.7
Bald Eagle	26061.6	43640.2	Wreck #10	26771.2	43557.7
Continent	26884.7	43637.4	Wreck #9	26859.7	43555.3
Shrewsbury Rock	26950.0	43635.0	X #1	26848.7	43553.1
Ranger	14719.4	43632.7	Wreck #7	26853.5	43550.9
B.A. Buoy	26876.5	43630.5	Across Wreck	26832.8	43550.1
Wreck #11	26722.5	43622.5	Wreck #8	26851.1	43548.8
Asfalto	26831.2	43620.8	Ayuruoca	26842.3	43547.7
Cindy	26831.2	43620.8	Oil Wreck	26842.3	43547.7
Rudder	26831.2	43620.8	Oil Wreck	26841.7	43547.6
Bomb	26831.2	43620.7	Larsen	26813.6	43547.0
BA Wreck	26874.7	43619.6	Miog	26844.0	43546.3
Skippy	26609.9	43609.7	Shark River S1	26943.0	43543.0
Gunboat	26608.9	43609.6	Southeast of Oil	26806.9	43540.3
Tarantula	26608.9	43609.6	Tug Boat	26842.1	43539.9
3 Fares	26651.5	43605.2	Barge #2	26838.1	43538.6
Three Pairs	26651.5	43605.2	Arundo	26796.9	43534.8
Wreck #3	26650.2	43604.4	Arundo	26796.3	43534.0
Monofilament	26878.5	43602.7	Twin Anchors	26796.4	43533.9
Happy Days	26674.8	43602.0	Ranger	14719.9	43532.7
59 Pounder	26632.4	43601.1	Eagle	26891.0	43531.0
Fifty-nine Pounder	26632.4	43601.1	X #3	26865.5	43526.4
Charles Morse (?)	26507.5	43600.9	Balaena	26799.8	43521.8
Linda	26507.9	43600.9	Crane Barge	26424.3	43516.1
Eureka	26752.3	43600.3	Edna	26705.9	43516.1
Broadcast	26752.3	43600.2	Austin W.	26705.9	43515.9
Adonis	26950.2	43598.8	Arundo (engine)	26791.8	43514.7
Dual Wrecks	26950.2	43598.8	Norness	25494.2	43510.8
Rusland	26950.2	43598.8	Sea Girt Reef	26905.0	43510.0
Farms	26887.0	43595.0	Bridge Rubble	26906.2	43509.9
Yankee (false)	26609.5	43592.0	Rockland County	26905.3	43508.5
Choapa	26863.6	43590.8	Blue Box	26814.7	43508.2
Greek	26863.6	43590.8	Dry Dock Reef	26908.8	43506.8
Junior	26863.6	43590.8	Bridge Rubble	26910.6	43506.7
South Yankee	26606.5	43589.4	Bridge Rubble	26910.5	43505.1
Immaculata	26801.8	43584.0	Small Tanker	26806.9	43504.3
X #2	26676.7	43580.5	Cranford Ferry	26906.3	43503.3
Pliny	26949.2	43579.8	Deck Barge	26911.1	43502.7
Coimbra	26203.6	43576.8	Car Float #52	26911.0	43500.7
Goulandris	26853.9	43576.8	Rock Pile	26490.5	43500.4
Ioannis P. Goulandris	26853.9	43576.8	Railroad Barge	26910.4	43499.2
Florence	26680.6	43574.7	Carlson II	26912.3	43497.6
G & D	26671.4	43574.3	Stainless Steel Drums	26912.1	43497.6
Gloria & Doris	26671.4	43574.3	Manasquan Wreck	26945.2	43497.3

Thistle	26945.2	43497.3
X #4	26855.0	43497.0
Bridge Rubble	26910.4	43495.1
Barge	26911.8	43494.5
Manasquan R "2"	26944.5	43494.3
Klondike	26914.0	43494.0
Boat Mold	26912.0	43492.6
Tanker (stern)	26803.0	43492.0
Wood Barge	26803.0	43492.0
Spartan	26910.7	43491.2
Wood Wreck	26854.0	43486.0
Mud Hole	26755.0	43485.0
Acid Barge	26794.8	43484.4
Algol	26794.8	43484.4
Galley	26788.0	43484.4
Stolt Dagali	26787.6	43484.4
Sam Berman	26792.8	43482.9
Alan Martin	26792.0	43482.4
Coney Island	26792.0	43481.3
Andrea Doria (stern)	26148.5	43481.0
Andrea Doria	25147.7	43480.0
Adelle	26883.4	43478.2
Brunette	26916.4	43476.0
Cadet	26916.4	43475.8
Logwood	26856.4	43474.6
Klondike Rocks	26844.8	43473.1
Sea Girt Wreck	26860.5	43471.6
Rock Pile	26480.4	43470.6
120 Wreck	26873.4	43468.3
Delaware	26928.4	43467.5
Park City Tug	26993.2	43461.2
Virginia	26425.9	43456.9
X #5	26425.0	43456.8
Sommerstad	26425.2	43456.5
Virginia	26425.2	43456.5
Steamer #1	26424.9	43455.7
Republic	14073.1	43453.4
Mohawk (north)	26875.7	43449.5
Riggy	26906.6	43449.4
Manasquan Ridge	26891.0	43444.0
Mohawk	26877.6	43444.0
Rock Pile	26440.4	43441.0
Mohawk	26878.0	43439.4
Rump	26918.9	43435.4
Holiday	26268.7	43434.0
Humpty Dumpty	26795.0	43434.0
Pan Pennsylvania	14073.1	43426.0
Pan Pennsylvania (bow)	26121.4	43425.5
Mohawk (south)	26881.0	43424.7
Ida K	26855.1	43422.5
Lana Carol	26859.9	43419.7
Lillian	26697.0	43419.4
Imperial	26873.6	43395.0
Emerald Wreck	26873.5	43394.8
Bonanza	26779.4	43363.5
Wreck (north)	26797.0	43363.5
Crane	26853.5	43361.0
Tolten	26815.9	43360.1
Irene	26871.3	43359.1
Anastasia	26853.5	43359.0
Maurice Tracy	26890.1	43358.9
Cassoon	26895.4	43350.1
Gov. Mansion	26926.4	43349.6
Hankins	26884.5	43340.6
Cedar Creek Wreck	26921.8	43339.2
Charlemagne Tower, Jr.	26921.8	43339.2
Tolten Lump	26813.0	43336.0
Anchor Chain	26847.7	43320.0
Gulftrade (stern)	26821.3	43318.3
Gov. Mansion	26918.1	43317.0
Bacardi	26308.1	43310.6
Durley Chine	26308.1	43310.6
Hammies Junk Pile	26911.0	43306.1
Northwest Barge	26883.2	43301.7
Unknown	26883.6	43301.6
Cornelius Hargraves	26854.8	43296.8
Northwest Barge	26878.9	43295.3
Spanish Wreck	26854.6	43295.2
Vizcaya	26854.6	43295.2
Atlantic Princess	26508.0	43294.0
Northwest Barge	26881.9	43293.2
Mildred	26829.1	43290.0
Bone Ship	26921.4	43289.8
Bone Wreck	26886.7	43289.7
Remedios Pascual	26886.7	43289.7
Northeast Wreck	26897.1	43287.4
Persephone	26897.1	43287.0
Sea Hag	26787.2	43286.7
North Ridge	26797.3	43286.5
North Ridge	26787.4	43284.3
Bidevind	26357.6	43280.4
Barnegat Inlet R "2"	26878.0	43278.0
R.P. Resor	26638.3	43277.2
Sumner	26916.8	43271.7
Wreck #1	26349.0	43268.0
Texas Tower #4	26313.5	43267.5
East Ridge	26788.3	43267.3
Fallon	26886.7	43266.5
South Ridge Wreck	26779.4	43263.8
Gulftrade (bow)	26886.8	43260.6
Southeast Wreck	26887.8	43260.5
Dragger	26806.6	43250.6
Brick Barge	26875.9	43245.4
Sailing Ship	26908.0	43243.4
H C Tank	26912.0	43241.7
William R. Farrell	26912.2	43240.7
Magnolia Wreck	26853.2	43240.6
San Saba (stern)	26853.2	43240.6
Southwest Barge	26853.2	43240.6
Barnegat Ridge North	26785.0	43240.0
Chaparra	26847.6	43239.9
Offshore Barge	26847.6	43239.9
San Saba (bow)	26853.8	43239.9

Books by the Author
Fiction

Vietnam
Lonely Conflict

Action/Adventure
Memory Lane
Mind Set

Supernatural
The Lurking

Science Fiction
Entropy
Return to Mars
Silent Autumn
The Time Dragons Trilogy:
  A Time for Dragons
  Dragons Past
  No Future for Dragons

Nonfiction

Advanced Wreck Diving Guide
Shipwrecks of New Jersey

Track of the Gray Wolf

Available (postage paid) from:

GARY GENTILE PRODUCTIONS
P.O. Box 57137
Philadelphia, PA 19111

Nonfiction

$25	*Andrea Doria: Dive to an Era* (hard cover)
$25	*Ironclad Legacy: Battles of the USS Monitor* (hard cover)
$20	*The Nautical Cyclopedia*
$20	*Primary Wreck Diving Guide*
$20	*Ultimate Wreck Diving Guide*
$20	*USS San Diego: the Last Armored Cruiser*
$20	*Wreck Diving Adventures*
$25	Video (VHS and PAL): *The Battle for the USS Monitor*

The Popular Dive Guide Series

$20	*Shipwrecks of New York*
$20	*Shipwrecks of Delaware and Maryland*
$20	*Shipwrecks of Virginia*
$20	*Shipwrecks of North Carolina: from the Diamond Shoals North*
$20	*Shipwrecks of North Carolina: from Hatteras Inlet South*

Wreck Diving Adventure Novel

$20	*The Peking Papers* (hard cover)

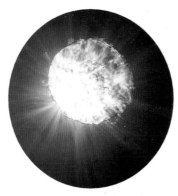